Philosophy of Social Science

B

Philosophy of Social Science

The Methods, Ideals, and Politics of Social Inquiry

Michael Root

BLACKWELL
Oxford UK & Cambridge USA

First published 1993
Reprinted 1994, 1996

Blackwell Publishers Inc.
238 Main Street
Cambridge, Massachusetts 02142
USA

Blackwell Publishers Ltd
108 Cowley Road
Oxford OX4 1JF
UK

Library of Congress Cataloging-in-Publication Data
Root, Michael, 1940–
Philosophy of social science : the methods, ideals, and politics of social inquiry / Michael Root.
p. cm.
Includes bibliographical references and index.
ISBN 0–631–19042–2 (pbk)
1. Social sciences — Philosophy.   2. Social sciences — Methodology.
I. Title
H61.R65   1993
300'.1—dc20
93–3213
CIP

British Library Cataloguing in Publication Data
A CIP catalogue record for this book is available from the British Library.

Typeset in 10 on 12pt Sabon
by Graphicraft Ltd, Hong Kong
Printed in Great Britain by
Hartnolls Limited, Bodmin, Cornwall

This book is printed on acid-free paper

To my mother and father

Contents

Analytical table of contents

He maintained that social scientists should not include judgments of moral or political value in their teachings or writings; but he did not maintain that the social sciences should or could be nonpartisan, for he allowed that practical reasons could not be excluded from the context of either discovery or justification in the social sciences. Moreover, Weber maintained that in justifying a theory containing ideal-types, the practical reasons would have to include judgments of cultural value.

3 Theories of development in psychology and political science

Theories of development in the social sciences assume that there is an end point or highest stage of development. The practice in which the end point is identified or defined introduces an element of partisanship. In the case of theories of moral development like Piaget's or Kohlberg's the partisanship involves judgments of moral value. Some social scientists who theorize psychological development also theorize limits to development and reason that some differences between subjects in the development of a trait are uneliminable. Their reasoning introduces another element of partisanship and relies on judgments of how resources ought to be deployed. Similar forms of partisanship are common in research in comparative politics and in theories of political development, despite their claim to value-neutrality.

4 Functional theories in sociology and biology

Functional theories and explanations in the social sciences and biology have a common form and draw on a common store of concepts, including the concepts of design and adaptation. Functional explanations have been criticized by methodological individualists for their ontology and by philosophers of science for being either incomplete or unnecessary. Functional explanations in sociology are said to be incomplete because they have no answer to the selection question, whereas functional explanations in biology are thought to be unnecessary because they assume causal explanations of the trait. In addition to being criticized on methodological grounds, functional explanations are criticized for being politically conservative. Though these political criticisms are mistaken, functional theories and explanations are partisan in that they rely on a distinction between fixed and variable features that favors some public policies over others. Moreover, functional explanations of moral or political attitudes are partisan when they assume that the attitudes are mistaken.

5 Rational choice theories in positive and normative economics

Economics has a positive side and a normative side. The core of the positive side is a theory of rational choice. The theory has a substantive and a procedural interpretation. While most economists favor the substantive interpretation, on this interpretation, their theories have little predictive or explanatory power. The positive side promises value-neutrality, but theories in positive economics are partisan in a variety of ways: in favoring narrow over broader conceptions of rationality and private or free market solutions to public problems and also in their identification of causes and their formulation of economic laws. Normative economics has sought neutrality by avoiding interpersonal utility comparisons; but the criteria offered, like the Pareto criterion, either do not avoid partisanship or do not measure well-being and are not welfare criteria at all.

6 Collecting data in the social sciences

The methods for collecting data in the social sciences are designed to assure that the data are reliable and valid. Social scientists assume that their data are reliable and valid only if the methods for collecting them are value-neutral; but, given the way they define "validity", their data are valid only if their methods are partisan. Neutrality leads the scientists to separate scientific protocols from codes of ethics. The separation permits social scientists to call their data "good" no matter how morally wrong the techniques for collecting them. Neutrality only prohibits calling them wrong. Milgram's research on obedience is an example of how the liberal ideals of good science influence codes of ethics and the moral reasoning of the scientist. Perfectionist approaches to the social sciences oppose the view that data can be good and the methods of collecting them morally objectionable and, as a result, can better serve the research subjects.

7 Sorting data into kinds

Many philosophers of science distinguish between natural and nonnatural kinds or between categories discovered and invented by science. The laws of science describe the behavior of discovered rather than invented kinds. Few of the kinds of the social sciences are natural, but some are discovered rather than invented by the social sciences. Though nonnatural, these kinds are real, for they support lawlike generalizations and enter into explanations of the subject's behavior. However, the kinds do not merely describe but also prescribe the behavior, for they are a basis on which the subjects are normalized. Their role in normalizing subjects makes the kinds partisan; but they are also partisan in favoring the values of those who invent or sustain the kinds, and, in employing the kinds, social scientists pass those values on to their own research.

8 Explaining the data

The subjects of the social sciences offer rational explanations of their own behavior. Many of the social sciences discount those explanations and offer explanations of their own which oppose the assumption that the subjects of the social sciences are agents and have a conception of the good. The practice of discounting is common to functional, covering-law, hermeneutic, and decision-theoretic explanations in the social sciences and is incompatible with the conception of the subject common to most moral reasoning. The subjects of these explanations are not the subjects of moral responsibility, Mill's utilitarianism, or Kant's kingdom of ends and are not individuals toward whom it is appropriate to have moral emotions or to whom it is appropriate to attribute moral attitudes. In discounting participant explanations, social scientists are not taking a particular moral stand, but rather a stand against our common conception of a moral subject and the moral judgments that rely on it.

9 The fact/value distinction

Liberals assume that statements of fact and value are entirely heterogeneous. The current language of most social sciences includes both kinds of statements, for it includes thick if not thin ethical terms. Value-freedom requires eliminating both kinds of terms. The belief that it is possible to eliminate thick ethical terms overlooks two truths about the meaning of words: the open texture of words and the interdependence of meaning and collateral information. In addition, value-freedom concerns not only the social scientists' words but also what they do with those words. Given what most social scientists do with their words, their acts of speech are partisan. Even if statements of fact and value were heterogeneous, given the contexts in which social scientists use their language, they would make value-judgments in using the presumably factual statements of the language.

10 Social science and perfectionism

On a perfectionist view, the quality of research in the social sciences is measured by the conception of the good the research advances as well as the methods it employs. Many perfectionist approaches are communitarian, in that they attempt to advance a conception of the good shared by the subjects of the research. One form of communitarianism in the social sciences is critical theory. The aim of a critical theory is to emancipate the subjects, and towards that end subjects are given a role in validating the theorists' descriptions or explanations of their lives. Participatory research is also a form of communitarianism, and many feminists in the social sciences have adopted its methods and ideals. The methods allow the researcher to join with her subjects to invent new kinds or categories into which to sort the facts of the subjects' lives. The new categories are important as part of a campaign for social change. Liberal universities and governments cannot openly support a perfectionist social science; as a result, social scientists who depend on their support have a reason to maintain that the teaching and research are value-neutral even if they are not and even if neutrality is a false ideal for the social sciences.

Bibliography

Author index

Subject index

Preface

This book is a description and criticism of the philosophy underlying much of the research and teaching in the social sciences. Though there are important differences between the many disciplines and schools that make up these sciences, a common thread runs through them and ties their different methods and ideals together.

Philosophers who write about the social sciences usually try to tie their methods to the natural sciences; but the thread joining the social sciences together, according to this book, is spun from the fabric of a political theory, and the question underlying the book is not whether the social sciences should resemble the natural sciences but whether they should emulate the ideals and practices of the liberal state and attempt to be neutral between competing conceptions of the good.

The book describes how theories are constructed and tested, how facts are predicted or explained, data collected and categorized, causes identified, and findings presented in the social sciences, and shows how the social sciences attempt, but fail, to be liberal or value-neutral. Though theory construction, confirmation, observation, prediction, and explanation in the social sciences are compared with similar practices in the natural sciences, the comparison is mostly with biology and the biomedical sciences; for they, like the social sciences, study human subjects and make human subjects the objects of their research.

Along with criticism of the present philosophy of the social sciences, this book offers an alternative, intentionally partisan philosophy for the social sciences – based on ideals and methods for research and teaching that favor one conception of the good over others. While the liberal approach is designed to separate the findings of research from their use, the partisan approach is designed to combine them. The book includes examples of partisan research – including feminist social science – and explains how the research combines a code of ethics with the methods or protocols for doing science.

The book is written for social scientists and philosophers. Early drafts were used to introduce undergraduate and graduate students to the philosophy of the social sciences. Most of the students were from the social sciences, and the book was written with special attention to their background and interests. My aim is that it be user-friendly but also provoke and challenge readers who believe that the social sciences and politics should be kept separate and that the social sciences should be value-neutral. The book can be read or taught cover to cover, but individual chapters stand on their own and can be read or taught to serve the following interests.

Readers whose primary interest is in the politics of the social sciences should read the introduction and chapters 1 and 10, for these compare the ideals of the social sciences with perfectionism and anti-perfectionism in politics and government. Chapter 2 is aimed primarily at readers interested in the work of Max Weber and the use of ideal-types in the social sciences. Readers whose primary interest is methodology or the standards of scientific inquiry should read chapters 2–8. Chapters 2–5 look at the forms which theories take in the social sciences and the standards used to test or assess them; chapter 6 discusses how data are collected and the means for determining whether they are reliable or valid; chapter 7 discusses how the data are sorted and whether there are any natural kinds in the social sciences; and chapter 8 is concerned with how the data are explained and how the explanations differ from those offered by the research subjects.

Readers with an interest in the relation between sociology and biology should read chapter 4, which focuses on functionalism and how the concept of adaptation influences these two sciences. Readers with an interest in the methods of economics should read chapter 5, which explains how positive and normative economics rely on a particular conception of rational choice and how the conception limits the explanatory and predictive power of theories in economics. Chapters 8–9 should be of interest to readers with an interest in ethics, for in chapter 8 I explain how many of the forms of explanation in the social sciences oppose our traditional view of morality and, in particular, our common conception of a moral subject, and in chapter 9 I discuss the distinction between facts and values and the possibility of a language of science free of values and limited to facts.

Chapter 10 offers ideals and methods for research and teaching in the social sciences very different from those accepted by most social scientists and is for readers with an interest in critical theory or who wonder how social science is conducted when the ideals are explicitly partisan rather than value-neutral or liberal. Chapter 10, together with chapters 6 and

7, are for readers with an interest in feminist research or those who are unhappy with the traditional distinction between theory and practice or pure and applied research in the social sciences.

The book includes an analytical table of contents designed to help the reader to pick and choose from the 10 chapters and survey the central claims and arguments of the book; it also includes an introduction that sets the theme and tone of the book and offers a summary of each chapter. The introduction develops the idea that there is a common thread running through the social sciences and shows how the thread is related to a prominent political ideal. The lengthy bibliography consists mostly of writings in the social sciences. They supply the many examples discussed in the book and, over the years, have helped introduce me to the ideals and methods of the social sciences.

Many people contributed to my writing of this book. Students and faculty who attended my course on the philosophy of the social sciences encouraged me to write about values in the social sciences and helped me to make my account of the methods and aims of the social sciences clearer. Here I owe a special debt to Tom Atchison, Dianne Bartels, Susan Bernick, Don Brunnquell, Andrew Davison, Chris Ferrall, Dick Levins, Kristina Rolin, and Dona Warren. A number of colleagues in the philosophy department at the University of Minnesota helped me in the early stages, but I owe special thanks to Naomi Scheman for her comments and criticisms of early drafts and John Wallace for his running commentary on the themes in the book. I also received encouragement and advice from colleagues at other universities and, in particular, Ernie Lepore. I received wonderful editorial help from Ruth Wood and much support and understanding from Tamara Goldstein Root. Part of the research for the book was supported by a Bush Sabbatical Fellowship from the University of Minnesota. Finally, I received splendid attention and assistance from my editors at Blackwell: Steve Smith, Jack Messenger, and Jean van Altena.

Introduction

Most social scientists today maintain that the social sciences should stand free of politics, but the philosophy that leads them to this view reflects a current political ideal – the ideal of liberalism – more than any truth about science. According to the political ideal, the state ought to be neutral on conceptions of the good and silent on questions concerning the nature of human perfection. Most social scientists believe that their methods and findings should be neutral and silent as well, and they have conducted their research with neutrality as a central ideal.

In the following pages, I survey the social sciences and explain how their methods are shaped by the liberal ideal. But I also criticize that ideal and, at the end of the book, present an alternative philosophy for the social sciences. My thesis is that while liberal ideals are appropriate for the state, they are not appropriate for the social sciences.

Liberalism is primarily a philosophy of government or the state, but many of its principles apply to other fields or areas of social life as well. A liberal philosophy is one which attempts to adhere to what has come to be called "the anti-perfection principle." According to this principle, nothing should be said or done within a given area of life to promote any one ideal of human perfection over another. The area of life can be politics, education, the media, the helping professions, the arts, or science. In the area of education, for example, the principle says that nothing should be said or done in the classroom to promote the ideals of one particular Church or moral community over another's; and in the area of politics it says that nothing should be said or done in government to favor the moral or spiritual values of one group of citizens at the expense of some other's.

The social sciences espouse the anti-perfection principle when they preach value-neutrality and tell us that teaching and research in their field should be neutral regarding ideals of the good life. According to a liberal philosophy of the social sciences, social scientists (in their capacity as social scientists) should not attempt to influence their subjects' judgments of the intrinsic superiority or inferiority of any conception of the good life or justify their methods on the basis of any such judgment. When they conduct their research and offer their findings, the social scientists should be nonpartisan and silent on questions of what morally ought to be.

Neutrality in any field is a matter of degree. Practices deviate from the anti-perfection principle to a greater or lesser extent; but there are some fields in which neutrality as an ideal is not coherent, for the very features that help to define the field preclude neutrality. The social sciences, I argue in this book, are such fields. Features of theory construction, theory choice, data collection, categorization, and explanation in the social sciences, by their very nature, make adherence to the anti-perfection principle impossible. The question is not whether the social sciences should be value-neutral but how they should be partisan and what they should favor.

If a liberal social science is not possible, what are the alternatives? The alternatives are some form of perfectionist science: one that aims at promoting or implementing the ideals of the good life of some individual or group. According to a perfectionist science, the practices of the science should include or be grounded on a view of the kinds of life worth pursuing. Of course, this leaves open the question of whose conceptions of the good the social sciences should pursue and how they should pursue it.

My special interest is in a variety of perfectionism that is framed in terms of the common good and defines the good life by the shared ends or aspirations of a community. This variety of perfectionism is communitarian. The community's way of life gives the social scientist a basis on which to rank conceptions of the good. However, there isn't just one community; there are many, and the social scientist must learn or discover to which one she owes her loyalties. Once she learns where she stands, she can conduct her science to promote or implement the view of human perfection that lies beneath her feet. Different communitarian social scientists can be expected to have different loyalties, and the differences will be reflected in their practice.

The image I had in mind while writing this book was that of a map. I saw myself drawing a map of the moral and political values displayed or assumed in some prominent work in a number of the social sciences. The map, I hoped, would highlight the ways in which the work was partisan and favored one conception of the good over another.

In drawing such a map of the social sciences, I looked to Max Weber and his distinction between value-relevance and value-freedom, and my survey of the social sciences begins with a discussion of Weber's distinction. However, teaching and writing in the social sciences can be partisan in areas and ways that Weber does not explore, and the work of the social scientist can favor a conception of the good in ways that Weber leaves unsurveyed and undepicted.

One of my major aims is to highlight some of the many forms of partisanship in the social sciences that Weber overlooks and, in particular, to show how, in collecting and sorting their data and choosing their theories, social scientists who intend to be neutral nevertheless practice in a partisan way. It is important to remember, as you read through the book, that teaching and research can be partisan without employing any value terms and that partisanship in the social sciences is not merely a matter of the language used in the findings but also a matter of how the research is conducted.

In chapter 1, I present a brief history of the concept of liberality and describe how it changed when the sciences split off from the arts. The aim of the chapter is to show how the ideal of neutrality is reflected in the workings of the state, life in the classroom, and the practices of the social sciences. Often partisanship in schooling, government, and social science is covert and unintentional. But, although at the level of the individual – namely, the teacher, the public official, or the scientist – the practice may be neutral, at the institutional level it is usually partisan.

Like institutional discrimination, partisanship in the social sciences does not depend on anyone's intentions but is written into the norms that govern the practice. University regulations protecting academic freedom offer an example of how a practice can oppose an intention. The regulations are intended to protect unpopular speech in the schools, but when combined with the norms for doing social science, they limit the political speech of the social science faculty. Contrary to many recent discussions of political correctness, academic freedom does not protect the free expression of values in the social sciences; but when combined with the ideal of neutrality, academic freedom can be invoked to censure it.

In chapter 2, I examine Weber's distinction between value-freedom and value-relevance and explain that while he believed that social scientists' findings should be free of value-judgments, he did not think that their research could be nonpartisan or silent on questions of the good; for, on his view, the discovery and justification of theories in the social sciences must rely on judgments both of what is and of what ought to be. Theories that contain ideal-types, in the sense of "ideal-types" that Weber had in mind, cannot be chosen solely on the basis of fit – how well they describe the data – but must be chosen on the basis of the researcher's judgments of cultural significance, and these are judgments of value. As a result, even if the theories themselves were free of all ethical language, they would not be value-neutral but perfectionist.

Weber does not survey the differences between theories in the social sciences or consider how the differences affect their partisanship. In chapters 3, 4, and 5, I continue my map of the politics of the social sciences and highlight the place of values in three prominent forms of social theory: developmental theory, functional theory, and rational choice theory. The idea is that personal, cultural, moral, and political values are included in each in a particular way. Though the social scientist intends the theories to be neutral, they are not, because of the reasoning used to confirm or assess them.

The focus of chapter 3 is developmental theories in psychology and political science. These are theories of how some psychological or political trait or competence changes and becomes more complex or more complete over time. The chapter focuses on theories of moral development and the work of Kohlberg and Gilligan, but the conclusions drawn about the role of value-judgments in their work apply to theories of perceptual, cognitive, emotional, and political development as well. Common to all these theories of development is a definition of competence, and definitions of competence rely on judgments of value in a number of important ways.

The focus of chapter 4 is functionalism in sociology and anthropology. The chapter begins with a discussion of how functional theories differ from other forms of theory and proceeds to an analysis of the relationship between functional theories in the social and the biological sciences. Many critics of functional theories have maintained that they are inherently conservative. The point of this chapter is to show that though this claim is mistaken, political value-judgments shape the direction of functional analysis in a number of places and, in particular, shape the analysis at the point of declaring which of the traits of the individual or group and the environment are fixed and which are subject to change or adjustment in response to needs.

The focus of chapter 5 is rational choice theory in economics. First, I explain how this form of theory is similar to and different from functional theory and how, although the version of choice theory behind neoclassical microeconomics is designed to exclude moral values, economists pass their own values through to their science when they choose *ceteris paribus* clauses in the formulation of economic laws. Next, I discuss partisanship in normative economics and how efforts to limit the ethical commitments of welfare criteria fail. The point of this chapter, like the preceding ones, is that despite efforts to keep theories in the social sciences nonpartisan and liberal, value-neutrality is compromised by the requirements of theorizing and that, as a result, such neutrality is a false, unobtainable ideal for the social sciences.

The social sciences consist of more than the practice of constructing and testing theories. They include the practices of collecting data, sorting the data into categories or kinds, and offering explanations of individual or group behavior. In chapters 6, 7, and 8, I explain how neutrality is compromised in each of these practices and how moral or political values pass through to them. Part of the problem with previous discussions of value-neutrality in the social sciences, including Weber's, is that they don't consider how each of the various practices within the science is connected to the surrounding moral and political landscape. The social sciences are discussed as if they could and should stand apart from the politics of the communities they study or serve. However, as I argue in these chapters, once we look closely at how data are collected, sorted, and analyzed, we see that the practice of social science does not stand apart but passes the values of the community through to the data and the kinds into which they are sorted.

Chapter 6 looks at the methods or protocols that guide the collection of good experimental and interview data. The ideal of value-neutrality in the collection of data allows that data can be collected in morally questionable or dubious ways and yet be good as data. Scientific norms can be value-free in Weber's sense even though they oppose the science's code of ethics. An experimental protocol that directs researchers to deceive their subjects is value-free, on Weber's account, as long as it is silent on whether the deception is morally desirable. As I explain in chapter 6 and later in chapter 9, most discussions of values in the social sciences focus on the words rather than the deeds of its practitioners and, as a result, ignore important ethical questions raised by the research.

Codes of ethics are not standards for measuring the quality of experimental or interview data, for good data are defined by the notions of reliability and validity. On the liberal view, if the data are reliable and valid, then they are value-neutral; but, as I argue in chapter 6, given the standards of reliability and validity in the social sciences, most data are reliable and valid only if they are not neutral but partisan. A test, for example, is a valid measure of ability or achievement if it predicts the performance of the subjects in other settings like a clinic, classroom, or occupation. If the assessment of their performance in these settings is itself partisan – for example, favoring some racial or cultural ideal over others – then a valid test passes the partisanship through. My point in chapter 6 is that although the standards of goodness for data in the social sciences are intended to be value-neutral, they pass moral and political values from sites like the office and the school to the data the scientists collect when they test, interview, or survey their subjects.

The social sciences do not merely collect data from their subjects; they sort the data into kinds. They do not collect data about individuals but about individuals as members of a certain class or category: as black or white, employed or unemployed, homeless or housed, single or married. The categories employed by the social sciences to classify their data do not carve the social world at its natural joints, because it has none. The cuts are due more to the knife than to the body of data. The categories impose an order on the data based on judgments of how things ought to be.

Chapter 7 is concerned with how the social sciences determine the kinds into which individuals, groups, and events are sorted and with the claim made by Michel Foucault and others that the kinds of the social sciences are not discovered but invented. Here I explain the distinction between the invention and the discovery of kinds and how it is related to value-neutrality. I argue that when social scientists identify and sort the subjects of their study as subjects of one kind rather than another, neutrality is betrayed at the outset; for values direct the choice of kinds, and kinds, in turn, direct the conduct and treatment of the subjects of these sciences. Not only are the kinds chosen to fit the subjects, but the subjects are taught and directed to fit the kinds. The scientists' practice of sorting is part of a larger practice of regulating and normalizing people and devising and maintaining a set of social roles.

Theory is not an end in itself but is used by science to predict, explain, or alter the facts of interest to the science. Chapter 8 is concerned with how the social sciences explain human behavior and how the explanations they offer are different from those offered by the subjects themselves. Subjects characteristically offer rational explanations of their own behavior, and the explanations offered by the social scientists typically discount them. In many cases, the explanations of the social sciences imply that there is no true rational explanations of the subjects' behavior or that most of the subjects' own rational explanations are mistaken.

The concept of the subject as someone whose behavior is seldom explained by her own rational explanations, I argue, is incompatible with the concept assumed by many moral theories and everyday moral practices. Whereas previous chapters look at the relationship between practices within the social sciences and particular judgments of moral value, this chapter looks at the relationship between the practice of explanation in the social sciences and the foundations of moral judgment. My point here is that explanations in the social sciences oppose most of our moral judgments by opposing the conception of the subject on which these judgments depend.

The ideal of value-neutrality rests on the assumptions that there is a logical gap between facts and values and that different values are consistent with the same body of facts. As a result, social scientists think that their science is value-neutral as long as it does not include any statements of value. The aim of chapter 9 is to call the assumption and the fact/value distinction into question. I discuss the distinction between thick and thin ethical terms and explain how value-neutrality requires that the social sciences exclude terms of both kinds. I argue from some features of the use of language that it is not possible to rid the language of the social sciences of all thick ethical terms, and go on to explain that even if it were possible, this would not assure that, in using the language, social scientists are not making judgments of value. Chapter 9 is intended to show that the prescriptive character of social science is often disguised or hidden behind the apparent or ostensible neutrality of the words its practitioners employ.

Not all social scientists believe in the ideals of liberal science or believe that social research ought to be neutral on questions of moral and political value. In chapter 6, I discuss some feminist criticisms of neutrality in the practice of collecting data. In chapter 10, I look at a number of different perfectionist alternatives to the liberal sciences. Perfectionist principles regulate the social sciences in ways openly designed to advance one conception of the good over another. In the first part of the chapter, I discuss the approach to social research associated with the Frankfurt school and with so-called critical theory. Critical theorists oppose the liberal ideal of social science, which they associate with positivism, and offer an alternative approach to social theory that has social criticism and change, rather than description, prediction, or explanation, as its objective.

Central to critical theory is the idea that a system of belief can be false but function to maintain inequalities of power between groups within a society. The aim of critical theory is to show that many of the institutions of a society are based on such a system of belief – that is, on false consciousness. The assumption is that once members of the society realize that their beliefs are benighted, they will try to revise them. In the first part of chapter 10, I examine the contrast between positive and critical theories and argue that though critical theories, unlike liberal theory, are openly rather than secretly partisan, they are not sufficiently communitarian or participatory, in that they often rely on a conception of the good that is imposed upon, rather than drawn from, the lives of their subjects.

In the second part of chapter 10, I discuss participatory research and some feminist approaches to the social sciences. Both oppose the liberal distinction between the researcher and the research subject; with participatory research, the people who do the research and the people on whom the research is done are the same. While the liberal approach is designed to separate pure from applied social science and the findings of research from their use, the participatory approach and many feminist approaches are designed to combine them. While on the liberal approach, research should precede and be kept separate from any program of education or political action that would use or apply the findings, on the participatory and feminist approaches, it should become a part of these programs. Many social scientists find such ideas loose, soft, or imprecise, but, as I explain in chapter 10, though the different perfectionist approaches are each committed to a single view of the good, they are not committed to any single way of pursuing it.

Most of my map of partisanship in the social sciences was drawn over a number of years in a class I teach in the philosophy of the social sciences. Often, students from the social sciences, in response to my discussion of the liberal ideal, would ask whether there was a better alternative. Scientists will hold onto hypotheses, frameworks, research programs, paradigms, and ideals in the face of anomalies or disconfirming evidence when there are no better candidates. I worried that no matter how compelling my case against the liberal ideal of social science, social scientists would continue to revere neutrality unless I described some alternatives. Chapter 10 offers some and tries to persuade you that they are reasonable.

The subject of this book is the social sciences, but some of what I say about value-neutrality in the social sciences applies to the natural sciences as well. The natural sciences are also committed to neutrality between differing conceptions of the good life. Parts of my map of political values in the social sciences apply to research in the natural sciences too. Some of my discussion in chapter 2 of Weber's notions of value-relevance and value-freedom, for example, and my discussion of the distinction between fact and value in chapter 9 apply equally to the social and the natural sciences.

However, much of the partisanship I discuss in this book is due to the fact that the subjects of the social sciences are also the subjects of moral and political life. They are not merely the objects of the social scientists' descriptions; they are subjects who interpret and comply with or resist those descriptions. They not only support the social scientists' interests but have interests of their own. Their values color and influence how they respond to the scientist, and even if the scientist attempts to limit their agency, the objects of the social sciences are agents and, as such, can act to support or oppose the science which attempts to predict, explain, or control their behavior.

Much has been written about the differences in subject matter between the natural and the social sciences. The usual question is whether the differences support a different aim or method for the social sciences. Some philosophers of social science argue that because human subjects are agents, or the creators or bearers of meaning or value, the aim of the social sciences should not be to explain behavior but to interpret it; others argue that because human subjects have wills and make choices, the aim of the social sciences should be not to discover laws of human behavior but to describe the norms to which the subjects conform their behavior. This book addresses these questions only indirectly, for my primary interest is not whether the social sciences should emulate the natural sciences but whether they should emulate the liberal state. Nevertheless, to the extent that the book promotes participatory and communitarian over liberal approaches to the social sciences, it supports an aim and method different from those of the natural sciences.

I do not think it is possible to recommend in very general terms what social scientists should or should not do except to say that they should not adopt a false ideal or present a false picture of what they do, and that they should highlight, rather than hide, the partisanship implicit in their practice. The map of partisanship drawn in the following pages is designed to correct the picture and encourage a more open, honest discussion of the aims of social research and the ideals for social science. Though I mean to encourage social scientists to adopt or attempt a perfectionist science (ideally with a politics I approve of), I would be pleased if they would tell a true story about their own supposedly liberal science.

1

The liberal ideal

What's in a name? In the eighteenth and nineteenth centuries, the disciplines of psychology, sociology, and economics were known as "human" or "moral sciences"; today, of course, they are known as "social sciences." Behind the change in name is a change in the way the disciplines are practised and the way we are invited to think about them. However, the name "social science" tells us little about the change; for, as I argue in the pages that follow, given the way the moral or human sciences are now supposed to be practised and the way we are now encouraged to think about them, they would be better called "liberal" than "social" sciences. That is, these disciplines endorse ideals that are more liberal than social, in much the way that ideals espoused by institutions like the modern secular state or university are more liberal than social. Let me explain.

The split between the arts and the sciences

The term "liberal" was originally an epithet for those arts and sciences that were considered worthy of free and noble men and were suited to a life free from everyday needs and toil.[1] In the Middle Ages, the term was applied to seven branches of learning: the trivium of grammar, logic, and rhetoric and the quadrivium of arithmetic, geometry, astronomy, and music. During the Renaissance, the term was used more broadly to cover general education, as against specialized or vocational training. The vocations, professions, trades, crafts, domestic arts, and most forms of work and commerce were associated with servility and a narrow, rigid, machine-like approach to life, whereas the liberal arts and sciences were associated with generosity, flexibility, imagination, and a free and open mind. The liberal arts and sciences were thought to inspire new ideas and to lead to progress and reform, while specialized and vocational training were thought to inspire the repetition of old ideas and lead to a slavish respect for the past.

At some point, the term "liberal" lost its association with the sciences while retaining its association with the arts.[2] The new, exclusive tie with the arts affected attitudes towards liberality. As art inclined toward freedom and freedom toward license, people came to see liberality as mere laxity and indulgence. Freedom in upholding rules and standards looked more like a vice than a virtue, and in comparison to the sciences, the liberal arts seemed to lack precision, rigor, and discipline. They relied more on invention and speculation than on observation and reasoning and were pliant and yielding where the sciences were solid, firm, and exacting. While the arts remained the liberal arts, the sciences became the empirical or exact sciences. Arithmetic, geometry, and astronomy were now more closely identified with wisdom and learning than were grammar, rhetoric, and music. The sciences had become hard, while the arts had grown soft and more worthy of a self-indulgent than a noble man.

The liberal state

The term "liberal" has another use that also connotes freedom, but freedom of the will rather than freedom of the understanding or imagination. In England and France in the seventeenth and eighteenth centuries, the term was a label for a particular conception of the relation between the individual and the state. A state was liberal if it left its citizens free to lead their lives according to their own lights.[3] Liberal principles were designed to regulate the basic institutions of the society without implying that any one member's moral or political ideals were better than any others or without taking sides on moral issues over which the members were divided.[4]

The rise of liberal thought in the seventeenth and eighteenth centuries in Europe was a response to historical circumstances: the passing away of a shared conception of the good in the form of the world view of the Church and the breakup of the feudal order.[5] The community of thought advanced and enforced by the Church dissolved and was replaced by a diversity of forms of life and a consciousness of self as separate from and set against the beliefs and desires of others. Rule by one on behalf of all seemed no longer possible, for there was no longer a body of common attitudes or outlooks binding all the members of society together in a single community. Liberalism was a political philosophy for a society whose members practised many religions, pursued many different occupations, and identified with many different customs and traditions.

Liberal theories of the state contrast with perfectionist theories like Plato's in the *Republic*, Aristotle's in the *Politics*, and the politics of civic virtue in Hegel's *Philosophy of Right*. Perfectionist principles regulate the basic institutions of a society in ways designed to reflect or advance a particular view of human perfection or the good life.[6] Whereas liberal principles assume the priority of an individual's freedom to lead his life according to his own lights, perfectionist principles assume the priority of a preferred light over the freedom of the individual to choose.[7] Liberal principles are designed to prohibit the state from requiring or even encouraging citizens to subscribe to one religious tradition, form of family life, or manner of personal or artistic expression over another; whereas perfectionist principles are designed to push or pull citizens in directions that reflect and sustain a particular set of values or traditions.[8]

The value of liberal neutrality

Liberal principles are designed to ensure value-neutrality, or neutrality between different conceptions of the good; but liberals differ as to why neutrality is necessary or appropriate. For skeptics, neutrality is necessary because there is no truth in matters of the good. On this view, there is nothing for judgments of value to be true of, and so no proper reason for the state to prefer or endorse some of these judgments over others. Liberals of the skeptical school are often noncognitivists in their interpretation of value. They believe that moral judgments have no truth-value and are expressions of feeling or personal preference rather than statements of moral fact.[9]

According to another school, pragmatism, neutrality is necessary because, given the differences in conceptions of the good, there is no way to win or maintain the cooperation or allegiance of the different individuals or groups within the state or social institution except by value-neutrality. Neutrality is seen as a means to earn and maintain the respect of all in a society in which differences in moral and political outlook are broad and well entrenched. Were the state to pursue a conception of the good favored by some over that favored by others, it would have a problem of winning the support and loyalty of many of its citizens.

Finally, for liberals like John Stuart Mill, neutrality is necessary in order to promote autonomy. According to this school, the good life includes the opportunity to plan one's life for oneself and "to be conscious of [oneself] as a thinking, willing, active being, bearing responsibility for his choices and able to explain them by reference to his own ideas and purposes."[10] Given this conception of the good, a person cannot be forced to be good, and the state should not dictate the kind of life a citizen should lead; it would be better for citizens to choose badly than for them to be forced by the state to choose well.[11] In linking liberalism and liberality with autonomy and freedom, liberals like Mill bring back the earlier link between liberality and freedom – the idea that the liberal arts and sciences are those worthy of free men. Liberal government, on Mill's view, is government worthy of free men and designed to inspire new ideas and free, open minds.

Liberal principles assume the priority of individual liberty or autonomy over the good, but liberals differ in their conception of liberty or autonomy. For the libertarian or classical school of liberalism, liberty is no more than the absence of constraint, and an individual is at liberty to live as he chooses if no other individual or no institution compels him to live otherwise. For the egalitarian school, liberty requires opportunities and resources necessary to live as one chooses. These differing conceptions of liberty are the basis for two very different conceptions of the liberal state. According to one, the state is a night watchman whose role is to supply those public goods that cannot be efficiently supplied by a free market; whereas, according to the other, the state is a benefactor whose role is to improve the prospects of the least well-off members of society. Ronald Dworkin distinguishes between liberalism based on neutrality, which "takes as fundamental the idea that government must not take sides on moral issues and . . . supports only such egalitarian measures as can be shown to be the result of that principle," and liberalism based on equality, which "takes as fundamental the idea that government treats its citizens as equals and insists on moral neutrality only to the degree that equality requires it."[12]

Though liberalism is primarily a theory of the state, its principles can be applied to any of the basic institutions of a society; for one can argue that the role of the clinic, the corporation, the scholarly associations, or professions is not to dictate or even recommend the kind of life a person should aim at. Neutrality can serve as an ideal for the operations of these institutions much as it can for the state. Their role, one can argue, should be to facilitate whatever kind of life a student, patient, client, customer, or member is aiming at and not to promote one kind of life over another.

Liberalism in education

The principles of liberalism are particularly applicable to the institutions of education, for the principles that regulate schooling can be designed to advance one view of a good and meaningful life at the expense of others or to be indifferent between the various views. The ideal of liberal education carries the ideals of the liberal state into the schools, where it limits the schools to informing students about the different views of the good and teaching them the facts, skills, and techniques required to successfully pursue them.[13] On the liberal view, as Amy Gutmann writes in her book *Democratic Education*:

> Schools should teach the capacity for moral reasoning and choice without predisposing children toward any given conception of the good life or toward a particular moral character (aside from one defined by this capacity). Just as a liberal state must leave its adult citizens free to choose their own "good" life, so must its schools leave children free to choose their own values. If public schools predisposed citizens towards a particular way of life by educating them as children, the professed neutrality of the liberal state would be a cover for the bias of its educational system.[14]

The choice between views is to be left to the students or their families; whereas the choice between facts, skills, and techniques is to be left to the schools and to the professionals who run them.

The ideals of liberal education complement and reinforce those of the liberal state. The liberal state permits both liberal and parochial education but does not endorse any one parochial school over another. When the liberal state finances or administers schooling through a system of public education, the schools are based on liberal principles and are designed to be silent on questions of religious and moral value, or at least on questions over which the community is sharply divided. The liberal state tolerates partisan education, but any education offered by the state is committed to the ideals of political neutrality and nonpartisanship.

Liberalism in science

Liberalism is also applicable to the institutions of science and, in particular, to the social sciences. The rise of the social sciences, as many historians have noted, overlaps the rise of the liberal state.[15] The dream of philosophers in Europe in the seventeenth and eighteenth centuries was to bring the methods of experimental reasoning – the methods that had proved so successful in the study of nature – to the study of "man" and society.[16] Behind that dream was the belief that knowledge in the social sciences would further the growth of the liberal state and enable every citizen to perfect and advance his own life according to his own plans. Though the state was not to promote one plan or project over another, it was to promote the mastery of those facts, skills, and techniques required by every project, and the social sciences were thought to offer such a mastery. Citizens were to supply the ends, and the social sciences, with the support of the state and the schools, were to supply the know-how or means for achieving them.

The liberal ideal of neutrality was shared by the state, the schools, and the social sciences. The social sciences, it was thought, should not favor or advance one conception of the good over any other, any more than the state or the public schools should. Because questions about the good were thought to lie outside the sciences, the social sciences were expected to remain silent on questions or disputes concerning ultimate moral values.

> Science does not attempt to formulate the end which social and moral conduct ought to pursue.[17]

> Science as such, is nonmoral. There is nothing in scientific work, as such, which dictates to what ends the products of science shall be used.[18]

> Economics deals with ascertainable facts; ethics with valuations and obligations. The two fields of enquiry are not on the same plane of discourse. Between the generalizations of positive and normative studies there is a logical gulf fixed which no ingenuity can disguise and juxtaposition in space or time bridge over.[19]

The social sciences were to speak to questions of means, for these are matters of fact for which science can be expected to provide an answer, but were to remain silent on questions of ends, for these are best left to the subjects or clients of the science to decide.

While the arts were allowed to advance a conception of the good life, the sciences were forbidden to. The sciences were to be limited to statements of what is, whereas the arts could express ideals of what morally or politically ought to be. The division of labor between the sciences and the arts in the liberal state is described by Mill in an essay on the methods to be used in doing political economy:

> Science is a collection of *truths*; art a body of *rules*, or directions for conduct. The language of science is, This is, or, This is not; This does, or does not, happen. The language of art is, Do this; Avoid that. Science takes cognisance of a *phenomenon*, and endeavors to discover its *law*; art proposes to itself an *end*, and looks for *means* to effect it.[20]

*scholar of mistake practice of science
for its ideology —even abstract ideology
come from scientists —*

While the sciences, on Mill's view, should be limited to an objective and disinterested pursuit of the truth, the arts should have an ethical dimension, engage in partisan proselytizing, and promote one view of the good life over another.[21]

I call the social sciences "liberal" because the dominant view of social scientists is that they ought to be silent on questions of the good, and silent for many of the same reasons that liberal political theorists believe the state and the schools should be silent: namely, that different subjects have different conceptions of the good and that, like the state and the schools, social science can offer no good or persuasive reason for preferring one conception to another or would be imprudent to try.[22]

Without endorsing any of the competing conceptions, the social sciences, like the state and the schools, are supposed to benefit or assist their subjects and clients; they are supposed to offer instruments that are suited for use in achieving the good life no matter how it is conceived.

> Have scientists, then, no special function or obligation in determining the ends for which scientific knowledge is to be used? As scientists, *it is their business to determine reliably the immediate and remote costs and consequences of alternate possible courses of action*, and to make these known to the public.[23]

The liberal state is forbidden to use the law; the liberal schools are forbidden to use the classroom or curriculum; and the liberal social sciences are forbidden to use teaching or research to endorse one conception of the good over another. Their function is to provide citizens, students, subjects, or clients with the opportunity or capacity to pursue their own life plans or projects but to leave the choice of plans or projects to them to decide. The social sciences and social scientific expertise, according to the liberal ideal, should inform public policy and direct the liberal state in its efforts to support its citizens in their pursuit of their visions of the good life, but they should not, any more than should the state, endorse one vision and condemn the others.[24]

Liberal science in comparison with the liberal state

Besides value-neutrality, the social sciences share other ideals with the liberal state. Methods in the social sciences must be objective. Observations must be free of bias, and the choice of theories must be unaffected by personal taste or prejudice. The standards of science must be administered with an even hand and without any hint of favoritism. The practice must be disinterested and concerned only with the truth. The practice of government, on the liberal view, must be equally disinterested. The methods used in administering and enforcing the laws and policies adopted by the state must be objective; the personal or political views of state officials – for examples judges, tax assessors, and bank regulators – must not be allowed to influence how they enforce the laws or apply the policies. The prosecution of justice under the law must be unbiased; the law must be executed with an even hand; the interests and claims of citizens must be considered without any hint of favoritism. The practice of government must be answerable only to fairness and the rule of law, just as the practice of social science must be answerable only to the standards of reliable and valid data and the rules of scientific reasoning.

In addition, the liberal sciences and the liberal state both rest on a distinction between popular authority and professional expertise. On the liberal view, society is composed of two realms: the public and the private. The legitimate interests of the state are limited to the public realm – to the area in which the actions of one person violate the rights or undermine the autonomy of others; but a distinction is drawn in the public realm between issues best left to popular authority – to be decided or influenced by citizens through public hearings, elections, or other expressions of public opinion – and issues best left to experts. Questions of means – how best to accomplish some popular objective – and matters concerning the enforcement of laws, management of programs, or administration of policies are reserved for professionals or people with publicly recognized expertise, and only questions of ends are reserved for the public to debate or decide.

A similar distinction is drawn in research in the social sciences. The conduct of research is to be left to the experts, while the direction and application or use of the research findings are to be left to ordinary men and women to decide. Untutored opinion can influence the problems studied, but only the experts, those trained in the methods of the sciences, can choose the techniques and tools with which to study them. The experts decide whether the findings are valid, and laymen whether and how to use them. In both the liberal practice of science and the liberal practice of government, matters of ends are left to popular authority and matters of means to people with special training or know-how.[25] The liberal sciences, like the liberal state, reflect a pervasive feature of modern life: the rise of professionalization and the division of labor into labor for experts and labor for the popular will.[26] So, for example, questions of whether a lower birthrate, an increase in employment, or a decrease in the rate of divorce is desirable are left to those on the street – to anyone who knows what she wants – to answer; whereas questions of how to *measure?*

secure such changes are assigned to scholars who have knowledge of the mechanisms of the market or the family.

As with the liberal philosophy of the state, there are three schools of liberalism in the social sciences: skeptical, pragmatic, and autonomous. Many social scientists believe that the social sciences should be regulated by liberal principles and remain silent on issues of morality or politics, because they believe that the aim of science is the discovery of truth and that there are no moral truths to discover. Max Weber's principle reason for maintaining that the social sciences should be free of judgments of moral and political value, for example, was his moral skepticism.[27]

> Even such simple questions as the extent to which an end should sanction unavoidable means, or the extent to which undesired repercussions should be taken into consideration, or how conflicts between several concretely conflicting ends are to be arbitrated are entirely matters of choice or compromise. There are no (rational or empirical) scientific procedures of any kind whatsoever which can provide us with a decision here.[28]

Weber also supported value-freedom for pragmatic reasons. He believed that the social sciences could not win support from the state and from a wide audience of citizens or bureaucrats if they included political judgments along with the findings of their research.[29]

Most social scientists today defend value-neutrality in the social sciences. Some are moral skeptics and believe that science cannot discover what is good or meaningful in life, because reason cannot decide questions of the good. Thus Robbins writes: "If we disagree about ends it is a case of thy blood or mine – live and let live, according to the importance of the difference, or the relative strength of our opponents. But, if we disagree about means, then scientific analysis can often help us to resolve our differences."[30] Social science, on this view, like the natural sciences, is concerned only with the discovery of truth, and there is no truth concerning ends, according to the moral skeptic.

Other social scientists are pragmatists. They believe that there is enough for science to do without taking on questions of value and that the social sciences will better enhance their credibility and authority if they leave such questions alone. They believe that progress in the social sciences depends on support and trust from competing interests within the surrounding community and assume that such support and trust are more likely to be achieved and maintained if the sciences are silent on questions of moral and political value.

Finally, some social scientists advocate neutrality out of concern for the autonomy of the individuals or groups they are hoping to serve. They are committed to a conception of the good life according to which the choice of ends ought to be left to the clients or subjects and not given over to their science to decide. The social sciences, as they see it, should encourage, or at least respect, the autonomy of the individuals they are designed to observe and understand. They should treat them as thinking, willing, active beings who bear responsibility for their choices and are free to choose their own life plans.

Not every argument for a neutral state is equally an argument for a neutral science. For example, one argument for neutrality in government is that the all-embracing authority of the state makes it an inappropriate institution through which to rank or favor a conception of the good life. Though the social sciences have considerable authority in most modern societies, they do not have the coercive power of the state, and an illiberal science is less threatening to those who do not share its conception of human perfection than an illiberal state. Similarly, not every argument for a neutral science is equally an argument for neutrality in government. For example, one argument for neutrality in science is that the methods of science do not provide a basis on which to rank or favor one conception over another. Though this view of the methods of science is debatable, there is no question but that governments have the methods to rank and favor conceptions of the good. A democratic form of government can favor a conception of the good preferred by a majority of its citizens, and a dictatorship can favor one preferred by the dictator.

The view that science should be value-neutral predates the seventeenth and eighteenth centuries and the rise of liberal thought. As Jürgen Habermas points out in *Knowledge and Human Interests*, the ideal of value-neutrality can be traced to accounts in ancient Greek and Roman philosophy of the nature and importance of theoretical thought – that is, *theoria* – or of a disinterested contemplation of the nature of things free from the contingencies of history or human interest.[31] But the ideal of a *social* science – an inquiry into the nature of society and social life which is independent of human interests – is more recent and emerges as part of the liberal project of fashioning the basic institutions of society to skirt differences in moral outlook and of employing the method of experimental reasoning to the study of social life. The idea that the study of nature should be limited to questions of truth and fact and be free of all considerations of what is morally or politically desirable is old; but the idea that the study of the moral or social world should be so limited is new and part of our modern era and our increasing moral and political skepticism or our elevation of freedom from institutional authority over other moral and political values.

Partisanship in the social sciences

Many political theorists have argued that the state cannot be totally neutral or avoid advancing or supporting some of its citizens' projects over others or influencing its citizens' views of what is morally good or politically valuable.[32] Their arguments do not show that neutrality is inappropriate as an ideal for the state, only that neutrality can only be an ideal. My thesis in this book is that neutrality is not even appropriate as an ideal for the social sciences; for the arguments for neutrality are more compelling when applied to the conduct of the state than to that of the sciences, and partisanship is required by the norms of the sciences, but not by the laws of the state. As a result, many of the virtues that liberalism offers as a philosophy for government, it loses as a philosophy for science.

I believe that social scientists have told themselves and their subjects a false story about the relation between science and politics, and although the story serves a purpose – namely, in supporting the scientists' claims of disinterestedness and objectivity – it offers a misleading picture of the nature of social inquiry.[33] My aim is to question liberalism as a philosophy for the social sciences and to show how the practice of social science favors some policy objectives and ends over others. I don't maintain that there is a single agenda or view of the good life advanced by all of the liberal sciences – a single way in which the various social sciences are partisan – but only that every bit of research and teaching in each social science is partisan on some matter of moral or political value. Though all the sciences assume or advance some politics, I don't believe, as some critics do, that there is some politics that is assumed or advanced by all. The many values that color the many social sciences are, in my view, less a motif than a motley – a ragbag of cultural, racial, religious, sexual, and economic allegiances and loyalties.

A central idea in the social sciences is that social life should be studied at two levels: the level of the individual agent and the level of the social organization or structure within which the agent perceives, thinks about, or acts on the world. Surprisingly, many studies of value-neutrality in the social sciences look solely at the individual level. Weber, for example, was concerned with the teaching and writing of individual social scientists and not with the organization of the classrooms, laboratories, libraries, journals, and publishing houses in which the teaching or research takes place or is disseminated. He admonished his colleagues not to include statements of value in their scientific lectures and articles but did not consider how the organization of a university, lecture series, journal, textbook, curriculum, department, or professional association could assume the values of the larger, surrounding political community.

Most discussions of value-neutrality are at the level of the social scientists' choices of what to speak or write and how to speak or write it. If their speech or writing does not contain any overtly evaluative words, their science is thought to be value-neutral. Arthur Pigou had the individual perspective in mind when he wrote of the value-neutral economist:

> Their effort, though it may well be roused to action by the emotions, itself necessarily lies within the sphere of the intellect. Resentment at the evils investigated must be controlled, lest it militate against scientific exactitude in our study of their causes. Pity however sincere and grief however real are here intruders to be driven ruthlessly away. Stirred by their appeal we have entered the temple of science. Against them its doors are closed, and they must remain for our return.[34]

What Pigou did not consider seriously enough is whether the intruders, the threats to scientific exactitude, are not so much brought into the temple of science by the economists who worship there as built into the architecture of the temple – into its altar, tabernacle, and pews. Economists can leave their own values outside the door, but once inside, they will encounter windows, walls, floors, and furnishings that reflect the values of many generations of congregants. No matter how free of values their own words, values are embedded in the pulpit from which they speak and the altar at which the daily service is conducted.

The issue of value-neutrality in economics or any other social science parallels the issue of race or sex discrimination in schooling, employment, or the law. There are a number of different, distinctive ways in which our legal system can discriminate on the basis of race or sex.[35] The least controversial and easiest to identify is overt, intentional discrimination. Here the law or a legal institution explicitly takes the race or sex of a person into account in assigning opportunities, privileges, rewards, and penalties, and by intention the law is not neutral on the value of the person's race or sex. Racial discrimination was the intention behind the laws that enforced racial segregation in the United States until the Supreme Court began to overturn them 40 years ago. Laws that denied black Americans the vote, property ownership, or schooling intentionally discriminated against them and placed a low value on their lives or life plans.

Overt, intentional legal discrimination against black Americans is mostly behind us, but legal discrimination continues in many covert or unintentional forms. These are what people have in mind when they talk about institutional racism. De facto segregation is the most familiar example of institutional racism. In school districts where there is no intention to discriminate among students on grounds of race, school attendance districts based on housing will lead to racial segregation of the schools if there is intentional racial discrimination in housing or if race is a major determinant of income and housing is segregated by income. The system of neighborhood schools passes on to the schools racial discrimination in the housing or labor markets, and even if neutral on the matter of race at the level of the intention of teachers and school administrators, is not neutral at the level of actual schooling.

The jury system offers another example of institutional racism.[36] The law prohibits the intentional exclusion of black citizens from juries, but it permits a race-neutral jury selection process that can, and in mostly white jurisdictions often does, lead to all-white juries. When there is widespread racial prejudice, black defendants face an unfair jury trial from the race-neutral selection process, for the process, like the race-neutral school selection process in the case of *de facto* school segregation, passes the racial prejudice and bias of the surrounding community on to the courtrooms. School or court officials need not intend any racial bias, and they can be scrupulous in keeping any of their own racial prejudices from influencing their work. Nevertheless, the system they administer is partisan on issues of race; for it is biased in the schooling provided to black children or the justice provided to black adults.

The least controversial way that the social sciences can fail to be value-neutral and the easiest to identify is overt, intentional partisanship. Here social scientists include judgments of moral or political value in their teaching or research. By intention their work is not neutral on questions of the good life, for they have chosen to use words that clearly favor one stand on some moral or political issue over others. Weber's call for value-freedom in the social sciences was to eliminate overt forms of partisanship. Nazi social science is an example of overt, intentional non-neutrality. Promoting the ideal of Aryan superiority was the intention behind much of the psychological and sociological research conducted by Nazi social scientists, and judgments of superiority were included in their "scholarly" lectures and publications.

Overt, intentional partisanship in research in the social sciences is rarer today, as a result of Weber's influence and the continuing campaign to hold science above politics; but partisanship continues in a number of covert or unintentional forms. I have these in mind when I speak of institutional partisanship or the values built in to the altar or tabernacle of the temple. For example, with *de jure* partisanship in favor of heterosexual marriage over homosexual partnerships, social scientists say that one is good and the other bad or include their moral estimate of these relationships in their studies of domestic life. With *de facto* partisanship, on the other hand, social scientists hold their own moral judgments back but pass on those of their subjects by sorting their data into categories like married, unmarried, widowed, or divorced rather than into more inclusive categories like domestic partners, single, survivor of a domestic partner or former domestic partner.

Social scientists, as I explain in chapters 6 and 7, attempt to avoid partisanship in collecting and sorting their data by holding back their own values from their practice, but the norms or standards they employ in collecting and sorting pass the values of their subjects or clients to their data and into their categories. Though their work may be free of any intentional or *de jure* partisanship, it is not free of institutional or *de facto* partisanship, and the latter is as great a threat to liberal neutrality as the former.

Liberalism and academic freedom

The liberal ideals of value-neutrality in the social sciences and the schools are mutually supporting. The social sciences offer theories of liberal or value-neutral education or learning that are a basis for the organization of the classroom, the design of the curriculum, and the management of the schools. According to these theories, the schools can teach about values without promoting or endorsing them and talk about religious worship, marriage and divorce, sexuality, birth control, patriotism and civil disobedience, wealth and poverty, and mental illness or physical disability without being partisan. In addition, the liberal sciences are included in the curriculum of liberal education, and most of what students learn in school about the social world they learn through their instruction in these sciences. Finally, the sites of most research in the liberal sciences are institutions of higher learning, and in some of these sciences the theories that develop are tested in primary or secondary schools. Students are often experimental subjects for theories of intellectual and emotional development in psychology, for example, and the theories, once tested, are used by the schools to affect the students' development.

Central to the practice of liberal education is the ideal of academic freedom, and the ideals of academic freedom and neutral science are related in an interesting and surprising way. Together they support a practice within the university that is not intended by the faculty or staff. Here again rules that govern an institution combine to produce effects different from those intended by the members.

According to the ideal of academic freedom, rewards and punishments should not be distributed to teachers or students of the sciences or arts on the basis of their moral or political values but only on the basis of their work as measured by the standards of the discipline. Students who write good lab reports or exams should not be graded down because their politics are disapproved of. Academic freedom requires that within the school individuals be at liberty to conduct their teaching, learning, or research without fear that their work will be judged by their political commitments. Faculty whose political views are offensive to students, parents, an administrator, school board, trustee, or legislator should not be harassed, denied raises or promotions, or fired for their views. The liberal ideal of neutrality in the classroom supports the ideal of academic freedom, for to be neutral on conceptions of the good, the schools must not reward or punish faculty or students on the basis of their conceptions of the good.

While academic freedom is designed to protect politically unpopular views and the teachers or students who espouse them, value-neutrality in the sciences is designed to limit the location of political speech; for it directs teachers and students not to voice their values in the lab or the classroom – in disciplinary spaces – but to save the expression of values for other more public or more private places. Proposing ideals for the disciplines of science or the arts different from the ideals of public or private life establishes a disciplinary space between public and private. The ideal of value-neutrality in the social sciences prohibits political speech in the new, disciplinary space, and academic freedom permits the regulation of speech that the neutrality imposes.

Academic freedom protects teaching and research in the liberal sciences from political attack and influence as long as the work is seen to be value-neutral and free of political influence. An American university can deny tenure to a sociologist for including her feminist politics in her teaching or research without violating her academic freedom; for academic freedom does not protect the political speech of faculty or students that steps beyond the bounds of their discipline, and feminist sociology steps beyond the bounds of sociology as long as the ideals of that discipline include value-neutrality.

The statements of my own university's policy on academic freedom in its regulations concerning faculty tenure make the limited nature of academic freedom clear.

> The Board of Regents of the University of Minnesota bears witness to its faith [in the traditions of higher education] by entering upon its record the following statements concerning academic freedom:
> 1. The University of Minnesota should not impose any limitation upon the teacher's freedom in the exposition of his own subject in the classroom or in addresses and publications.

2. No teacher may claim as his right the privilege of discussion in his classroom [of] controversial topics that are not pertinent to the course of study that is being pursued.
3. The University of Minnesota should not place any restraint upon the teacher's freedom in the choice of subjects for research and investigation undertaken on his own initiative.
4. The University of Minnesota should recognize that the teacher in speaking or writing outside of the institution upon subjects beyond the scope of his own field of study is entitled to the same freedom and is subject to the same responsibilities as attach to all other citizens but in added measure.[37]

The statements continue, but the idea remains the same: academic freedom does not protect speech that is excluded by a faculty member's discipline, and therefore, given the ideal of value-neutrality, a member whose discipline is science cannot claim any right to engage in political speech in her lab or classroom.

As Amy Gutmann writes in her discussion of the relationship of academic freedom to democratic education:

> The core of academic freedom is the freedom of scholars to assess existing theories, established institutions, and widely held beliefs according to the canons of truth adopted by their academic disciplines, without fear of sanction by anyone if they arrive at unpopular conclusions. Academic freedom allows scholars to follow their autonomous judgment wherever it leads them, provided that they remain within the bounds of scholarly standards of inquiry.[38]

The proviso of remaining within the bounds of scholarly standards, she notes, is sometimes overlooked, but academic freedom rests on the idea that scholars have a duty to remain within those bounds: "Scholars must recognize a duty to observe scholarly standards of inquiry as a condition of their social office."[39] As long as the standards of inquiry in the social sciences include value-neutrality, scholarship in the social sciences must appear to be neutral for scholars to deserve their office, and scholars who include what their colleagues see as politically partisan judgments in their teaching or research are out of bounds and can be sanctioned or disciplined for their words.

When combined with academic freedom regulations, the norms of the social sciences can be a basis for punishing political speech within the university. According to historians of higher education, the norm of neutrality has often been cited to justify the dismissal or censure of faculty during times of political conflict.

> Academics were unwitting accomplices in [the Communist witch hunts] by virtue of the fact that, beginning in the last decade of the nineteenth century and continuing up until virtually the present day, they insisted on deluding themselves with the false idea of "objectivity" (as contrasted with, say, fairness and compassion). Once it had been established as a kind of natural law of the profession that professors were supposed to be resolutely objective and therefore of necessity above the battle, it was simple enough for state legislators, trustees, and administrators to fire them for taking unpopular "partisan" positions on controversial issues.[40]

The legislators, trustees, and administrators who censured the professors cannot be faulted for violating their academic freedom but can be praised for defending the liberal, scholarly standards of the social sciences against social science teachers who use the classroom to promote their political ideals.

In showing how values inform the social sciences, I oppose those scholarly standards and hope to remove a threat to openly partisan research and teaching in the university. Proper scholarly standards, I argue, are not violated by political speech, and scholars who include such speech in their work are not flouting their duty to observe scholarly standards of inquiry. Their work can be protected by their university's policy on academic freedom if the academic community can be persuaded that liberalism in science is not possible or desirable. As I suggested earlier, the liberal sciences have added another space – a disciplinary space – to the distinction within the liberal state between public and private arenas. Political speech, according to the liberal approach, is permissible in public and private, but not in any disciplinary spaces. A perfectionist approach would place the social sciences in the public space and increase the academic freedom of the social sciences.

Academic conservatives like Allan Bloom, William Bennett, Roger Kimball, and Dinesh D'Souza who oppose efforts to diversify the curriculum or critically interpret the canon complain that such efforts are politically partisan, and they appeal to the ideal of a value-neutral or liberal university to try to discredit them. Though, typically, their objection is to the introduction of political judgment into the humanities rather than the social sciences, they use university policies on academic freedom, just as the critics of leftist social science did in the 1950s, to bolster their case. Academics, they argue, have a duty to observe the scholarly standards of inquiry that are a condition of their office. The scholarly standards for teaching and research in the humanities, on their view, forbid politics in the interpretation and evaluation of works of art.[41] Only considerations of fact and aesthetic value should enter into literary or artistic interpretations or evaluations. Judgments of aesthetic value have a place in the classroom, but judgments of political value do not.

Feminist scholars and other "illiberal" members of the faculty fail to observe these standards and, so, on the conservatives' view, are failing in their academic duties. The conservatives exploit liberal ideals to attack scholars who promote the political values they oppose. University policy on academic freedom allows them to censure the scholars for failing in their academic duties; for universities have an obligation to uphold scholarly standards and enforce academic responsibility, and academic freedom permits them to do so.[42]

Many proponents of the new critical approaches to the humanities and social sciences do not understand that, should their scholarly discipline maintain a standard of value-neutrality, the liberal ideal of academic freedom gives them no right to practise the new teaching and scholarship and no protection from those who would censure them. In a recent exchange with John Searle over the "politicization" of the humanities, Gerald Graff, for example, writes: "What I did defend is an individual teacher's right to endorse any belief in the classroom, including a belief in 'social transformation' or 'the politics of the left.' I take it to be merely a restatement of a basic principle of academic freedom."[43] Graff is mistaken if the University of Minnesota's policy on academic freedom is any guide, for that policy states that no teacher may claim as his [sic] right the privilege of discussion in his classroom of controversial topics that are not pertinent to the course of study that is being pursued; and, on Searle's view and that of other critics of politics in the humanities and the university, the controversial topics that Graff and others are introducing into the classroom are not pertinent to the course of study – namely, the humanities – that is being pursued. To the extent that Searle's views on pertinence are favored on Graff's campus or favored by those in the university or scholarly community with the most power and prestige, Graff will be seen not to have any right to endorse the politics of the left in his classroom but to have a duty not to do so.

In short, the liberal ideals of the university are expressed in its policies of academic freedom, but these policies do not permit political expression when the expression is excluded by the norms of the academic disciplines. The norms of the liberal sciences exclude political expression, and, as a result, in order to enforce its own liberal ideals, the university can forbid the faculty from advancing a view of the good life or a conception of human perfection in their academic writings or their classrooms. Their academic freedom does not give them any right to practice an illiberal science. The ideal of neutrality within their discipline limits the freedom granted them by the ideal of neutrality within their university.

Conclusion

The liberal ideal of neutrality has been applied to the intellectual disciplines as much as to the state and to education. The idea in each case has been to limit the overt, intentional promotion of standards of human perfection or conceptions of the good to private spaces – to families, churches, civic organizations, and political parties. However, the proponents of the ideal have not appreciated the extent to which the architecture of the state, the schools, or an intellectual discipline like the social sciences is partisan and colors the practices that occur there with value. Still, neutrality can be defended as an ideal for the state. The aim of this book is to show why it cannot be equally defended as an ideal for the social sciences and to offer a number of alternative ideals that allow social scientists to join with families, churches, civic associations, and political parties to promote and advance a standard of human perfection.

NOTES

1 *The Compact Edition of the Oxford English Dictionary* (Oxford University Press, 1971), vol. 1, p. 1612.
2 Our word "science" comes from the Latin *scire* which means to know or to discern. Up through the seventeenth century, "science" was used to cover any body of interrelated beliefs that could be easily remembered or applied. However, in the eighteenth and nineteenth centuries, lexicographers came to distinguish science from the arts and from philosophy. The word "science" then came to mean a body of knowledge having an exact, objective, systematic basis.
3 J. Gray, *Liberalism* (University of Minnesota Press, 1986), pp. 7–26.
4 See B. A. Ackerman, *Social Justice in the Liberal State* (Yale University Press, 1980), p. 10. As Ackerman explains it, liberal principles imply that "nobody has the right to vindicate political authority by asserting a privileged insight into the moral universe which is denied the rest of us." See also R. Dworkin, *A Matter of Principle* (Harvard University Press, 1985), p. 205; B. Barry, *Political Argument* (Routledge and Kegan Paul, 1965), p. 66, who writes: "Classical liberalism has had other strands than this one, no doubt, but one was certainly the idea that the state is an instrument for satisfying the wants that men happen to have rather than a means for making good men (i.e., cultivating desirable wants or dispositions in its citizens)"; and A. Gutmann,

"Communitarian Critics of Liberalism," *Philosophy and Public Affairs*, 14 (1985), pp. 308–21.

5 J. Gray, *Liberalism*, p. 82.

6 For a discussion of perfectionism, see J. Rawls, *A Theory of Justice* (Harvard University Press, 1971), pp. 325–32.

7 Because male pronouns were used in the classics of political philosophy exclusively rather than inclusively – i.e., to include all males but no females – there is a problem in choosing pronouns today to paraphrase these classics. I don't want to reproduce the attitudes towards women assumed or expressed there, but neither do I want to misrepresent the classics by washing those attitudes out. My solution is to use male pronouns whenever it seems that the authors had only or mostly males in mind and female pronouns (inclusively) whenever I am speaking for myself.

8 Some political philosophers dispute whether there is an idea or principle that is shared by the variety of approaches to political life that are called "liberal," or whether all the approaches display some unity. With Dworkin and Ackerman, I believe that there is; but I will assume rather than argue for this view here.

9 Dworkin maintains that liberalism based on neutrality finds its most natural defense in some form of moral skepticism (*Matter of Principle*, p. 205), but John Stuart Mill and John Locke, fathers of the liberal theory of the state, did not rest their liberalism on any form of moral skepticism. As Brian Barry points out, Mill did not doubt that some conceptions of the good were better than others; he recommended only that the state act as if they were of equal merit. The most prominent examples of liberalism based on moral skepticism are in economics, where the idea is common that all judgments of value are mere expressions of personal preference or taste and, as a result, are not open to rational assessment. See, e.g., M. Friedman, *Capitalism and Freedom* (University of Chicago Press, 1982), pp. 110–15.

10 I. Berlin, "Two Concepts of Liberty," in *Four Essays on Liberty* (Oxford University Press, 1969), p. 131.

11 J. S. Mill's *On Liberty* is the source of this school of liberalism; but, as critics of Mill's argument for liberalism have pointed out, if neutrality is based on the goodness of autonomy, then the ideal of a neutral state is not, itself, neutral between competing views of the good; and the state, in remaining neutral on moral questions in order to encourage or preserve autonomy, is enforcing one conception of the good over others.

12 Dworkin, *Matter of Principle*, p. 205.

13 The word "liberal" in "liberal education" can be understood in either of two ways: as it was in the Renaissance to cover general as against specialized or vocational training or as it was in the eighteenth century to cover policies or institutions that emphasized neutrality and autonomy. Here it is intended in the second sense. Not all theories of liberal education emphasize neutrality. In *Democracy and Education*, John Dewey, e.g., maintained that the schools, public and private, should develop in children the habits or virtues of fair-mindedness and courage; still, these virtues are relatively formal, and Dewey did not think that even these should be taught so much as inspired or encouraged.

14   A. Gutmann, *Democratic Education* (Princeton University Press, 1987), p. 55.

15   The most provocative and, to my mind, interesting account of the relations
     between the rise of the liberal state and the social sciences is given by members
     of the Frankfurt school of social thought – see, e.g., P. Connerton (ed.), *Critical
     Sociology* (Penguin, 1976) – and by Michel Foucault, *Discipline and Punish: The
     Birth of the Prison*, tr. A. Sheridan (Random House, 1979). They argue that
     the ideals of the social sciences derive from the ideals and practices of the state.
     That is not my claim. I am not trying to explain how the social sciences came
     to be liberal but only to show that they have attempted to be liberal in much
     the same sense as has the state.

16   The subtitle of David Hume's *Treatise of Human Nature* is "Being an Attempt
     to Introduce the Experimental Method of Reasoning into Moral Subjects."

17   G. H. Mead, "Scientific Methods and Moral Sciences," in *Selected Writings*,
     ed. A. J. Reck (University of Chicago Press, 1964), p. 256.

18   G. Lundberg, *Can Science Save Us?* (Longmans, Green and Co., 1947), p. 28.

19   L. Robbins, *An Essay on the Nature and Significance of Economic Science*, 2nd
     edn (Macmillan and Co., 1952), p. 148.

20   J. S. Mill, *Essays on some Unsettled Questions of Political Economy* (Longmans,
     Green, Reader and Dyer, 1874), p. 124; emphasis original.

21   Mill's distinction between the sciences and the arts is opposed by critics of the
     multicultural university. According to many critics of the growth of minority
     and feminist scholarship and instruction in American universities, the new
     scholarship and instruction is political, whereas traditional scholarship and
     instruction are not. They recommend that scholars in the arts and humanities
     study, interpret, or appreciate a work of art or literature without allowing
     political values to intrude, just as proponents of a value-neutral social science
     recommend that the social scientist study, interpret, or theorize the behavior
     of an individual or group without allowing such values to intrude. See, e.g.,
     D. D' Souza, "Illiberal Education," *Atlantic*, 267 (1991), pp. 51–79, and my
     discussion of recent attacks on partisanship in the arts and humanities at the
     end of this chapter.

22   Not all social scientists subscribe to the ideal of nonpartisanship. Some soci-
     ologists and economists have proposed perfectionist approaches to their sci-
     ence. For a discussion of perfectionist ideals in sociology, see L. Bramson, *The
     Political Context of Sociology* (Princeton University Press, 1961); and for ex-
     amples of perfectionism in economics, see T. W. Hutchinson, *"Positive" Econ-
     omics and Policy Objectives* (Allen and Unwin, 1964), pp. 23–50.

23   Lundberg, *Can Science Save Us?*, p. 29; emphasis original.

24   The liberal sciences can reveal inconsistencies in the goals or preferences of a
     subject – i.e., they are allowed to comment on the form but not the content or
     substance of the goals or preferences. See M. Weber, *The Methodology of the
     Social Sciences*, tr. and ed. E. Shils and H. Finch (Free Press, 1968), pp. 52–4.

25   Today we associate liberalism with democracy; but there is no necessary
     connection between the two. Whereas, for a time, ancient Athens had a demo-
     cratic government (for male citizens), the government was never liberal.
     The idea that on questions of virtue – the nature of piety, justice, courage,

temperance, and wisdom – the state should be neutral was no part of Greek political thought. Conversely, the state or any other social institution can be liberal but undemocratic. A constitutional monarchy is governed by royal command rather than popular will, but the monarch can be bound to rule according to liberal ideals and principles. Hobbes's Leviathan was such a monarch. I return to the relation between liberal and democratic ideals in chapter 10.

26 See R. N. Bellah, R. Madsen, W. M. Sullivan, A. Swidler and S. M. Tipton, *Habits of the Heart: Individualism and Commitment in American Life* (University of California Press, 1985), pp. 226–7, for a discussion of the growth of expertise in relation to a number of American institutions, especially religion. For a discussion of the nature and significance of professionalization, see A. Abbott, *The System of Professions: An Essay on the Division of Labor* (University of Chicago Press, 1988). Professionalization links the social sciences with the liberal state in the following way. Central to the development of the social sciences is their emergence as professions, and a hallmark of the professions is their role as learned servants to the public. Members of professions like medicine and law and disciplines like economics and psychology develop or acquire specialized knowledge with the hope or aim that such knowledge will further the ends of their public – viz., their patients, clients, or subjects. Public service is also the function of the liberal state, a function that is carried out by professionals who are often, by training, social scientists and whose clients or subjects are citizens of the state. With both the social sciences and the state, the servants are expected to defer to their masters, the public, for purpose and direction, and remain neutral on questions of value over which the masters disagree.

27 As I explain in chapter 2, although Weber maintained that the social sciences should be value-free, he did not claim that they should be value-neutral; and while he is often seen as a proponent of liberal science, his ideal of value-freedom is not the liberal ideal that all aspects of a social science, including the methods of reasoning, should be neutral concerning the nature of the good or standards of human perfection. That is, I will offer an interpretation of Weber as a philosopher of the social sciences who supports, rather than opposes, most of my own illiberal views. Weber's views, as I interpret them, are still somewhat puzzling, however; for, although he believed that the practice of the social sciences must rely on the scientist's own judgments of cultural significance, and, as a result, his conception of the good, he was nevertheless a moral skeptic, believing that reason could not resolve disputes concerning the ultimate good.

28 M. Weber, *Methodology*, pp. 18–19.

29 See M. Weber, *Max Weber on Universities*, tr. and ed. E. Shils (University of Chicago Press, 1973).

30 Robbins, *Essay*, p. 150.

31 J. Habermas, *Knowledge and Human Interests*, tr. J. J. Shapiro (Beacon Press, 1971), p. 303.

32 See, e.g., B. Barry, *Political Argument*, p. 75.

33 See Habermas, *Knowledge and Human Interests*, p. 311.

34 A. C. Pigou, *Unemployment* (Home University Library, 1913), pp. 10–11.

35   See R. Wasserstrom , "Racism, Sexism and Preferential Treatment: An Approach to the Topics," *UCLA Law Review*, 24 (1977), pp. 581–622, for a discussion of the different ways in which the laws can be biased against the members of one race or sex.

36   This example is from ibid.

37   *Regulations Concerning Faculty Tenure*, University of Minnesota, July 1, 1985. The male pronouns are a reflection of an earlier practice in the University of Minnesota of discriminating against women. The language is currently being revised to reflect the University's present commitment to affirmative action.

38   Gutmann, *Democratic Education*, p. 175.

39   Ibid.

40   Page Smith, "Letter," *New York Review of Books*, 33 (1987), pp. 60–1.

41   In maintaining that value-neutrality should be an ideal of research and teaching in the humanities, the academic conservatives seem to reject the earlier view, advanced by Mill and others (see n. 20), that although the social sciences should be prohibited from advancing a conception of the good life, the arts and humanities should be encouraged to do so. I owe this point to Doug Lewis and Naomi Scheman.

42   Feminist scholars do not accept the view that scholarly standards in the humanities forbid the introduction of politics in the interpretation of texts. They are not proponents of the philosophy of value-neutrality for either the social sciences or the humanities, and they attempt to get their own scholarly standards accepted by editors, publishers, university officials, and leaders of their professional associations. However, where they are not successful, they cannot turn to traditional policies on academic freedom to oppose the conservatives. These policies offer no more protection from attacks from the right today than they did during the McCarthy era.

43   Gerald Graff, " 'The Storm over the University': A Further Exchange," *New York Review of Books*, 38 (1991), p. 62.

2

Max Weber and the methodology of the social sciences

It is common today for social scientists to maintain that their work is or should be free of judgments of personal, cultural, moral, and political value. They attribute this idea to Max Weber, who, in a number of essays written between 1904 and 1917, argues against the promotion of values in economics and sociology.[1] Weber is not the first to warn against values in the social sciences; Mill, Sidgwick, Marshall, and John Neville Keynes before him each fathered the idea that ethical and political judgments are not the business of the social sciences.[2] Keynes, for example, wrote in 1890: "It is not . . . the function of science to pass ethical judgments; and political economy regarded as a positive science may, therefore, be said to be independent of ethics."[3] Nevertheless, Weber nurses the distinction between social science and politics and makes it robust, and many social scientists today credit him with the view that the social sciences should be value-neutral and turn to his methodological writings for the reasons.

Weber's own liberal view of science rests on his distinction between value-freedom and value-relevance. When it comes to discovery, Weber concedes, personal, cultural, moral, or political values cannot be eliminated from the social sciences; what social scientists choose to investigate or discover, they choose on the basis of the values they expect their investigations to advance. But Weber called on the social sciences to be value-free. They should not present their values, he said, as part of their findings – part of what they have discovered through their investigations. The findings should be value-free; and they *are* value-free, on Weber's view, if and only if they do not contain any judgments of personal, cultural, moral, and political value.

Weber's call for value-freedom assumes that research in the social sciences *can* be value-free. In chapter 9, I argue, against Weber, that the language of the social sciences cannot be cleansed of moral or political values. However, my aim in this chapter is to show that theories in the social sciences, like Weber's, that rely on ideal-types would be partisan even if they were value-free in Weber's sense.

Weber's distinction between value-freedom and value-relevance does not capture the full play of values in the social sciences; so I employ a broader distinction – namely, that between neutrality and partisanship, where value-neutrality means neutrality between competing conceptions of the good. Weber's value-freedom is a proper part of neutrality, for a body of teaching or writing can be value-free, in Weber's sense, and yet partisan. For theories to be value-neutral, their language must be free of values, but so too must the grounds on which they are confirmed or justified. Whatever words they employ, if the reasons for choosing between two or more theories are practical, the theories are not value-neutral but partisan; for practical reasons include judgments which, from Weber's perspective, are judgments of value, and the practical reasons for choosing one theory in the social sciences over another include moral and political values.

Weber's concept of value-relevance

Weber says that the social sciences should be value-free, but he also says that they should be value-relevant. He does not believe, as some social scientists do, that teaching or writing in the social sciences should or can be disinterested or unbiased. Values have to be implicated in parts of the practice of the social sciences if the practice is to be purposeful or rational. Without a desire to serve some personal, cultural, moral, or political interests over others, social scientists would have no reason to teach or write at all. "An attitude of moral indifference," Weber writes, "has no connection with scientific objectivity."[4]

A study is value-relevant, on Weber's view, if a judgment of value rationalizes an interest in the study. Since an interest can be rationalized only by a judgment of value, if an interest in a study can be rationalized at all, the study is value-relevant. Weber writes:

> The problems of the empirical disciplines are, of course, to be solved "non-evaluatively." They are not problems of evaluation. But the problems of the social sciences are selected by the value-relevance of the phenomena treated. . . . It should only be recalled that the expression "relevance to values" refers simply to the philosophical interpretation of that specifically scientific "interest" which determines the selection of a given subject matter and the problems of empirical analysis.[5]

In the social sciences the stimulus to the posing of scientific problems is in actuality always given by practical "questions." Hence the very recognition of the existence of a scientific problem coincides, personally, with the possession of specifically oriented motives and values.[6]

It is due to the evaluative ideas with which he unconsciously approaches his subject matter, that he has selected from an absolute infinity a tiny portion with the study of which he concerns himself. . . . To be sure, without the investigator's evaluate ideas, there would be no principle of selection of subject-matter and no meaningful knowledge of the concrete reality. Just as without the investigator's conviction regarding the significance of particular cultural facts, every attempt to analyze concrete reality is absolutely meaningless, so the direction of his personal belief, the refraction of values in the prism of his mind, gives direction to his work.[7]

Weber uses the phrase "relevance to values" to refer to the values that give social scientists a reason to favor one question or study over another; but the values need not be their own. There are psychologists at the University of Minnesota, for example, who study the relation between intelligence and genes but have no interest in eugenics. Yet, the Prime Minister of Singapore has such an interest and endorses their study because he believes that their findings will serve it. As a result, whatever the ends that guide the psychologists in Minnesota, their study is relevant to the Prime Minister's plans to promote eugenics.

Some charges of bias in the social sciences can be understood in terms of value-relevance. Feminist critics of the social sciences have claimed, for example, that the social sciences are biased against women.

Critics argue that traditional social science has begun its analyses only in men's experiences. That is, it has asked only the questions about social life that appear problematic from within the social experiences that are characteristic for men (white, Western, bourgeois men, that is). It has unconsciously followed a "logic of discovery" which we could formulate in the following way: Ask only those questions about nature and social life which (white, Western, bourgeois) men want answered.[8]

The interests which rationalize the choice of questions in the social sciences, according to the critics, are much more often those of men than women; men's interests decide what gets picked out as a problem and studied much more often than women's do; or, whatever the reasons behind the choices, the interests of men are better served by these choices than the interests of women. As a result, much that is written in the social sciences is more relevant to the values of men than of women.

A recent book on corporate crime argues that sociology is biased in favor of corporations over customers and employees; for, while sociologists have conducted only a handful of studies of corporate violence, they have conducted many studies of street and family violence.[9] The lack of attention to corporate crime, the book suggests, serves the interests of corporations that engage in crime over the interests of their victims. The decision to study street rather than corporate crime supports the public policy of policing the streets more assiduously than the corporate boardrooms.

Again, the point can be put in terms of value-relevance: writing on crime in sociology is more relevant to the values of corporate criminals than to those of the victims of corporate crime. This is not to say that the corporate values are what lead sociologists to study one form of crime over another, for the sociologists who study crime may not share those values; but whether they share them or not, if their studies serve them better than they serve the values of the victims, then, in at least one perfectly clear and significant sense, they are biased in favor of criminal corporations.

When Weber speaks of value-relevance, he has more in mind than the values that rationalize the choice of questions asked. He is also thinking of the values that rationalize the way we ask the questions and the direction we take in answering them. According to Weber, values not only give social scientific work direction; they also give it content. The social scientist not only chooses what social phenomena to study; he chooses a particular point of view from which to study them, and that point of view influences how they are theorized or explained. For, "there is no absolutely 'objective' scientific analysis of culture or ... of 'social phenomena' independent of special and 'one-sided' viewpoints according to which – expressly or tacitly, consciously or unconsciously – they are selected, analyzed and organized for expository purposes."[10] In order to understand or explain the social or cultural phenomena they study, social scientists must relate the phenomena to their interests.

> The number and type of causes which have influenced any given event are always infinite and there is nothing in the things themselves to set some of them apart as alone meriting attention. . . . Order is brought into this chaos only on the condition that in every case only part of concrete reality is interesting and significant to us,

because only it is related to the cultural values with which we approach reality.[11]

In the empirical social sciences ... the possibility of meaningful knowledge ... is bound up with the unremitting application of viewpoints of a specifically particularized character, which, in the last analysis, are oriented on the basis of evaluative ideas.[12]

They do this by employing what Weber calls "value-concepts."

The significance of a configuration of cultural phenomena and the basis of this significance cannot however be derived from and rendered intelligible by a system of analytical laws (*Gesetzesbegriffen*), however perfect it may be, since the significance of cultural events presupposes a value-orientation towards these events. The concept of culture is a value-concept. Empirical reality becomes "culture" to us because and insofar as we relate it to value ideas. It includes those segments and only those segments of reality which have become significant to us because of this value-relevance.[13]

By employing value-concepts in their work, social scientists allow their interests to guide not only their selection of questions to ask but also the way in which the questions are answered.[14]

Because the social sciences must employ value-concepts or include judgments of cultural significance, they are relevant to values in a way that the natural sciences are not. The aim of the natural sciences, according to Weber, is knowledge of general laws governing all empirical phenomena.[15] The aim of the social sciences, by contrast, is knowledge of the phenomena of life in terms of their cultural significance. The social sciences study reality under the guidance of values which lend it significance, whereas the reality studied in the natural sciences is a matter not of cultural interest or perspective but only of the natural world itself.[16] In short, studies in the social sciences are relevant to values in at least two ways: values rationalize the decision to undertake the study and are included in the judgments of significance necessary to carry it out.

Values, on Weber's view, must direct investigation in the social sciences, and so the social sciences must be value-relevant. However, at the same time, Weber thinks that they should be value-free. What does Weber mean by value-freedom, and how is it possible that studies in the social sciences can be both value-free and value-relevant?

Weber's concept of value-freedom

By "value-judgment" Weber means "practical evaluations regarding the desirability or undesirability of social facts from ethical, cultural or other points of view."[17] Value-freedom is simply a matter of the language used in the social sciences. The social sciences are value-free, on Weber's view, if their language is free of value-judgments. Weber calls on social scientists to exclude value-judgments from their writings and teachings, but his call for value-freedom is not one call but two. He exhorts them not to present their personal, cultural, ethical, or political values in their lectures or publications; but he also exhorts them not to suggest that these values follow from their facts. It is a fundamental imperative of scientific freedom, he writes, to make it "constantly clear to readers ... exactly at which point the scientific investigator becomes silent and the evaluating and acting person begins to speak."[18] "What is really at issue is the intrinsically simple demand that the investigator and teacher should keep unconditionally separate the establishment of empirical facts ... and his own political evaluations."[19]

On Weber's view, there are two questions of value-freedom, a practical and a logical question. The practical question is whether social scientists should include value-judgments in their teachings or writing.[20] Weber maintains that this question is one of practical policy and cannot be discussed scientifically. The answer depends on one's value system, and one's value-system, according to Weber, is not rationally debatable.[21]

The logical question is whether there is a logical connection between fact and value, between what is and what should be,[22] and whether social scientists should speak or write as if their values followed from their facts.[23] This question, according to Weber, is one not of practical evaluation but of logical or scientific truth: is it true that values can be inferred from facts, or are judgments of fact and value entirely distinct? On Weber's view, values cannot be inferred from facts, and honesty in science prohibits social scientists from claiming or suggesting otherwise.

Weber's position on value-freedom has been adopted by most recent defenders of ethical and political restraint in the social sciences. Kurt Klappholz, in his paper "Value Judgments and Economics," and Lionel Robbins, in his book An Essay on the Nature and Significance of Economic Science, for example, espouse Weber's position on the "logical question" of values in the social sciences.[24] According to Klappholz and Robbins, economics is independent of all value-premises, for it is not possible to infer proposals from hypotheses. There is a logical gap between the statements of positive or descriptive studies, like economics, and normative or prescriptive studies, like ethics and political philosophy.

Klappholz traces the logical claim back to Hume's observation that "ought" cannot be inferred from "is."[25] Since the scientific part of economics, Klappholz writes, consists exclusively of descriptive statements, it cannot have any ethical entailment and is independent of all value-premises. Klappholz and Robbins believe, as did Weber, that it is an imperative of intellectual honesty for economists to make it clear that no value-judgments are entailed by the descriptive part of their studies.

Milton Friedman, in his paper "The Methodology of Positive Economics," and Lionel Robbins espouse Weber's position on the "practical question" of values in the social sciences.[26] According to Robbins and Friedman, economics should exclude all value premises and include only descriptive statements. Their reasons for calling for such an exclusion is practical. With descriptive statements, differences of viewpoint, in principle, can be eliminated by the progress of positive economics, while fundamental differences over basic values are, according to Friedman, "differences about which men can only fight";[27] or, as Robbins writes:

In the rough-and-tumble of political struggle, differences of opinion may arise either as a result of differences about ends or as a result of differences about the means of attaining ends. Now, as regards the first type of difference, neither economics nor any other science can provide any solvent. If we disagree about ends it is a case of thy blood or mine – or live and let live, according to the importance of the difference, or the relative strength of our opponents. But, if we disagree about means, then scientific analysis can often help us to resolve our differences.[28]

Irreconcilable differences are the reason for economists to exclude value-judgments from their teaching and writing, for differences between economists on questions of ultimate value cannot be resolved by any form of scientific reasoning, so their inclusion can only leave economists divided.

Robbins and Friedman share Weber's view that all scientific reasoning is reasoning about means to given ends[29] and that there is no scientific reasoning about ends. Like Weber, they believe that all judgments of ultimate value are irrational. Weber writes:

Even such simple questions as the extent to which an end should sanction unavoidable means, or the extent to which undesired repercussions should be taken into consideration, or how conflicts between several concretely conflicting ends are to be arbitrated are entirely matters of choice or compromise. There are no (rational or empirical) scientific procedures of any kind whatsoever which can provide us with a decision here.[30]

Judgments of ultimate value, on Weber's view, are not the conclusion of any act of reasoning but the expression of a personal commitment.

> Only on the assumption of belief in the validity of values is the attempt to espouse value-judgments meaningful. However, to judge the validity of such values is a matter of faith. It may be a task for a speculative interpretation of life and in the quest of their meaning. But it certainly does not fall within the province of an empirical science in the sense practised here.[31]

Science and empirical analysis, according to Weber, can provide an answer only to a question of means or a "technical criticism" of a person's ends in the sense of providing a clarification or explication of the relation between them.[32]

The practical question of value-freedom is not rationally debatable, for it is a question of ultimate ends.[33] As a result, Weber believes that it is not within the province of the sciences to settle it. Only if the question is whether inclusion of a value-judgment is a means to a given end is it a question for which the social sciences can offer a solution.

Weber's ideal of value-freedom is narrower than the liberal ideal. The point can best be made using the distinction between the context of justification and the context of discovery.[34] According to the liberal ideal, values cannot be excluded from the context of discovery; but they can and should be excluded from the context of justification. Values should be relevant to discovery but not to justification. On Weber's view, by contrast, values should be relevant to both. Value-freedom requires that values be excluded from the formulation of the findings of the research, but value-relevance requires that they be relevant to the context of discovery and also to the context of justification; for, as I explained earlier, when Weber speaks of value-relevance, he means that values rationalize the scientists' choice of questions and also their choice of answers. For Weber, value-freedom is a matter of what social scientists say, not why they say it; as a result, his approach to the social sciences is much less liberal than most of his followers and admirers think.

The practical and logical questions of value-freedom

Weber's own practical reasons for opposing the use of judgments of value in teaching and writing in the social sciences included his own ultimate political values and, in particular, his commitment to a more rational organization and management of the German economy and state. At the time when Weber called upon his colleagues not to include judgments of value in their teaching or writing, few of the offices in government or industry in Germany were held by people who were well trained to solve questions of means. Weber thought that the best way to increase the power and economic prosperity of Germany was to train a new managerial class, a class learned about means and silent about ends. The mission of the university, on Weber's view, should be to offer such training.[35] A faculty that limited its teaching and writing to questions that science can settle would contribute more to this mission, he thought, than one that tried to inculcate political, ethical, or cultural values.[36]

At the time of his writing this, value-freedom was especially important to Weber, because, on his view, (a) university hiring in the social sciences was controlled by political officials; (b) only if the faculty in the social sciences refrained from making political judgments critical of these officials or their policies would they relinquish their control; and (c) only if they relinquished their control would the faculty be able to effectively train students to solve questions of means. In particular, so long as these officials had control over who taught at the universities, the teachers would be chosen not on the basis of their scientific know-how but on the basis of their political commitments. However, so long as the faculty included political judgments in their teachings and writings, the officials had a reason to maintain their control.[37]

One incident that, for Weber, forcefully demonstrated the state's control was "the Bernhard affair."[38] In 1908, Ludwig Bernhard was appointed on the initiative of Friedrich Althoff, head of the Department of University Affairs in the Prussian Ministry of Education, to a full professorship of economics at the University of Berlin. The appointment was made without consultation with the university faculty.[39]

Weber's objection to Althoff's action was that it took the appointment decision out of the hands of those with the know-how – namely, the faculty of the university. Had the faculty been allowed to decide, their judgment would have been a scientific one, a knowledgeable and objective assessment of the intellectual merits of the various candidates. Althoff's decision, by contrast, was based not on the facts of academic merit but on Althoff's own political preferences and values; yet, in the circumstances, Althoff's decision was reasonable, for, given that members of the faculty used their pulpits to oppose him, it was understandable that, in an effort to protect his position, he should use his power to put a friend rather than an opponent in a university chair.

The way to convince officials like Althoff to give up their control and grant academic freedom to the universities of Prussia, Weber thought, was to convince the professors to free their professional teachings and writings of political judgments. "This privilege of freedom from outside control seems in any case to be appropriate only to the sphere of specialized qualifications of the professor. There is, however, no specialized qualification for personal prophecy, and for this reason it is not entitled to that privilege from external control."[40] Weber allowed, however, that reason was not entirely on his side; for if preaching politics was an ultimate end for the professors, there was no line of reasoning that would convince them not to use their pulpits to oppose Althoff or vent their politics. Therefore, Weber concluded that the question of whether to include political value-judgments in the social sciences could not be definitively settled and was not, for that reason, scientifically resolvable.

While the practical question of value-freedom, on Weber's view, is not rationally resolvable, the logical question is. The social scientist should not offer value-judgments in the name of science, because value-judgments cannot be inferred from or fully rationalized by science.[41]

> It is simply naive to believe . . . that it is possible to establish and to demonstrate as scientifically valid "a principle" for practical social science from which the norms for the solution of practical problems can be unambiguously derived.[42]

> The validity of a practical imperative as a norm and the truth-value of an empirical proposition are absolutely heterogeneous in character.[43]

Weber did not appeal to any empirical evidence or logical reasoning to show that judgments of fact and value are absolutely heterogeneous in character. Apparently he believed that the distinctness of fact and value was obvious to his audience. Nevertheless, the question of their distinctness, on Weber's view, is a question of fact rather than of value and so is susceptible to rational settlement. As a result, Weber is committed to there being, in principle at least, a means of convincing a skeptic, no matter what his or her values or cultural point of view – whether he is a German or she is a Chinese – that judgments of fact and value are distinct.

> It has been and remains true that a systematically correct scientific proof in the social sciences, if it is to achieve its purpose, must be acknowledged as correct even by a Chinese – or more precisely stated – it must constantly strive to attain this goal, which perhaps may not be completely attainable due to faulty data.[44]

A Chinese, Weber tells us, can lack a sense of our ethical imperatives, but he or she cannot lack a sense of our logical or scientific truths.[45] The Chinese can lack Weber's sense that teachers should not vent their politics in the classroom but not his sense that their political judgments and judgments of fact are absolutely heterogeneous.

There are, of course, people everywhere who doubt that facts and values are distinct and believe that values can be inferred from facts; but Weber assumes that there is some reasoning that, in principle at least, could convince them otherwise. Here I note only that the presence of a substantial and long-standing disagreement over the logical question should have made Weber suspicious. The long-standing, unresolved disagreement over whether facts and values are entirely heterogeneous should have been reason for him to suspect that whether they are is not a question of fact but of value.

Value-freedom and value-neutrality

Value-freedom, for Weber, is a matter of the words used in a theory, not of how the theory is chosen or justified.[46] Weber did not believe that a choice among value-free theories was simply a matter of fit between theory and data. He realized that disagreements in science over the acceptability of theories are common and that often no appeal to the data or evidence can resolve them. All the evidence may support the competing theories equally well, and he knew that the history of even the natural sciences is marked by extended disagreement over rival frameworks which were equally well supported by the available evidence.[47] Because theories are underdetermined by their evidence, there is a gap between what a theory says and what the data show.

What closes the gap are theoretical virtues. Choice between empirically equivalent theories is based on the judgment that one is more fruitful, more explanatory, more predictive, simpler, or more conservative than another and a judgment that more fecundity, simplicity, or explanatory or predictive power is desirable.[48] However, the judgment that the simpler or more conservative of two theories is the more desirable is value-laden, and so the premises that rationalize the choice of one scientific theory over another include a judgment of value: the judgment that one should choose the simpler or more conservative of two empirically equivalent theories. In short, differences between scientists or scientific communities in value commitments can affect their scientific analyses of a body of empirical data or choice of a theory; so practical imperatives – for example, opt for simplicity – are part of the reasoning in support of one theory and against another, and a theory is not value-neutral but partisan if the rationalization of the choice of the theory relies on a judgment of value.

The question is not whether a choice between theories in the natural or social sciences relies on judgments of value but whether the values are nonscientific (cultural) – for example, moral or political – values. Defenders of the liberal ideal maintain that theories should be neutral on questions of nonscientific, rather than scientific, value. The theoretical virtues are values, but, on the liberal view, they are the values of science. Neutrality in science cannot preclude practical reasoning but should preclude reasoning based on "practical evaluations regarding the desirability or undesirability of social facts from ethical, cultural or other points of view."[49] The dependence of theoretical facts on the value of simplicity or predictive power is not proof of partisanship, a liberal would say; for simplicity and predictive power are scientific values.

Weber's objection to judgments of value is that disputes over them are not rationally resolvable, since ultimate values, on his view, are irrational. But ultimate scientific values are no better off, in this respect, than ultimate cultural values. As a result, from Weber's perspective, there should be no more objection, in principle, to relying on cultural values than to relying on values like predictive power in the choice of theories in science. Nevertheless, proponents of liberal science do distinguish between scientific values – the theoretical virtues – and cultural values or virtues. They argue that a commitment to predictive or explanatory power, simplicity, or fecundity does not favor one conception of the good over others.[50] Social scientists who disagree over the nature of human perfection, they would say, nevertheless agree that accurate predictions are a virtue.

Weber, however, does not believe that the theoretical virtues are sufficient for theory choice in the social sciences. On his view, the choice must look to cultural values as well. The social sciences, according to Weber, should employ a special kind of theoretical term – what he calls an "ideal-type" – and the choice of ideal-types relies on judgments of cultural value in addition to the theoretical virtues. That is, for the conduct of the social sciences, the theoretical virtues are not virtue enough, and the choice of theory must look to other values as well.

Ideal-types and value-neutrality

Weber does not assume that all judgments in social science should be of empirical fact; rather, he maintains that some should be of ideal-types.

> Pure economic theory in its analysis of past and present society, utilizes ideal-type concepts exclusively. Economic theory makes

certain assumptions which scarcely ever correspond completely with reality but which approximate it in various degrees and asks: how would men act under these assumed conditions, if their actions were entirely rational? It assumes the dominance of pure economic interests and precludes the operation of political or other non-economic considerations.[51]

All specifically Marxian "laws" and development constructs are ideal-types – in so far as they are theoretically sound.[52] = internally consistent

A social science in our sense is concerned with practical significance. This significance however can very often be brought unambiguously to mind only by relating the empirical data to an ideal limiting case.[53]

Judgments of ideal-types are not of empirical fact, for they are about some ideal and not any empirical reality. They are assessed on the basis not of their fit with the cultural phenomena but on how well they make the significance of the cultural phenomena clear.

Ideal-types are defined by traits that are not possessed by any actual individual or group. Some individuals or objects may possess some of the traits that make up the type, but no individual or group possesses all of them. In this respect, ideal-types are different from ordinary class-terms. A class-term can be true of the data; an ideal-type cannot be, for it offers a standard or norm against which the data can be measured, rather than a description to which they can be fitted.[54] An individual may be compared to an ideal-type, but he or she cannot be an instance of one.[55]

An ideal-type is a synthesis or idealization which the investigator constructs for certain heuristic purposes. The primary purpose of an ideal-type, according to Weber, is to enable the social scientist to offer a causal explanation of the facts of social life. "Its function is the comparison with empirical reality in order to establish its divergences or similarities, to describe them with the most unambiguously intelligible concepts, and to understand and explain them causally."[56] Social scientists want to study social phenomena in a way that makes the causal relations between the phenomena clear.[57] Ideal-types are a means to this end. To the extent that they wish to understand their data in causal terms, social scientists, on Weber's view, must relate them to an ideal limiting case.[58]

When social scientists use a term like "capitalism," "mercantilism," "individualism," "democracy," "bureaucracy," "public opinion," or "rational economic man," they are using it as an ideal-type. The features that define the economist's "rational economic man" are not common to any class of real consumers or producers. The beliefs and preferences of the rational economic man satisfy axioms that are not satisfied by the beliefs and preferences of real people.[59]

The selection of the ideal-type "rational economic man" for a study of economic life rests on certain values or interests. The selection of class-terms rests on values or interests too; but the interest is in the truth. Social scientists rationalize their decision to use one class-term over another by an interest in a true description of reality. However, ideal-types are not true of reality; so the choice of one ideal-type over another is not rationalized by valuing the truth. Ideal-types have "heuristic significance for the assessment of reality but are not empirically valid and hence do not describe what is real."[60] A choice of ideal-types must be rationalized by values other than truth, and a study that employs the type is relevant to these values.

For example, according to the equi-marginal "law" in microeconomics, a rational economic man will consume units of a good as long as the marginal benefit of the next unit exceeds the marginal cost. The test of this "law" is not whether it corresponds to the way that real consumers think or behave but how well it portrays what, on the economists' view, is significant about consumers' behavior. The economists' judgment of significance depends on their point of view, which, in the last analysis, is oriented on the basis of their evaluative ideas.[61]

In recommending that social scientists employ ideal-types in their studies, Weber is opposing what he calls "scientific naturalism." Scientific naturalism, Weber tells us, is the view that the end and goal of science is "to order its data into a system of concepts, the content of which is to be acquired and slowly perfected through the observation of empirical regularities, the construction of hypotheses and their verification."[62] The goal of science, according to the naturalist, is the reduction of reality to laws. The naturalist maintains that every concept in the social sciences should be similar to those in the exact natural sciences, and the function of every concept should be to mirror empirical reality.[63]

Weber offers an alternative epistemology for the social sciences, according to which social scientific concepts are primarily analytical instruments for understanding the meaning of, and causal relations between, elements of social and cultural life.[64] The validity of such concepts is always relative to the point of view and interests on the basis of which the social scientist selects them.

> The objective validity of all empirical knowledge rests exclusively upon the ordering of the given reality according to categories which are subjective in a specific sense, namely, in that they present the

presuppositions of our knowledge and are based on the presuppositions of the value of those truths which empirical knowledge alone
is able to give us.[65]

Weber uses the concept of ideal-types to respond to the positivist view
of science as the discovery of laws and the use of those laws to predict
and explain the facts. According to Weber, there are few social laws to
discover, and explanation is a matter of interpreting the facts in light of
their meaning for the subjects of the science rather than subsuming the
facts under general laws. Moreover, on his view, interpretation relies on
the values of the interpreters, for they cannot elicit meaning without
employing their own subjective categories. As a result, theories that include ideal-types cannot be expected to mirror or fit reality. Their validity
depends instead on whether they order reality to suit the scientists' cultural
interests and values.

Though Weber admits that the choice of an ideal-type is based on a
judgment of value – that is, that the choice is value-relevant – he denies
that the types are value-laden. "The constructs of pure economics which
are useful for analytical purposes cannot, however, be made the sources
of practical value-judgments."[66] Ideal-types are value-free, according to
Weber, because to use an ideal-type is not to claim that individuals or
groups in the social world ought to conform to the type. Weber maintains
that ideal-types can be distinguished from judgments about what ought
to exist and, in particular, from the judgment that to approximate the
ideal-type is desirable.[67] That is, on Weber's view, there is a distinction
between an ideal-type as an idealization useful for empirical analysis and
an ideal-type as a normative ideal, or between concepts with which reality
is compared and ideals by which it is exhaustively judged.

> The elementary duty of scientific self-control and the only way to
> avoid serious and foolish blunders requires a sharp, precise distinc-
> tion between the logically comparative analysis of reality by ideal-
> types in the logical sense and the value-judgment of reality on the
> basis of ideals.[68]

> An "ideal-type" in our sense, to repeat once more, has no con-
> nection at all with value-judgments, and it has nothing to do with
> any type of perfection other than a purely logical one. There are
> ideal-types of brothels as well as religions.[69]

> The idea of ethical imperatives – of a "model" of what "ought"
> to exist – is to be carefully distinguished from the analytical con-
> struct, which is "ideal" in the strictly logical sense of the term.[70]

The term "rational economic man" is an idealization useful in the analysis of prices in competitive markets. To use the term for this purpose is not to imply that actual consumers or producers ought to be rational economic men, since there is no implication that individuals who best approximate this ideal-type are better or more admirable than those who do not approximate it at all. But this does not mean that ideal-types are laden only with the theoretical virtues or that types can be chosen on the basis of their predictive or explanatory power alone.

Weber allows that ideal-types are laden with more than the theoretical virtues, for a decision as to whether one ideal-type is more useful than another relies on the values with which the researcher approaches the events in a culture's economy.[71] The model of the rational economic man enables an economist to analyze the behavior of her subjects as a series of economic transactions or as efforts to maximize individual marginal utility; but whether this is the best way to analyze that behavior, on Weber's own view, depends on the value-concepts with which the economist approaches the culture. Weber would call this a matter of value-relevance; but now we can see that value-relevance is not a matter merely of the values that lead researchers to ask a question but also of those that influence their answers, and that, for Weber, cultural or ethical values not only rationalize discovery in the social sciences, they also rationalize justification.

Disputes over the choice of ideal-types

With the use of ideal-types in theories or explanations in the social sciences, nonscientific values rationalize the choice of questions and the choice of types with which to answer them. They rationalize the choice of types, in that a type is chosen in order to exaggerate features of a culture that the researcher finds most significant. Though Weber asks social scientists not to offer judgments of value as part of their research, he expects that values will lead them to their research and to the ideal-types or idealizations with which to conduct it. Values not only lead social scientists to the temple; they also influence how they pray when they get there. Weber would not agree with Pigou that economists must leave their values outside when they enter the temple of science and must not allow those values to influence their form of worship. On Weber's view, even the rituals of theory choice are informed by values carried by worshipers into the sanctuary.

Research is value-neutral only if it is value-free (in Weber's sense) and the grounds that support the research do not favor any one conception of the good – that is, are themselves value-free. A theory that contains ideal-types cannot be value-neutral, for the choice of type favors one view of what is most significant in a culture over others. Weber does not call upon his colleagues to free their scientific writing and teaching of idealizations or ideal-types. To the contrary, he maintains that there can be no science of cultural phenomena without them, and his own work on the rise of capitalism is rich with ideal-types. He maintains, for example, in *The Protestant Ethic and the Rise of Capitalism* that the ethic of early Protestantism was the central force in shaping the capitalist spirit[72] and in *Economy and Society* that religion functions to legitimize the lives of those with social and economic privilege.[73] Terms like "capitalist spirit" and "Protestant ethic" are, for Weber, ideal-types, and the thesis that the capitalist spirit in seventeenth-century Europe was affected by the rise of Protestantism is tested not only by observation or by how well it fits the facts of European history but also by its power, as part of a theory of the relation between religion and economics, to reveal the significance of the economic history of Europe to someone with Weber's interests.

Ideal-types are widely employed in Weber's social science, but they are employed widely in today's social science as well. Key terms in current research and teaching in political science like "democracy," "liberalism," "sovereignty," and "the public interest" are ideal-types rather than simple class-terms. In economics, terms like "household," "firm," "market supply," and "market demand" are ideal-types; and, in sociology, "gang," "neighborhood," "delinquent," and "leader"; they do not describe the facts but offer a standard against which the facts can be compared or understood.

Terms do not carry their type on their face, for whether a term is an ideal-type or a simple class-term is partly a matter of how it is used. For example, some critics of opinion research maintain that the research favors conservative political values.[74] Even if the findings are value-free, they are not value-neutral but partisan, the critics would say. One reason for thinking that the research is partisan is the use of the term "public opinion," for as the term is used in opinion research, "public opinion" is not a class-term but an ideal-type.

Most political scientists would balk at the idea that "public opinion" is an ideal-type. They see it as a statistical concept – that is, an aggregate measure – in the form of summary statistics of collected responses to a questionnaire; but that view ignores how measures of public opinion are used in discussions of public policy.

For example, according to George Gallup, public opinion in 1983 supported President Reagan's decision to invade the island of Grenada. Gallup's findings appear to be value-free, for he is not recommending

Reagan's policy or agreeing with the opinions he collects. The methods Gallup uses to measure public opinion suggest that "public opinion" is a simple class-term, a collection of responses to a series of survey questions. But a mere collection of responses has no bearing on issues of public policy. Only if the responses are equated with the *vox populi* do they support or oppose a political decision; but "the voice of the people" is not a simple class-term but an ideal-type.

As an ideal-type, "the voice of the people" has cultural significance and can be cited in support of Reagan's policy. Opinion research seems to be important or interesting, because the findings are understood to have such a significance; but this assumes that "public opinion" is more than a statistical concept, that it does not merely reflect a collection of responses but also imposes a political significance on those responses.

Conclusion

Social scientists look to Weber's methodological writings for a defense of value-neutrality in the social sciences, but the writings offer reasons for partisanship. As his discussion of ideal-types shows, a theory with ideal-types must favor some cultural values over others, and ideal-types are a prominent and desirable feature of theories in the social sciences. Weber's methodological writings are usually read to support the liberal ideal, but, on my view, they can be better read to oppose it. For, although Weber argued that theories in the social sciences could and should be value-free, he did not argue that they could or should be value-neutral. In fact, given his nonnaturalistic view of the social sciences, he believed that the social sciences, unlike the natural sciences, could only be partisan. While many proponents of liberal science turn to Weber for support, on my interpretation of Weber's views, he opposes a liberal philosophy for the social sciences.

NOTES

1 These essays are collected in Weber, *Methodology*. For a discussion of Weber's influence on the methodology of the social sciences and, in particular, on the ideal of neutrality, see D. Kasler, *Max Weber: An Introduction to his Life and Work* (University of Chicago Press, 1988), pp. 211–16, and D. H. Wrong, "Max Weber," in *Max Weber*, ed. D. H. Wrong (Prentice-Hall, 1970), pp. 1–76.

2 For a discussion of the history of the ideal of value-freedom, see Hutchinson, *"Positive" Economics*.

3 J. N. Keynes, *The Scope and Method of Political Economy* (Kelly and Millman, 1955), p. 60.
4 Weber, *Methodology*, p. 60.
5 Ibid., pp. 21–2.
6 Ibid., p. 61.
7 Ibid., p. 82.
8 S. Harding, *Feminism and Methodology* (Indiana University Press, 1987), p. 6.
9 S. Hills (ed.), *Corporate Violence* (Rowan and Littlefield, 1987).
10 Weber, *Methodology*, p. 72.
11 Ibid., p. 78.
12 Ibid., p. 111.
13 Ibid., p. 76.
14 Ibid., p. 102.
15 Ibid., p. 72.
16 Ibid., p. 76.
17 Ibid., p. 52.
18 Ibid., p. 60.
19 Ibid., p. 11.
20 Ibid., p. 2.
21 Ibid., p. 3.
22 Ibid., pp. 8, 51, and 54.
23 Ibid., p. 30.
24 K. Klappholz, "Value Judgments and Economics," in *The Philosophy of Economics*, ed. D. M. Hausman (Cambridge University Press, 1984), pp. 277–8, and Robbins, *Essay*, pp. 136–58.
25 See D. Hume, *Treatise of Human Nature* (Doubleday, 1966), pp. 373–8, 412–24, esp. p. 423. For a discussion of how to interpret Hume's statements, see J. L. Mackie, *Hume's Moral Theory* (Routledge and Kegan Paul, 1980), pp. 51–63.
26 M. Friedman, "The Methodology of Positive Economics," in *Philosophy of Economics*, ed. Daniel Hausman (Cambridge University Press, 1984), pp. 210–44.
27 Ibid., p. 212.
28 Robbins, *Essay*, p. 150.
29 Weber, *Methodology*, p. 52.
30 Ibid., pp. 18–19.
31 Ibid., p. 55.
32 Ibid., pp. 53–4.
33 Ibid., pp. 52–3.
34 The distinction between discovery and justification is central to the philosophy of science of the logical positivists. Weber was not a positivist, and in his own methodological writings he does not recognize such a distinction. Nevertheless, the distinction helps in understanding what Weber did and did not mean by "value-freedom."
35 Weber, *Weber on Universities*, pp. 4–30.
36 Weber, *Methodology*, p. 3.

37 Weber, *Weber on Universities*, pp. 4–8.

38 Ibid., p. 19.

39 The legal authority of the minister was based on the fact that the faculty were members of the civil service. As a civil servant, a professor in a Prussian university served at the pleasure of the Prussian Ministry of Education.

40 Weber, *Methodology*, p. 4.

41 Ibid., p. 4.

42 Ibid., p. 56.

43 Ibid., p. 12.

44 Ibid., p. 58.

45 Ibid.

46 As I explained earlier in this chapter, on Weber's view, values influence how a question is answered as well as what question is asked. As a result, the role of values within the context of justification is a matter of value-relevance rather than value-freedom.

47 For a discussion of disagreement in science, see L. Laudan, *Science and Values: The Aims of Science and their Role in Scientific Debate* (University of California Press, 1984), pp. 7–22.

48 M. Hesse, *Revolution and Reconstruction in Science* (Harvester Press, 1980), p. xxiii.

49 Weber, *Methodology*, p. 52.

50 The claim that the theoretical virtues are neutral between different conceptions of the good is more plausible for some of these virtues than for others. E.g., predictive power seems not to favor the good life as a life of contemplation any more than the good life as life of pleasure; while explanatory power seems to favor the former by assuming that understanding rather than mere enjoyment is valuable. Moreover, the idea of a good explanation – i.e., the standard by which explanations are judged – can carry with it a conception of the good. Thus, if a good explanation in the social sciences is one that reveals the meaning of an event in relation to a background of cultural values, then good explanations are partisan in the sense of favoring these values.

51 Weber, *Methodology*, pp. 43–4.

52 Ibid., p. 103.

53 Ibid., p. 94.

54 Ibid., p. 102.

55 Ibid., p. 90.

56 Ibid., p. 43.

57 Ibid., p. 93.

58 Ibid., p. 94.

59 Ibid., pp. 43–4.

60 Ibid., p. 103.

61 Ibid., p. 111.

62 Ibid., p. 106.

63 Ibid., p. 88.

64 Ibid., p. 106.

65 Ibid., p. 110.

66 Ibid., p. 37.
67 Ibid., p. 44.
68 Ibid., p. 98.
69 Ibid., pp. 98–9.
70 Ibid., p. 92.
71 Ibid., pp. 72, 76, 78, and 111.
72 M. Weber, *The Protestant Ethic and the Rise of Capitalism* (Allen and Unwin, 1930), p. 40.
73 M. Weber, *Economy and Society*, ed. G. Roth and C. Wittich (Bedminster Press, 1968), p. 491.
74 See F. Pollock, "Empirical Research into Public Opinion," in *Critical Sociology*, ed. Paul Connerton (Penguin, 1976), pp. 225–36.

3

Theories of development in psychology and political science

A central question in the social sciences is the extent to which they can or should emulate the natural sciences. On one side of the question are philosophers of the Enlightenment and fathers of the liberal sciences like Condorcet and Hume who maintain that the aim and form of reasoning in the natural and the social or human sciences should be the same: the discovery of causal laws whereby events can be predicted or explained and the method of experimental reasoning for the discovery or justification of those laws. On the other side are philosophers of history like Herder and Dilthey who maintain that the aim and form of the social or human sciences should be different: the discovery of the meanings of social events whereby they can be explained though not predicted and a method of interpretation for the discovery of those meanings.

Weber falls between these two extremes. He believed that the social should emulate the natural sciences in looking for the causes of events. However, he believed that they should be different from the natural sciences and employ a method of interpretation to discover the meaning of the events. Nevertheless, on his view, the question of value-freedom is the same for both the social and the natural sciences. In both, judgments of fact and value are absolutely heterogeneous, and the scientist is obliged to make clear to his audience at what point the scientific investigator becomes silent and the evaluating, acting person begins to speak.[1] As Weber sees it, the reasons for excluding judgments of value from teaching and writing apply equally to the social and the natural sciences.[2]

Weber's account of values in the social sciences is limited, however, for it pays too little attention to differences between the sciences and to practices within the sciences other than explaining and theorizing. A fuller account would look at the different approaches or schools within the various social sciences and ask how a conception of the good is assumed or advanced by each of them. While Weber offers a useful elevated or bird's-eye view of partisanship in the social sciences, my map of the field calls for a more close-up view – a smaller scale and a finer level of resolution.

In this chapter, I look particularly at one area of psychology, developmental psychology, and one area of political science, comparative politics and theories of political development, and show how, in theorizing psychological and political development, social scientists rely on judgments of value beyond the judgments that appear in the ordinary course of discovery or justification in science. In particular, I explain how, in theorizing moral development among children and political development among nations, values play a role in theorizing differences and theorizing limits in reducing the differences. In the course of my account, I describe a role for values in theorizing that Weber does not write about and show how developmental theories differ from other theories in the social sciences.

Theories of mental development

Theorizing in psychology includes theorizing how individuals develop a personality, a family of emotions, or a set of abilities or skills, like the ability to speak a language or do mathematics, as a result of normal maturation or on the basis of some course of experience or instruction. Theories of development explain that mastery comes in stages rather than all at once. Later stages are theorized as more adequate and closer to full mastery than earlier ones, and the succession of stages provides a scale on which any individual's level of competence can be measured and compared with another's.

For example, in theorizing the acquisition of a first language, psychologists offer a theory of cognitive development. They attempt to explain how native speakers acquire the knowledge that enables them to speak and understand the language; and they theorize that speakers progress through stages, from knowledge of some part or aspect of the grammar of the language to knowledge of more of it until they reach the stage of knowing it all.

The first task in constructing a theory of development is to describe what full competence or mastery consists in – that is, to describe the end point or final stage of development. When mastery is an intellectual ability or skill, the psychologist assumes that the end point is a body of knowledge, not merely a habit or a set of conditioned responses. The first question that the psychologist must answer is what is known by a subject who is fully competent that is not known by one who is not. The second task in constructing a theory of development is to describe how those who lack mastery proceed to build it up: the stages they pass through and how they negotiate the passage.

Noam Chomsky has made popular the idea that in theorizing language development, psychologists should get their descriptions of the end point – that is, of competence – from the linguist; for what competent speakers know, according to Chomsky, is a grammar of the language, and the task of the linguist is to describe these grammars. A grammar is a set of rules that pair the sounds of a language with their meanings, and a description of the grammar answers the question, on Chomsky's view, of what people learn when they learn to speak and understand a language.[3] The task of the linguist, on his view, is to discover the rules, and the task of the psychologist is to discover how people learn those rules. Most psychologists theorize that speakers do not learn the grammar of a language all at once, but in stages. At each stage, the speaker acquires a grammar that more closely approximates the knowledge of a competent speaker than the grammar acquired at a preceding stage.

Values in the definition of competence

In trying to discover what the competent speaker knows, the linguist constructs a theory using as data the intuitions of fluent speakers. The intuitions are the evidence that linguists use to rationalize their choice of one description of competence or one grammar over another. The theory is not intended to be a description of the mind or understanding of any one of the speakers, but an idealization of the state of mind of each of them. The understanding of each actual speaker will differ somewhat from that of every other, and no actual speaker will have complete understanding of the language; for the notion of a common language is itself an idealization, based on intuitions shared by some but not all the speakers and on features that exceed the intuitions of all of them.

For example, while the grammar the linguist theorizes will define well-formedness for any sentence of the language regardless of length or complexity, the intuitions of well-formedness of actual speakers of the language will be limited to short or only moderately complex sentences. Moreover, the intuitions of well-formedness of actual speakers will sometimes conflict, and the grammar the linguist theorizes will fit the intuitions of some but not all of them.

The subject of the linguist's theory is an ideal-type. The grammar the theory describes is not understood by any actual speaker but is an ideal which the understanding of even the most fluent actual speakers will only approximate. Chomsky's use of ideal-types in linguistics is similar to

Weber's use of them in economics and sociology. That is, the subjects of the theory are defined by a set of traits that is not possessed by actual subjects, though actual subjects have some of the traits, and they can be compared to the ideal-type and their actions understood in relation to it.

A theory of the development of an intellectual skill or competence depends on a definition of the competence; but if the competence is an idealization of what actual subjects understand rather than a description of the state of mind of a real subject, then the definition, in some measure, will be arbitrary or nominal, and the choice of one definition over all others can be rationalized only by appealing to practical reason. That is, even if linguists knew all there was to know about the state of mind of each speaker of the language, the selection of the ideal-type "competent speaker" would be open; for the linguists' knowledge would not rationalize the choice of one definition or grammar over others. The test of the linguists' grammar or theory of what the idealized speaker knows is not that it corresponds to what an actual speaker knows, for there is no correspondence, but that it serves the linguists' interests better than other theories that fit the intuitions or speech of actual speakers equally well.

To the extent that the linguists' definition of competence or choice of grammars is influenced by their interests, the psychologists' theory of the development of that competence will be influenced by them as well. That is, the rationalization of a theory of the development of a competence rests on whatever rationalizes the choice of one definition of the competence over others. Since some of the reasons that rationalize the definition of competence are practical, some of the reasons rationalizing the choice of the theory of development are practical as well; and since practical reasons include judgments of value, the theory of development is not value-neutral but partisan.

Values play a role in any theory of psychological development that employs ideal-types, but this does not distinguish theories of psychological development from other theories in the social sciences that employ ideal-types. However, theories of cognitive development are employed in programs of education in ways that other psychological theories are not, and, as a result, the types that are included in these theories are not merely idealizations used for empirical analysis but idealizations used for normative analysis as well.

One aim in theorizing linguistic or mathematical development is to guide a program of linguistic or mathematical education. That is, the psychologist's aim is to increase the likelihood that an individual approximates the highest stage of development; and the definition of that stage and the theory of how to get there provide the psychologist with a directive for action. The psychologist wishes to stimulate the development of linguistic or mathematical competence in some children or adults and uses the definition of competence as a yardstick for measuring the accomplishments of her subjects or·for selecting a course of instruction or treatment. Looked at as part of a program of education, the statements of a theory of cognitive development are judgments of value in the sense that Weber had in mind. That is, they contain "binding norms or ideals from which directives for immediate practical activity can be derived"[4] or statements that "express the desirability or undesirability of some course of actions from ethical or cultural or other points of view."[5]

Defenders of Weber's ideal of value-freedom would say that theorizing development can and should be distinguished from prescribing or encouraging it. That is, even if theories of development are seen as a means of moving subjects up the ladder from lower to higher stages of mastery, the definitions of competence and the description of how to attain it are separate from the judgment that competence is desirable or that subjects ought to be helped to achieve it. For a psychologist to say that later stages represent a higher or more integrated form of functioning than earlier ones does not imply that it is desirable for someone to move from an earlier to a later stage unless the psychologist adds that the more integrated forms of functioning are more desirable than those that are less so.

Though developmental theories include terms like "better", "superior," "more developed," and "more competent," these terms are not value-laden, the liberal would say, unless the theories are used prescriptively to develop or encourage the development of competence rather than merely descriptively to show how competence develops. A theory of the development of burglary competence, for example, would describe what the competent burglar knows that bungling burglars don't know and describe the stages on the way to mastery. In saying that knowledge at later stages is more advanced or better than knowledge at earlier ones, however, psychologists would not be making judgments of the value of burglary. Only if they used their theory in a school for scoundrels would there be any reason to say that the theory contained such judgments of value.

The view that theorizing development can be distinguished from prescribing or encouraging it seems plausible. After all, can't the knowledge that a science offers always be distinguished from the use to which that knowledge is put? I invent something. You use it to accomplish a bad end. In inventing it, I am not endorsing your end or recommending your use of my invention. I will argue in chapter 9 that offering knowledge is often to endorse a use of the knowledge and, in particular, that, in theorizing, a social scientist can be prescribing or recommending a course of action. However, for now I will drop the question, for I want to consider a variety of theories of cognitive development in which theorizing and prescribing are combined.

Theories of moral development

An interesting class of theories of cognitive development in psychology are theories that attempt to explain moral development. The assumption is that individuals who are able to make moral judgments and engage in moral reasoning have a competence or some knowledge that those who are not able to do so lack. The task for the psychologist is to explain how individuals acquire this competence, and psychologists who propose developmental theories assume that the knowledge is not acquired all at once, but in stages. That is, according to their theories of how we learn to make moral judgments and engage in moral reasoning, we pass through a sequence of stages from lower to higher levels of knowledge or understanding.

The first task in constructing a theory of moral development, as with any other theory of development, is to describe the end point or competence that is the final stage in the process and represents full mastery. The psychologist must describe what morally competent people know before she can describe how they come to have that competence.

Morality, on the view of some psychologists, is no more than the values or norms adopted by a given culture or a dominant group within a culture. They think of morality the way that Thrasymachus did in Plato's *Republic*. On matters of morality, there is no difference, they would say, between what is true and what seems to most of the members or the more powerful members of the culture to be true. For them, moral or social development is merely the internalization of the external norms of the group or culture.

For the Thrasymachan psychologist, the task of defining the end point of moral development is no different from that of defining the end point of any form of intellectual development. The psychologist would base his or her definition on the intuitions of whichever subjects the members of the group or culture believe to be competent moral speakers. However, for psychologists who view morality as Socrates does in the *Republic* and do not identify moral knowledge with community standards but believe that community standards themselves can be right or wrong, the task is quite different. For them, the task requires that they make their own judgments of moral right and wrong.

Jean Piaget theorizes moral development in children.[6] He models his work on the theories he had already offered of the development of mathematical and spatial reasoning. Moral competence, according to Piaget, consists in mastering a system of rules. Piaget assumes that the rules at the highest stage of moral development are not merely the standards of his or the child's community but the expressions of moral truth. He appeals to his own moral intuitions to define moral competence and uses the intuitions of children to identify their stage of development and measure their level of moral competence. He gathers his data by asking children questions about a series of games and stories.

Piaget thought he discovered three stages in the development of moral judgment in children. In the first stage moral judgments are based on the child's own interests, in the second on the norms and values shared by members of the community, and in the third on principles of mutual respect and cooperation. However, Piaget's discovery of these stages and their occurrence in the development of children are based on his belief in his own moral competence. That is, he relied on his own moral judgments in deciding how many stages there are and how they are ordered.

Kohlberg's theory and the alleged moral inferiority of women

Lawrence Kohlberg follows Piaget's lead in theorizing moral development.[7] Like Piaget, he believes that moral knowledge is knowledge of rules, and, like Piaget, he believes that theorizing the rules of morality is theorizing what is rather than what merely seems to some community to be. That is, like Piaget he thinks of morality in Socrates' way rather than Thrasymachus's. He presents his theory as a theory of the development of morality in a community, not a theory of the development in the community of what the members take morality to be.[8]

Piaget theorizes moral development in children, Kohlberg in children, adolescents, and adults. According to Kohlberg, there are six stages that a subject can pass through on the way to moral maturity, each representing a different level of understanding of morality. The understanding represented by a higher stage is more adequate – is an expansion of moral understanding – than that represented by a lower one.

Kohlberg maintains that it is the task of moral philosophy rather than psychology to define the ethically optimal end point of moral development and full moral competence. He writes: "Science, then, can test whether a philosopher's conception of morality phenomenologically fits the psychological facts. Science cannot go on to justify that conception of morality as what morality ought to be."[9] The philosopher stands to the psychology of moral development, on Kohlberg's view, as the linguist stands to the psychology of language development on Chomsky's. The philosopher and the linguist tell the psychologist what counts as competence. However, whereas the linguist bases her advice on empirical data – the intuitions of native speakers – the philosopher bases his advice on his own intuitions.[10]

Kohlberg turns to Kant and Rawls to learn the nature of moral competence and to define the final, "ethically optimal" stage of moral development. In the sixth or highest stage, according to Kohlberg, moral judgments are based on a reflective perspective, and the principles employed by moral subjects at that stage are the principles of a moral theory like Rawls's theory of justice as fairness.

> [The] principles [at this stage] are universal principles of justice: the equality of human rights and respect for the dignity of human beings as individual persons. Right is defined by the decision of conscience in accord with self-chosen ethical principles appealing to logical comprehensiveness, universality, and consistency. These principles are abstract and ethical (the golden rule, or the Categorical Imperative); they are not concrete moral rules like the Ten Commandments. At heart, these are universal rules of justice, of the reciprocity and quality of human rights, and of respect for the dignity of human beings as individual persons.[11]

Kohlberg's conception of morality as directives for action chosen under conditions of equality is, of course, only one conception among many. Kohlberg does not explain why he believes that it is the true or best conception. He leaves us with the impression that he picks one philosopher's conception from the many (Rawls's rather than Aristotle's or Mill's, for example) on the basis of his own convictions. The question is why anyone should trust Kohlberg's moral convictions over the convictions of subjects who, according to Kohlberg, are at a lower moral stage. The answer cannot be that his convictions echo Rawls's or Kant's, since, on Kohlberg's view, moral competence does not consist in mimicking other members or even authoritative members of the society, but grasping the moral truth.

Equipped with a belief about which conceptions of morality are better and worse, Kohlberg finds that some cultures are more morally developed than others and that within our own culture middle-class conceptions are more developed than lower-class conceptions and male more developed than female. He says, for example, that the moral judgments of women in our culture are at the third stage of moral development and that the two highest stages are absent in preliterate or semiliterate village culture: "Our finding that our two highest stages are absent in preliterate or semiliterate village culture, and other evidence, also suggests to us a mild doctrine of social evolutionism, such as was elaborated in the classic work of Hobhouse [*Morals in Evolution* (Chapman and Hall, 1906)]."[12] Kohlberg believes that he is able to make such claims about women or village cultures because he thinks that he knows which of two opposing moral judgments – for example, Rawls's or the semiliterate villager's – is closer to the truth.

Kohlberg's mistake

Carol Gilligan criticizes Kohlberg's findings for relying initially on a study of boys rather than both boys and girls.[13] She assumes that Kohlberg built a measuring stick to match the judgments he found in boys and then used it to measure the judgments of both girls and boys. On Gilligan's view, Kohlberg's mistake lies in reasoning from a bad sample, from the morality of boys to the morality of children. He is like an ornithologist who limits his observations to birds he can sight from his own window, such as crows; then, on the basis of his observations, forms a definition of the entire biological class – namely, Aves – and, using the definition as a field guide, concludes that other avian varieties – for example, starlings – are underdeveloped or immature forms.

There is much to object to in Kohlberg's theory, but Gilligan is mistaken in saying that Kohlberg reasons from an atypical sample, for he doesn't reason from any sample at all. Kohlberg did not build his measuring stick to match the moral convictions of the boys in his studies. He built it to match his own convictions, or the convictions of moral philosophers who equate morality with justice as fairness.

Kohlberg's error was to apply a false measuring stick, a too narrow conception of morality, to boys and girls. Kohlberg's stick leaves inches off the moral height of everyone. It equates a part of morality with the whole of it. As Gilligan points out, moral maturity is not simply adherence to rules or principles of fairness but includes, for example, personal ties and loyalties. The value of Gilligan's work is to draw attention to forms of moral thought that are neglected by the conception of morality on which Kohlberg bases his theory. She contributes to a growing body of writing about morality that explains how particularistic commitments and a wide range of feelings and emotions are part of the fabric of moral life.

Kohlberg simply assumes that lower scores on his tests show lower morality. He does not consider the alternative – that lower scores might show higher morality – or that the tests are not measuring morality at all. The different scores of girls and boys can be interpreted in at least two ways: to damn the girls or to damn the scoring. A study of girls would not have given him a different measuring scale, for his scale was fixed before he undertook any study of boys. The units and end points of Kohlberg's scale are brought to, rather than taken from, his empirical psychology.

Had Kohlberg studied girls rather than boys, he would have made the same mistake; for what rationalizes his belief that some children are less morally mature than others is not his choice of children to study but his choice of philosophers to listen to. Imagine what Kohlberg would have found in measuring moral development if his conception of morality had been Nietzsche's conception in *Beyond Good and Evil* rather than Rawls's conception in *A Theory of Justice*. Had Kohlberg held boys and girls up to Nietzsche's measuring stick, he would have found that children are most morally mature at the first, egoistic stages of development and become less mature as they internalize the moral norms of their community and adopt the principles of justice as fairness. Moral maturity, Kohlberg would have discovered, is lost rather than won with age. The theory he would offer us – on the basis of the same experimental evidence – would not be a theory of moral development in children but a theory of moral decline or corruption as children become adults.

Only if Kohlberg were to equate morality with popular moral opinion or community standards of morality could he make the mistake of reasoning from a faulty sample. To discover popular opinion, the psychologist would have to query a fair sample of the population whose morality he is studying. If he sampled entirely from one portion, and the thoughts about morality of members of other parts were very different, his generalizations would be faulty. Clearly Kohlberg does not equate morality with popular opinion or community standards, for he believes that the standards of preliterate or semiliterate village cultures fall short. If boys' thoughts about morality were as different from girls' thoughts as Kohlberg says they are and morality were a matter of popular opinion, the differences Kohlberg claims to have discovered would be evidence of different moralities, girls' morality and boys' morality, not of different levels of mastery of some common body of principles.

Thrasymachus did not equate morality with popular moral opinion but with the opinion of the most powerful members of society. In a society in which men are more powerful than women, a moral psychologist who brought Thrasymachus's philosophy to his psychology might well find, as Kohlberg did, that women are less morally developed than men. That is, a moral psychologist who equated morality with the will or commands of the mighty would have a stick for measuring and comparing levels of moral development. At the highest stage would be subjects whose thoughts of right and wrong were closest to the mighty's, and at the lowest stage would be subjects whose thoughts were furthest away. In a society in which men are more mighty than women, women do not share the judgments of men, and morality is seen through Thrasymachus's eyes, women are seen as less morally developed than men. This is hardly a surprising result, but it is not the result that Kohlberg claims to have found.

The distinction between theorizing and prescribing

I share some of Kohlberg's convictions. I agree with him that morality is not simply a matter of popular opinion or conformity to community standards and that the standards of a community are themselves a proper object of moral judgment and evaluation. However, a theory of moral development that begins with such a conception of morality is value-laden in a very direct sense, for the description of the end point of development that such a theory offers is also a recommendation or an endorsement of the principles or judgments identified with the highest stage. In other words, psychologists cannot say that Kant gives a truer account of morality than Nietzsche does, that Kant's principles represent a higher stage than Nietzsche's, and still claim to be silent on questions of moral value and neutral between conceptions of the good.

With theories of moral development like those offered by Kohlberg and Piaget, there is no distinction to be drawn between theorizing and prescribing. To say, in the context of such theories, that subjects at the highest stages believe that they have a moral duty not to lie implies that their belief is true. Kohlberg cannot say that in describing moral beliefs he is not endorsing them or making any judgment about them; for part of what he means by "highest moral stage" is the stage closest to the moral truth.

There is no separating Kohlberg's own moral convictions from his descriptions of the moral convictions of his subjects. His descriptions assume them. Psychologists who view theorizing moral development the way Kohlberg and Piaget do must endorse the moral principles and judgments of the subjects they place at the top of the measurement scale, because they are theorizing not the development of morality as it looks to some members of a community but morality as (on their view) it really is. Kohlberg and Piaget are moral realists; as a result, when they describe boys as more morally developed than girls, they are trying to say what is, while relying on their own views of what ought to be.

— way too easy a target.
How about Piaget or cognitive development?

Theories of natural differences

Piaget and Kohlberg believe that boys and girls differ in moral capacity, but they believe that the differences are due not to any differences in male and female nature but to differences in the way boys and girls are socialized or raised. There are, however, theories of cognitive development that theorize such differences as differences in nature or inheritance, and, from the belief that these differences are inherited, some social scientists theorize that it is not possible or practical to eliminate them.

Stephen J. Gould, in his book *The Mismeasure of Man*, discusses the history of theorizing natural differences in intelligence.[14] According to some of the fathers of IQ testing, people differ in their level of intelligence, and most of the difference is due not to how they are raised or what they have been taught but to their genes. As Gould explains, in theorizing differences in scores on IQ tests, these psychologists took the differences as a measure of natural differences and reasoned that because they were natural, there was a limit to how much they could be narrowed. According to these psychologists, no matter how much we improve the schooling of children with low IQ scores, they will be plagued with a low intelligence. Gould calls the theory of intelligence that these psychologists offered "a theory of limits," for it takes the measure of natural differences as a measure of inevitable differences and predicts that any success in eliminating or significantly reducing the differences will be limited.[15]

In theorizing limits, the social scientist describes some psychological differences between individuals or groups of individuals, offers an explanation of the origin of the differences, and finds in the explanation a reason to believe that the differences cannot be otherwise – that they are in some respect necessary. The sociobiologists Charles Lumsden and Edward Wilson offer a limit theory in their book *Genes, Mind and Culture* when they theorize that genetic natural selection operates to keep culture on a leash.[16] Genes, they argue, limit what culture can teach us. The members of a culture arrive with genetic predispositions, and there are limits to how far culture can oppose these dispositions. Members can be taught to resist their natural inclinations, but only within limits. Whenever members of a culture "go against their nature," they impose on themselves a cost, and sometimes the cost is more than the members of the culture can bear.

Many differences in skill, attitude, or sentiment between men and women, on the view of sociobiologists, have evolved through natural selection. By nature, women are disposed to devote more time to caring for children and managing the household than men are. Culture teaches women, through approbation and disapprobation, that childrearing and household management are their roles; but culture is only following nature's lead, according to the sociobiologists, and though culture can resist her lead and try to teach childrearing or household management to men, the teaching is seldom effective, the effects are short-lived, and in time the old, sex-linked patterns reappear.

> Even with identical education and equal access to all professions, men are more likely to play a disproportionate role in political life, business and science.[17]

> [This line of reasoning] also suggests why women have almost universally found themselves relegated to the nursery while men derive their greatest satisfaction from their jobs. For example, reversion to standard sexual division of labor has even occurred in Israeli *kibbutzim*, despite an overt ideological commitment to behave differently.[18]

As the quotations make clear, in theorizing that differences between men and women are natural, sociobiologists judge that success in erasing or reducing them will be limited. These sociobiologists make judgments not only about current practice but also about whether an alternative practice is possible.

Theories of limits and judgments of value

Psychologists and sociobiologists who theorize that differences between individuals or groups in skill, attitude, or sentiment are inevitable or uneliminable maintain that their theories are value-free. David Barash writes, for example, that "Sociobiology has no inherent political or social bias and . . . is as value-free as any other science."[19] Limit theorists tell us that no statement of what *is* implies anything about what *ought* to be, and that to suppose that it does is to commit the naturalistic fallacy.

> The philosopher David Hume made a valuable distinction when he emphasized that "is" does not imply "ought." Many of the political objections to human sociobiology are the result of the "naturalistic fallacy." When we describe and seek to understand the natural world, we are not seeking to condone it. What is biological is not necessarily good. As Ogden Nash pointed out, "small pox is natural; vaccine ain't." In recent years, there has been a healthy human bias in favor of things that are "natural" – natural foods, natural

childbirth – and such. But being natural is not synonymous with being good. When we study pneumococci, it is with the hope of better understanding this natural organism and its effects, not to condone pneumonia![20]

Social scientists who, like Barash or Lumsden and Wilson, naturalize psychological differences maintain that the term "natural," as it appears in theories in natural or social science, is a descriptive term with no prescriptive implications. Biological theories of behavior, they maintain, are no more partisan than any other theory in the social or natural sciences.

Biological theories of behavior, however, not only say what is, but also how it came to be. The word "natural" is supposed to explain the origin of behavior whose existence has already been noted or recorded. These biological theories share the word "natural" with theological theories like the theory that every animal species, including man, was specially created by God. In theological theories the term "natural" is also meant to explain how things came to be. The explanation is that they are the result of the will of God. The judgment that some behavior is the result of God's will, for many speakers of our language, is a judgment of both fact and value; for, as they use or understand the term "God," God is good, and what is due to his will is good. The term "natural" in biology, however, is free of this theology. God's will is replaced by the gene. Behavior is natural when caused by a gene(s); but to judge that genes are the cause is a judgment of fact. As a result, according to the biologist, to say that the sexual division of labor is natural is to explain it but not to endorse it.

Nature and necessity

According to a theory of limits, there is more to the claim that differences are natural than that they are due to our genes; there is also the suggestion that what is natural is somehow inevitable or necessary. Here the theological and scientific uses of "natural" overlap. When religious conservatives say that differences between men and women are due to the will of God, part of what they mean is that the differences will survive human efforts to remove them; likewise, when Lumsden and Wilson say that these differences are due to genes, part of what they too mean is that the differences will survive human efforts to remove them. According to religious conservatives, there is no possible world that conforms to God's will in which men are not different from women in the way that the conservatives suppose. Perhaps Lumsden and Wilson have a similar idea: namely, that there is no possible world that conforms to the present state of our genes in which men are not different from women in the way they suppose. But what sense of "possible" could they have in mind here?

Even if male and female differences must remain so long as God's will or our genes are unchanged, we can ask whether God's will or our genes must remain unchanged. Is a present inability to change the genes of our own or any other species a matter of history or necessity? In Darwin's day, we altered the genes of varieties of plants and animals through artificial selection. In our own day, with the development of molecular biology, we can alter the genes of present plants and animals as well as influence the genes of future offspring. If what Lumsden and Wilson mean by "must remain unchanged" is that there is no scientifically possible world in which the male or female gene pool is different from this one, they are clearly mistaken; for artificial selection and gene splicing enable us to create worlds in which the gene pool is different.

When Lumsden and Wilson theorize the limits of sexual equality and judge that sexual inequalities are inevitable, they don't mean, I assume, that there is no biologically possible world in which the distribution of child care is any different from that known in this world. I assume that they mean something weaker – perhaps that, given existing resources or commitments, it is not possible to alter the present division of sexual labor. What is clear is that, on their view, the distinction between biology and upbringing imposes some type of modal distinction on the current state of the sexes. Differences due to upbringing can be changed, whereas differences due to biology cannot be in some sense of "cannot be." In theorizing the limits of sexual equality, Lumsden and Wilson judge that we are stuck with the inequalities whether we approve of them or not.

Necessity and value

Critics like Richard Lewontin and Stephen J. Gould have shown, I believe, that the theories of limits offered in psychology and sociobiology rest on mistakes in reasoning.[21] Gould explains that in identifying differences in IQ, the theorist reifies the performance of children on tests and interprets the performance as a trait of the child and differences in performance between children as differences in the trait. Next, the theorist converts the trait into a scalar magnitude, a thing that can be ranked along a scale from higher to lower, and judges that some children have more of the trait than others.[22] The theorist then appeals to studies of twins to show that differences among children in the trait are mostly due to differences in their genes and concludes that, given our inability to alter a child's genes for intelligence, the differences in intelligence among children are inevitable. Against this reasoning, Gould argues that the differences in performance on tests cannot be identified with differences in a mental trait and that the study of identical twins reared apart is not evidence that differences in the trait are hereditary.[23]

Richard Lewontin offers a similar objection to the sociobiologists' theories of sexual difference.[24] According to Lewontin, sociobiologists first identify differences in behavior between males and females with a difference in traits. Next, they tell a story to show that the difference in traits is adaptive – that is, that it enhances the reproductive fitness of males and females. From such a story they conclude that the difference in traits is due to differences in male and female genes. Lewontin argues that differences in behavior cannot be identified with a difference in traits and that the story of how a difference in traits enhances fitness is not evidence that the differences are hereditary.

I endorse the criticisms of Gould and Lewontin. Many who study the psychology or biology of our own species and theorize limits have been guilty of bad science. They reduce differences between members to differences in traits and conclude that the traits are hereditary or adaptive on the basis of inadequate evidence. Sociobiologists like Wilson and Lumsden lump a wide variety of behavioral dispositions together as a single trait and then ask whether the trait is inherited or acquired. Their decision to lump the variety of dispositions together encourages the idea that the dispositions are expressions of a single gene or gene cluster; conversely, the idea that they are the expression of a gene encourages the idea that they constitute a single trait. But the dispositions do not form a natural kind but only a class of disparate things grouped together in response to the biologist's interest.[25] Parenting is no more a single trait than intelligence is. Wilson and Lumsden reify the variety of efforts to aid or support offspring and turn them into a single thing. They treat them as if they were naturally related when they are related only by someone's interest in grouping them together; the efforts are related by interest rather than nature, and the traits Wilson and Lumsden see as inherited are in fact neither inherited nor acquired, for the idea that they are traits is invented in order to find a biological basis for a sexual division of labor.

My interest, however, is not whether theorizing limits is bad science but whether theorizing limits brings into science judgments of value or forms of partisanship that are not brought in by every act of theorizing in science. Lumsden and Wilson maintain that (a) women are naturally disposed to care for infants and children and men are not, and that (b)

because women are and men are not naturally disposed, efforts to educate men and women to share equally in child care must fail (in some
sense of "must" which they don't specify but which we are supposed to
take seriously). They also maintain that to theorize (a) and (b) is not to condone the inequalities between men and women. The question I want to
consider is whether they can maintain that the inequalities are inevitable
(in their sense of "inevitable") and, at the same time, deny that they are
making any judgment about whether the inequalities ought or ought not
to be. Is it open to them to maintain that the inequalities cannot be
reduced or eliminated and, at the same time, to claim that they are silent
on whether they ought to be or on the nature of human perfection?

Even if we adopt the language of traits and assume that a phenotypic
trait has a biological basis – even if the etiology or causal chain leading
to the presence of the trait has a gene or gene complex among its links
– the biological basis tells us nothing about whether the trait can be
modified or eliminated. Phenylketonuria, for example, is a recessive inherited disease. If a child receives a certain faulty gene from both parents,
she will suffer from a liver enzyme deficiency that will cause mental
retardation if not recognized in time and treated by a special diet. But
in the biologically possible world in which a child receives the faulty
gene from both parents and receives the special diet, there is no retardation. Though the retardation has a biological basis, it can be prevented,
and the effects of the faulty gene eliminated.

Clefts of the lip and the palate, to cite another example, occur when
the embryo's facial folds fail to unite in the palate or the upper region
of the lip. According to current wisdom, the failure is due to a genetic
predisposition combined with a special agent such as rubella contracted
during pregnancy. If left untreated, a cleft lip or palate causes disfigure-
ment; but the condition can be treated through surgery early in childhood.
Though the clefts have a biological basis, they can be prevented through
treatment during pregnancy or surgery later on.

There are some genetic disorders for which, at present, there is no
treatment. Huntington's chorea is a dominant inherited disease involving
a progressive degeneration of the nervous system. A person who inherits
the faulty gene from either parent will develop the nervous disorder at
some point during adulthood. However, although there is no means at
present for repairing the faulty gene or preventing the disorder from
developing in those with the gene, it is likely that one day there will
be a way to repair the gene or counter its effects on the nervous system.
Though Huntington's chorea is at present inevitable in those who inherit
the faulty gene, this tells us nothing about whether with more effort we
will eventually be able to repair the fault or treat the disorder caused

by the gene. The question is whether to make the effort, and this question is not answered by the fact that the nervous disorder is inherited.

Let us assume with Lumsden and Wilson – in spite of the absence of any genetic evidence – that differences in parenting strategies between males and females in our species have a biological basis. An aversion to child care, we might say, is a genetic disorder or pathology – "a parenting disorder" – that exclusively affects males in much the way that some other disorders like prostate cancer do. Humans with a Y chromosome develop a distaste for caring for infants and children and are unable to acquire the skills of caretaking. Let us then assume with Lumsden and Wilson that there is no treatment for the genetic, parenting disorder common to the male members of our species and that efforts to treat this disorder or pathology, like those in the Israeli kibbutzim that Barash mentions, have all failed. Still, none of these assumptions gives us a reason to say that the male disorder is inevitable. As in the case of Huntington's chorea, our present inability to treat the disorder is no reason to conclude that the disorder is beyond the means of science to treat. Of course, only if we understand that it is a disorder will we have an interest in seeking to treat it.

What Lumsden and Wilson mean when they say that the sexual division of labor is necessary or inevitable is not that we cannot eliminate it, but that it is not a disorder and they do not morally approve of efforts to treat or eliminate it. When they judge that the differences are natural, they don't mean that efforts to eliminate them must fail – that is, that the laws of nature preclude the elimination of the differences – but that they oppose efforts to tamper with nature and eliminate them. Natural differences are often no more difficult to eliminate than acquired ones; but even if they were, the decision not to eliminate them or to try to eliminate them is ours, not nature's. Limits imposed from without, as Gould explains, are falsely identified by biologists like Lumsden and Wilson as lying within.[26]

To reason from the claim that differences between individuals or groups in skill, attitude, or sentiment are natural to the conclusion that they are desirable is to commit the naturalistic fallacy; but to reason from the claim that the differences are necessary or inevitable to the conclusion that they are desirable is not, if "necessary" means ought not to be otherwise – that is, that although there is a biologically possible world in which the differences are absent, we should exclude that world from consideration because of the undesirable changes that would be needed to make the possible world actual.

An analogy may help to make the point. Economists often say that the goal of full employment is impossible and that a significant amount of unemployment – they call it "structural unemployment" – is necessary or uneliminable. If they mean that there is no logically possible world in which there is no unemployment, then they are obviously mistaken; so too if they mean that there is no physically possible world or even any politically or economically possible world in which there is no unemployment, for there have been centrally planned economies that have achieved full employment. What the economists mean is that unemployment is necessary in any economy that conforms to their own cultural values or ideals. Centrally planned economies aren't contenders, for the economists do not approve of them.

Nothing in economics or biology shows that efforts to eliminate structural unemployment or a male aversion to parenting is a waste of time or effort. Still, economists and biologists talk about limits. They talk as if no world with full employment or a male preoccupation with parenting is consistent with our knowledge of economics or biology. They could misunderstand their science; but it is more likely that they understand their science but add their politics to it in their talk about limits. When economists say that there is a limit to how much unemployment can be reduced, they mean that they would not vote for a world with full employment; and when biologists say that there is a limit to how much a parenting difference between men and women can be reduced, they mean that they would not vote for a world with parenting equality between men and women. As a result, talk about limits in the social sciences is not neutral but partisan. As Condorcet recognized many years ago, biologists "make nature herself an accomplice in the crime of political inequality."[27] But biologists are not alone in this. The practice of blaming nature for human injustice is common to the whole range of social scientists who traffic in limit theories.

Theories of political development

Just as some psychologists have theorized the development of psychological skills or competence in children, so some political scientists have theorized the development of political capabilities in nations.[28] The political systems of nations change over time, and political scientists have looked for a framework within which the changes could be charted and the system of politics of a nation at one time compared with its political system at another time or with the political system of different nations. Their interest led them to develop the field of comparative politics and theories of political development.

Enlightenment philosophers were apparently the first to offer such theories.[29] They maintained that changes in forms of government were progressive and that nations were moving closer to the form of government we associate with liberal democracies. Political change, as they saw it, was unilinear, with a direction that brought each successive political system closer to the political system they most admired and approved of. They thought that democracy was the best form of government, on the grounds that it was ordained by natural law or best provided for the development or expression of what they saw as human nature.[30]

Theories of political development like those offered during the Enlightenment explain that political maturity or mastery comes in stages, rather than all at once. Later stages are theorized as more adequate and closer to the best form of political system than earlier ones, and the succession of stages provides a scale whereby any nation's level of political development can be measured and compared with another's. But the first task in constructing such a theory is to describe the end point or final stage in the process of change. The end point is an idealization rather than a description of any actual political system. It is an ideal-type in Weber's sense: defined by a set of traits that is not possessed by actual governments, though actual governments have some of them. According to the theorists of the Enlightenment, democracy was the end point or final stage of political development; but "democracy" was an ideal-type of political system rather than a term that could be expected to accurately describe any real government.

Today theories of political development do not assume that development is unilinear or that change is always toward some one ideal-type such as democracy.[31] The criterion of political change is a difference in some capability, but there is no assumption that new capabilities are always acquired; it is now allowed that capabilities can be lost as well as gained and that not all political systems begin and progress through the same set of stages.

> . . . political systems acquired and lost capabilities and their associated, cultural, structural, and performance characteristics in anything but a unilinear, evolutionary way.[32]

> We still begin with the enormous variety of cultural and structural starting points in the emerging nations, and even though they are confronted with all four problems of political growth simultaneously, the dosages of each vary from case to case, and the responses of elites to these challenges differ from one country to the next. Thus, while we can say that there will be some common content

in the outcomes of these processes of change, this is far from arguing that there will be one common outcome.[33]

Although there is no longer thought to be one common outcome, there is still thought to be a fixed set of stages through which a political system can pass. In the recent literature, for example, political systems in the contemporary world are said to fall into one of seven broad classes or types: traditional systems, modernizing authoritarian systems, tutelary democracies, immobilist democracies, conservative authoritarian systems, totalitarian systems, and stable democracies.[34]

Moreover, social scientists who today offer theories of political development cling to the belief that some political systems are more competent than others.

> The stable democratic systems are more versatile in their performance capabilities than other political systems. The structural and cultural autonomy of their capabilities enables them to cope with a variety of political problems with relative efficiency and without disruptive system changes. . . . They cannot solve some problems as well as totalitarian systems.[35]

But competence for today's theorists, as compared to the theorists of the Enlightenment, is no longer an absolute notion. The competence of a system is now measured in relation to the social or international environment. In some environments, a democracy may be less competent than an authoritarian system. Today's theorists also try to avoid the partisanship of the theorists of the Enlightenment and to avoid drawing conclusions about the moral worth of one system by comparison with another. They question whether a developmental theory ought to include a normative assessment of the changes or terms suggesting that one political system is better than another in any categorical sense.

In keeping with the ideal of liberal neutrality, proponents of comparative politics would deny that, in theorizing political change, they are recommending or prescribing what ought to be rather than merely describing what is; but their denial is opposed by their practice, for the practice includes more than discovering differences between political systems. It also involves evaluating them; for an ideal of improvement and a voice of approval is included in the very notions of modernization and development – for example, in the terms "backward," "undeveloped," "underdeveloped," and "primitive." The theorist can say that no judgment of virtue or superiority or virtue is intended; but intentions are not all that matter in assessing the force of a person's words.

Contemporary theorists allow that one of their principal goals is to measure and evaluate the performance of different political systems; but they maintain that they achieve their aim without being normative.[36] But even if the standards do not themselves imply that one type of system is morally superior or more virtuous than another, the theorists have to select their standards and decide what priorities to give them; and whether they merely take them over from existing political elites or offer their own, the decision, to the extent that it can be rationalized at all, cannot be rationalized by the facts alone but must rely on the values of the elites or on their own personal, cultural, or political values. To avoid being normative, theorists must not only avoid employing normative standards; they must avoid choosing standards on the basis of their own cultural and political values.

not necessarily

Conclusion

what about how to promote or recognition development?

Because theories of development rely on a concept of mastery or competence, they introduce judgments of value in ways that Weber's discussions of value-freedom ignore. The judgment that one person is more psychologically competent than another or that one political system is more developed than another is a judgment of both fact and value; and if the competence is moral or political competence, it is a judgment of moral or political value. Theories of development are also very often limit theories; that is, they theorize a limit to the course of development, and, as I have argued, in one sense of limits, such a theory is clearly false, while in another sense, it is clearly partisan. In addition, I have shown that the way in which sociobiologists like Lumsden and Wilson talk about limits, their limit theories trade on the second sense and, as a result, are partisan. Though value-freedom and value-neutrality are seen as ideals for theories of development in the social sciences, there are features of these theories that preclude neutrality and require a high degree of partisanship.

His targets are way too easy —

NOTES

1 Weber, *Methodology*, pp. 12 and 62.
2 Though, as I explain in chapter 2, on Weber's view, theories are partisan in the social sciences in a way that they are not in the natural sciences, insofar as theories in the social sciences include ideal-types whose selection or definition depends on judgments of cultural significance.

3 N. Chomsky, *Aspects of the Theory of Syntax* (MIT Press, 1965), pp. 3–9.

4 Weber, *Methodology*, p. 52.

5 Ibid., p. 10.

6 J. Piaget, *Moral Judgment of the Child* (Free Press, 1932).

7 L. Kohlberg, "Moral Stages and Moralization: The Cognitive Development Approach," in *Moral Development and Behavior: Theory, Research and Social Issues*, ed. T. Lickona (Holt, Rinehart and Winston, 1976), pp. 31–53.

8 See L. Kohlberg, "From Is to Ought: How to Commit the Naturalistic Fallacy and Get Away with it in the Study of Moral Development," in *Cognitive Development and Epistemology*, ed. T. Michel (Academic Press, 1971), pp. 151–235.

9 Ibid., p. 223.

10 Philosophers disagree on how moral judgments or principles are to be tested. John Stuart Mill seems to have thought that the truth of the greatest happiness principle was evident to everyone, and Kant that the categorical imperative could be given a proof. Rawls recommends considered judgments and the thought experiment of the original position and likens his method to Chomsky's; but Rawls's actual practice is to rely primarily on his own moral convictions, and the way he argues for his principles of justice over other principles – e.g., utilitarian principles – is different from the way a linguist argues for one grammar of a language over another.

11 Kohlberg, "Moral Stages," p. 35.

12 Kohlberg, "From Ought to Is," p. 178.

13 C. Gilligan, "Do the Social Sciences have an Adequate Theory of Moral Development?," in *Social Science as Moral Inquiry*, ed. N. Haan, R. N. Bellah, P. Rabinow and W. M. Sullivan (Columbia University Press, 1983), pp. 33–51.

14 S. J. Gould, *The Mismeasure of Man* (Norton, 1981).

15 Ibid., p. 28.

16 C. Lumsden and E. O. Wilson, *Genes, Mind and Culture* (Harvard University Press, 1981), p. 13.

17 E. O. Wilson, "Human Decency is Animal," *New York Times Magazine*, Oct. 12, 1975.

18 D. Barash, *Sociobiology and Behavior* (Elsevier, 1977), p. 301.

19 Even if all the statements of sociobiology were value-free, that would not mean that they were value-neutral and did not have any inherent political or social bias. For the distinction between value-freedom and value-neutrality, see chapters 1 and 2.

20 Barash, *Sociobiology*, p. 160.

21 R. C. Lewontin, "Adaptation," in *Conceptual Issues in Evolutionary Biology*, ed. E. Sober (MIT Press, 1984), pp. 235–51, and Gould, *Mismeasure*, pp. 250–2.

22 On my account of theories of moral development, developmental theorists do the same. They identify differences in moral judgment between subjects, reify those differences as if they were differences in a trait, and treat the trait as something that can be ranked along a scale from higher to lower.

23 Gould, *Mismeasure*, pp. 19–29.

24 Lewontin, "Adaptation," pp. 240–4.
25 See chapter 7 for a discussion of natural kinds.
26 Gould, *Mismeasure*, pp. 28–9.
27 Quoted in ibid., p. 21.
28 See, e.g., G. A. Almond, *Political Development: Essays in Heuristic Theory* (Little Brown and Company, 1970).
29 Ibid., p. 160.
30 Ibid.
31 Ibid., p. 170.
32 Ibid., p. 169.
33 Ibid., p. 170.
34 Ibid., p. 173.
35 Ibid., p. 178.
36 Ibid., pp. 291–2.

4

Functional theories in sociology
and biology

In chapter 3, I added to Weber's map of values in the social sciences by showing how social scientists rely on values in the discovery and justification of theories of psychological and political development. In this chapter, I want to add another feature to the map and show how, in theorizing that a trait is adaptive and in offering a functional explanation of the presence of the trait in some individual or group, sociologists and biologists rely on values in ways that Weber did not consider. First, however, I offer a general account of functionalism in the social and biological sciences and consider the issue of methodological individualism and the criticisms that are commonly made of functional explanation.

The form of functional explanation

Many theorists in sociology and biology make heavy use of the concept of adaptation. They treat some cluster of characteristics of an individual or group as a trait and theorize that the possession of the trait has some beneficial consequences or function. Durkheim and Radcliffe-Brown, for example, explain the division of labor within a group by showing how it contributes to the proper functioning of the group;[1] Malinowski by showing how the trait contributes to the well-being of the individual members;[2] and Marx by showing how the trait sustains the growth of the forces of production.[3] Each offers a theory about the functional effects of some social practice and attempts to explain the practice by describing the function.

Evolutionary biologists also treat the division of labor within a group as a trait and maintain that the effects of the division are functional.[4] The trait, the biologists explain, contributes to the reproductive success of the members. For example, biologists explain why the male members of a species hunt and the females care for the young by speculating that the differences are due to a gene and showing how the differences in behavior increase the likelihood that both male and female members will pass on their genes to future members of the species.

The form of a functional or adaptive explanation in sociology and biology is the same. The theorist observes that the individual members, I, of a group, G, possess some trait, T. For example, the sociologist observes that Andaman Islanders engage in turtle rituals, or the biologist that black-headed gulls engage in sanitation "rites" – that is, they remove broken eggshells from their nests after the eggs have hatched. The task is to explain why all the I's in G possess T.

According to the biologist, black-headed gulls remove the broken eggshells because this protects the young from predators, and the advantage of protecting the young is that more survive to reproduce. According to the sociologist, the Andaman Islanders engage in turtle rituals because this keeps them from over-hunting a valuable food supply. Both the sociologist and the biologist explain the presence of T by describing some of T's effects and arguing that they are functional or adaptive; or, as Richard Lewontin explains, both explain the presence of T as the solution to a hypothetical design problem – namely, the problem of designing a trait to assure that the needs of the individual or the group are satisfied.[5]

For Radcliffe-Brown, the problem is designing the rites and rituals of the Andamanese to ensure the survival of the turtle and, as a result, the culture. For the biologist, the problem is designing the rites of the gulls to assure the survival of their offspring and, as a result, their genes. Both explain a trait by theorizing that it is a good solution to a hypothetical problem, or, in other words, by showing how the trait is functional or adaptive.

Design without a designer

The design problems in biology and sociology are make-believe, for the biologist and the sociologist do not assume that the members of a species or group consciously design their institutions or choose their traits. That is, neither maintains that T is intentional. Their explanations of T go beyond the intentions of the members of G or don't assume that the members have any intentions at all.

There was a time in the history of biology, however, when design problems were not seen as make-believe. In the eighteenth century, naturalists thought that nature was designed by God and offered intentional explanations of functional or adaptive traits as part of God's intentions. Nature, they thought, was God's design problem, and his creations are his solutions. They assumed that a natural trait could be functional or adaptive for an individual or a species only because God intended it to be.

Darwin subsequently undermined their assumption; for, with his theory of evolution by natural selection, he was able to offer a non-intentional explanation of the good designs in nature. The forces of selection, he explained, operate as if the designs were intended by an agent. Darwin's theory enables biologists to explain traits like the sanitation rites of black-headed gulls by showing how the rites contribute to the gulls' fitness without attributing any intentions or imputing any agency to the natural world at all.

Levels of explanation

Functional explanations can be offered at any number of different levels of organization. While some are at the level of the group, others are at the level of the individual or even the gene. Each explains the presence of T by showing how it enhances some kind of object, but the kinds of object are different – for example, species, organism, and gene. Species are a level of aggregation higher than organisms, while organisms are higher than genes. At what level of aggregation, philosophers ask, should social scientists or biologists attempt to explain the facts of human or animal life? While some say at the level of groups, others say at the level of individuals.[6]

According to the methodological individualists, every fact of social life is nothing other than the effects of the characteristics of a number of interacting individuals and is explained only when the characteristics of these individuals are explained. "[The principle of methodological individualism] states that social processes and events should be deduced from (a) principles governing the behavior of participating individuals and (b) descriptions of their situations."[7] Some functional explanations in the social sciences seem to be individualistic, for they speak only of benefits to individuals; while others seem not to be, for they talk about benefits to groups. Moreover, the explanations of some evolutionary biologists seem to be individualistic with a vengeance, for they reach below the level of the individual organism to that of the gene(s).[8]

But the distinction between individual and group is relative. Relative to her species, the hen is an individual; but relative to her genes, she is a group. As a result, the requirement of individualism, for biology at least, is not clear. Does the principle, for example, require evolutionary explanations at the level of the gene or at the level of the organism?[9] The participating individuals can be participating organisms or participating genes. On the first view, the principle directs biologists to offer explanations with the unit of selection as the gene; on the second, with the unit of selection as the organism.

To require that explanations be at the level of the individual rather than the group leaves the question of level open; for we can ask: "At the level of what kind of individual should we offer our explanations?" The kinds can be arranged in a ladder of descending levels – species, organisms, genes, molecules, on down into the world of subatomic particles. Methodological individualists need to tell us which rung has explanatory primacy; but, even more important, they need to tell us why, for the purpose of explanation, there is only one rung to stand on.

The individualist seems to assume that, other things being equal, the lower the rung on the ladder the better; but when explanations are offered at different levels, other things are seldom equal. Functional explanations in evolutionary biology at the level of the gene, for example, assume that natural selection can select among genes directly; but, as critics have suggested, there is no gene or cluster of genes for each of the different traits for which the biologist offers an explanation.[10] The issue of the unit of selection or level of explanation in biology is not settled by deciding whether species, organism, or gene is more basic but by assessing the different theories of natural selection that each explanation relies on. The same might be said about the levels of explanation in the social sciences. The issue between the individualist and the holist is not settled by deciding whether groups or individuals are more basic but by assessing the different theories of individual or social adaptation which support each of the competing explanations.[11]

The adequacy of functional explanation

The principle of methodological individualism is not only about the level of the explanation, however; it is also about the form. According to the principle, the facts of social life should be deduced from laws or principles. Functional explanations do not seem to include any laws or principles, and the facts they seek to explain – namely, the presence of a trait – cannot be deduced from what they do include – a description of the way in which the trait is adaptive or functional.

To deduce the presence of the trait, we need more than information that the trait is adaptive; we need a principle, a "covering law," or a mechanism to assure that whenever a trait is adaptive, it is present in the individual.[12] However, as a general principle, adaptiveness does not assure presence; for what biologists call "adaptive failure" is a fact of natural and social life. That is, there are many traits that the individual members of a species or a social group lack which, if possessed, would enhance survival but which, for any number of reasons, aren't possessed by the members.

A trait will not evolve, whenever the evolution would be adaptive, for example, unless the trait is heritable; for unless heritable, it will not be the subject of biological evolution. Moreover, even if the trait *is* heritable, individuals may fail to acquire it; for natural selection is not the sole evolutionary force acting on the transmission of the gene(s). An individual may fail to acquire the gene(s), for example, because the gene(s) is subject to genetic drift; that is, because individuals with the trait move from the region and take the genes for the trait with them and out of the gene pool.

The evolutionary biologist must offer a less general and more qualified adaptive principle that is true and supports the inference from the fact of a trait's adaptiveness to the fact of the trait's presence. However, to do so, she must identify the nonevolutionary forces and the countervailing selection pressures on the trait that could prevent the evolution of the trait in the population. But when biologists explain the presence of a trait by showing how it is adaptive, they are able to identify only some of the forces or pressures and are in no position to formulate a principle indicating when the trait will be present. Sociologists are worse off, for where traits are social, adaptive failure is even more common; and they have no theory as rich and as well supported as the theory of evolution by natural selection to even begin to explain when the adaptive traits will be present. Neither Durkheim nor Radcliffe-Brown offers a theory of how adaptive traits are passed on or maintained, and nothing they offer in their explanations of the rites and rituals of social life amount to a principle from which the presence of those rites or rituals could be deduced.[13]

A second concern over functional theories is whether they are empirically testable.[14] Philosophers of science differ on how theories are to be put to an empirical test; but, to the extent that a theory in the natural or social sciences is empirical, it must, in some fashion, face the tribunal of sense. In the case of a functional theory, for example, there must be evidence that a cluster of attributes constitutes a trait and that the trait is adaptive. Functional theories seldom satisfy this condition, for the hypothetical design problem is seldom well defined enough to show that the trait is the best solution. As Lewontin says in his criticism of functional theories in evolutionary biology: "By allowing the theorist to postulate various combinations of 'problems' to which manifest traits are optimal 'solutions,' the adaptationist program makes of adaptation a metaphysical postulate, not only incapable of refutation but necessarily confirmed by every observation."[15]

When evolutionary biologists say that a trait is adaptive or the best solution, they mean that, in the circumstances, it contributes more than other possible traits to the survival of the gene(s); but genes survive for greater and lesser lengths of time, so to make their statements testable, the biologists must specify the period of time – for example, the number of generations – they mean to be tracking the gene. Moreover, they must describe the circumstances in which the trait will and will not contribute most to survival. Removing broken eggshells may contribute more than leaving them in the nest when climatic conditions are not considered among the circumstances, but less when they are. Lewontin's point is that so much is open-ended that a story could be told about any trait that would make it seem adaptive.

Functional theories in sociology do not meet the testability requirement any better. Radcliffe-Brown writes, for example: "My own view is that the negative and positive rites of savages exist and persist because they are part of the mechanism by which an orderly society maintains itself in existence, serving as they do to establish certain fundamental social values."[16] The taboos among the Andamanese, for example, on the use of animals and plants for food persists, on Radcliffe-Brown's view, because they do more to maintain the Andaman society than would a use of animals and plants that was free of such ritual avoidances. We can ask whether anything could show that the taboos contribute *less* to the maintenance of the Andaman society than a use of animals and plants unconstrained by the taboos. Unless Radcliffe-Brown tells us more about the circumstances surrounding the use of animals and plants and indicates the length of time he is talking about (for example, the taboo might do more to maintain the society for five years but less to maintain it for six), we will have to conclude, following Lewontin, that the talk of functions is more a metaphysical article of faith than a statement of empirical fact.

The selection problem

A functional theory attempts to show that a trait is a solution to a design problem; but it replaces one question with another: namely, why of all the solutions that might have been selected T was selected. Even if the funeral rites of the Andaman Islanders were, in the circumstances, the most effective means to maintain the Islanders' culture, why or how was the most effective means selected?

One obvious answer to this question is ruled out by the sociologist: that the behavior is the outcome of a process of intentional choice. Functional theories are meant to be an alternative to, and not dependent on, intentional choice. Had the Andamanese, for example, chosen the funeral rites with the intention of solving a problem, their intention would explain their choice; but Radcliffe-Brown believes that the beliefs and desires of the Andamanese don't explain their ritual behavior, and so he looks for a different account. On his view, the Andamanese don't choose the rites because they believe they are solutions to a problem. They don't think of themselves as facing a problem at all or of rites as a solution to anything.

> The very common tendency to look for the explanation of ritual actions in their purpose is the result of a false assimilation of them to what may be called technical acts. In any technical activity an adequate statement of the purpose of any particular act or series of acts constitutes by itself a sufficient explanation. But ritual acts differ from technical acts in having in all instances some expressive or symbolic element in them.[17]

Radcliffe-Brown looks to functions because, on his view, the Andamanese don't intentionally choose their ritual behavior. Consequently, he can't turn to their intentions to explain how such behavior has come to be selected.

Neither can the biologist turn to intentional choice to answer the selection question. The biologist who is attempting to explain the behavior of the black-headed gull can't turn to intentional choice to answer the question, because the gulls are assumed not to have any intentions. So, for example, the biologist can't explain how the gull comes to select removing the eggshells over leaving them by citing the gulls' thoughts – for example, by maintaining that the gull desires that its genes survive its death and believes that removing the eggshells will contribute more to that end than leaving them in the nest.[18]

The selection question remains. How do we explain behavior of an individual that looks to be directed to a goal but is produced by an individual unable to articulate such a goal, behavior that seems designed to achieve an objective but is performed by an individual to whom no such objective can be attributed? The selection question asks the social scientist to theorize a mechanism that would cause behavior (that seems designed to achieve an objective) to be chosen when the choice is not the result of any intention.

The common opinion is that biologists (since Darwin) have an answer to the selection question, while sociologists do not, and, for that reason, that functionalist theories in biology are more scientifically respectable than those in sociology. The biologists' answer to the selection question is natural selection. What causes design in the absence of a designer or adaptation in the absence of an adapter is random variation and differential reproduction. According to the biologist, a trait is adaptive because it is inherited; its first appearance was due to random variation, and its distribution in the present population is due to differential reproduction – that is, to the fact that individuals with this trait were able to leave more offspring than individuals without it. What causes the black-headed gull to do what contributes most to the survival of its genes is the mechanism of natural selection. The agent of selection is not the gull whose behavior is to be explained, for gulls are not agents, and their behavior is not the effect of any process of intentional choice or deliberation. Nor is God the agent of selection, for the black-headed gull and the eggshell-removing trait were not specially created by God or the result of God's intention. The agent of selection is no agent at all, but only random variation and selection pressures. Hostile forces like food shortages, bad weather, predators, parasites, and disease prevent more individuals without the trait from producing or bearing offspring than individuals with it.

Sociologists cannot appeal to the mechanism of natural selection to explain how traits that contribute more to the maintenance of a group or culture are selected over those that contribute less, for they assume that such traits are not inherited but culturally acquired. To stand even with the biologist, they need a mechanism that explains how culturally acquired traits are transmitted and how more culture-conserving than culture-transforming traits are transmitted to members of the culture. As one critic of functional explanation in the social sciences put the objection:

> If functionalistic explanations are to have any explanatory value, then it is not enough simply to *assume* that social institutions arise in response to actual social needs. Rather, one also has to be in a position to point out the specific *social mechanism* (or mechanisms) by which these social needs supposedly give rise to institutions satisfying these social needs.[19]

Since no mechanism of "cultural selection" has been offered, functional explanation in sociology is commonly thought to fall short of functional explanation in biology or to be no explanation at all.[20]

My own view is that adaptiveness does not explain the presence of a trait even when the trait is inherited. An answer to the selection question must include a description of how the trait is transmitted from some members of the group to others. The biologist explains how, first by theorizing that the trait is the effect of a gene and next by describing the process by which genes are inherited. However, this answer to the selection question replaces a functional explanation with a causal one; for what explains why a black-headed gull removes the broken eggshells is not that removing the eggshells is adaptive but the fact (if it is a fact) that the removing of the eggshells is caused by a gene and the gene was transmitted to the gull through the mechanism of sexual reproduction.

Functionalism faces a dilemma. If it doesn't offer an answer to the selection question, then it doesn't explain the presence of the trait; but if it does provide such an answer, then the answer, rather than the functional fact, explains the presence of the trait. Add the causal facts needed to explain the selection of the trait, and the fact that the trait is functional is trimmed from the explanation; for the causal rather than the functional fact now explains the presence of the trait. In short, functional explanations seem to be incomplete in sociology and unnecessary in biology.

The problem of functional equivalents

The problem of functional equivalents is another reason to doubt that functional facts explain the possession by an individual of a particular trait. Given any adaptive trait T, there is another trait, T′, that is functionally equivalent to T; as a result, the fact that T is adaptive can't explain the presence of T rather than T′ and so can't explain why the individual possesses T. For black-headed gulls, for example, removing the broken eggshell functions to protect the nest from predators and, in turn, helps transmit the genes of the adult to a succeeding generation. However, the same effect could have been achieved by other strategies to foil detection and protect the nest – for example, by camouflaging the broken eggshells. Consequently, the fact that removing the eggshells is adaptive does not explain the presence of the removing but only the presence of a trait that protects the nest from predators. The functional explanation does not explain why one way of protecting it is present rather than another.

One response to the problem of functional equivalents available to both the evolutionary biologist and the sociologist is generality. Evolutionary biologists can maintain that their task is to search for and explain traits that are common to different varieties or species and not to identify or explain the traits that distinguish them. What different varieties of gulls share are strategies for protecting their nests. What they don't share is a common strategy for protecting them. As a strategy for protecting the nest, there is no difference between removing and camouflaging the broken eggshells and so no differences for biologists to explain. The fact of functional equivalents, the biologist might say, is no problem for functional explanation, because, given the way in which evolutionary biology identifies and individuates its facts, there are no facts that functional explanations leave unexplained.

The sociologist can answer in a similar way that the task of sociology is to search for and explain the presence of traits common to different societies or cultures. The fact that every society engages in the practice of some religion is something that sociology needs to explain; but it does not need to explain why a society practices in one of the religions of the world rather than another. The sociologist explains why the members of a society practice a religion by showing how the practice contributes to the society's maintenance. The fact that the practice of some other religion might have had the same effect does not matter, for the aim is not to explain why one religion rather than another, but why any religion at all.

But to make their answers convincing, the biologist and the sociologist have to tell us why the aim of their science should be to explain sameness but not difference. Why isn't it the business of the science to explain why different varieties, societies, or cultures offer different solutions to the same problem of design? The fact that functional explanations can offer no more is not a very good answer. The boundaries of the science need to be rationalized in a way that does not merely trace the limits of some favored mode of explanation.

There is another answer to the problem of functional equivalents that does not hide the differences – namely, that only traits subject to selection are explained by their adaptive effects. However, to offer this answer, social scientists must have an answer to the selection question. They must understand what causes one adaptive trait to be selected over equally adaptive others. Here the biologist and the sociologist are not on equal ground, for while one has a mechanism – namely, natural selection – the other has none.[21]

The evolutionary biologist understands how selection works and so can locate some factor in the evolution of a trait that shows why it, rather than some equally adaptive alternative, came to be transmitted from one generation to another. The biologist can explain, for example, why the black-headed gull removes rather than camouflages the broken eggshells by citing something about the evolutionary history of the gull that made the selection for camouflaging rather than shell-removing gulls impossible – for example, the fact that at no point was a gene for the camouflaging trait in the population's gene pool.

However, the explanation that the biologist offers of the differences between functional equivalents is not a functional but a causal explanation – namely, that the difference is due to the presence of a gene for T but not for T'. Neither the fact that the trait is adaptive nor the mechanism of natural selection needs to be cited to explain why any individual gull removes rather than camouflages broken eggshell, for the explanation is that the gull has a gene(s) for removing shells but no gene(s) for camouflaging them. What functional theories in evolutionary biology explain, if they explain anything at all, is not the presence or absence of a trait in an individual but changes in the distribution of traits in a population of individuals. Functional theories are not about the traits of individuals at all, but about differences in the distribution of traits within groups or populations over time, and, as a result, properly understood, functional theories are not individualist even when the unit of selection is the individual or the gene.

Doubts about functional explanations in the social sciences are not new; philosophers of science raised them years ago. But years ago, philosophers were more confident and more in agreement over what counts as an adequate explanation in the sciences. Today there is less confidence and no consensus, and so it is harder to say that functional explanations don't measure up. "Measure up to what?," the social scientist might wonder. Moreover, the aim of functionalism need not include explanation. That is, a functional analysis of a trait could be understood as part of a thick description rather than as an explanation of a trait.[22] In citing the functional effects of a trait, the social scientist, on this view, is not attempting to explain why the trait is present but to describe how the trait is related to other traits of the individual or group. However, my aim here is not to resolve questions of the scientific status of functional analysis in social science but to set the stage for a political assessment of functionalism. *just what we need (more)?!*

Functional explanations and conservatism

Philosophers of science have not been the only critics of functional theories in biology and sociology. Political philosophers have also been critical. A common political criticism is that functional explanations are inherently conservative.[23] According to this criticism, the explanations offer a defense and a rationalization of the status quo. Functional explanations of rites of sexual passage like decorating the bodies of children by scarification or of female initiation rituals like cicatrization is to condone them, the critics say, because the explanations imply that the rites or rituals satisfy an important human need and, as a result, are morally excusable and thus that the status quo is morally acceptable.

Richard Lewontin offers such criticism of functionalism in evolutionary biology.[24] According to him the program in evolutionary biology of seeking functional explanations of most of an individual's traits is a program of apologetics, for when a trait is explained as contributing to an optimum, it is made to seem legitimate. Consequently, according to Lewontin, when biologists explain a pattern of behavior by telling how it is adaptive, they endorse the status quo by condoning the present way of doing things.

Most functionalists dismiss the criticism that their program is conservative. To show that a trait is adaptive, they say, is not to show that it is legitimate, and to show that a trait is necessary is not to judge that it is desirable. The judgment that ritual scarification is necessary to maintain the structure of the society of the Ndembu of Central Africa is a judgment of fact, and it is a fallacy, they say, to infer from any fact about the practice any judgment about whether the practice is desirable or ought to be continued.

The functional explanation of a rite, most sociologists would say, is completely silent on whether the rite is desirable. All that follows from the fact that the initiation rite is functional is that if it is desirable to maintain the structure of the society of the Ndembu, it is desirable to maintain the rite; but the sociologist (being committed to value-freedom) is silent on whether maintaining the structure of the society of the Ndembu is desirable, and so there is no basis for saying that the explanation is a defense of anything, let alone the status quo.

There is a tradition of conservative political thought that does base judgments of policy on a functionalist analysis. Patrick Devlin, for example, argues against proposed reforms in Britain's laws on homosexuality that legal toleration of sodomy would tear apart the fabric of British society and, as a result, should be resisted.[25] Devlin assumes that any tearing of the fabric is undesirable, but, of course, proponents of the reform believe that if changing the law did tear the fabric, well and good, for, on their view, a fabric woven from threads of intolerance is tawdry and not worth preserving. The use Devlin makes of functionalist theorizing encourages the belief that the theorizing is itself conservative, but there is nothing in functionalism itself that supports Devlin's conservative political philosophy.

Even if some functionalist analyses do have a static or equilibrium bias, such a bias is not part of every such analysis. Marx and Engels's theory of history does not have such a bias and yet is a form of functionalism.[26] Moreover, Marx and Engels use their theory to condemn, rather than condone, the social and economic structures they are attempting to explain.

The rise of Protestantism in Europe in the sixteenth and seventeenth centuries, Marx and Engels claim, is to be explained by showing how it contributed to the growth of the forces of production; but Marx and Engels do not believe that the fact that the Protestant religion contributed more than the Catholic religion to the growth of these forces was any reason to prefer one over the other or to judge that the rise of Protestantism was desirable. They attempt to explain the facts of social life by showing that they are adaptive but do not maintain that because they are adaptive, they are desirable.

Marx and Engels viewed history as if it were a design problem – the problem of placing nature at the service of human needs – and they tried to explain most traits of human society or culture as a solution. They did not believe, however, that at each moment in history the solution was a trait that conserved the prevailing social order. At times when the social or economic organization of a society prevents the forces of production – nature's power to serve – from growing, an adaptive trait helps to overturn rather than conserve the basis of the society.

During the Middle Ages, for example, prohibitions against money-lending were adaptive, because they helped to maintain the economy of feudalism; and at that stage in human history, such an economy enabled the forces of production to grow. However, during the sixteenth and seventeenth centuries, these prohibitions were no longer adaptive, because the economy of feudalism now constrained rather than sustained the forces of production. The solution was a more permissive attitude towards money-lending. Thus, on Marx and Engels's view, the function of a trait is not always to conserve the prevailing social or economic arrangements but sometimes to change them.

There are two reasons, then, to resist the idea that in theorizing the function of a trait the social scientist is condoning the status quo. First, the social scientist can theorize that the function of the trait is to upset the status quo, and, second, she can theorize that the trait is to conserve the status quo and judge, without any inconsistency, that the trait is undesirable because she judges that the status quo is undesirable.

Ideology and theorizing functions

An ideology is a body of widely held but false beliefs that has the effect of making a practice or institution that is not legitimate seem so.[27] The Protestant "ethic," on Marx and Engels's view, is an ideology. According to that ethic, in a capitalist society, as long as every market is free, every member has an equal opportunity to acquire any of the society's prizes. Hard work and diligence are all that is needed for poor boys or girls to become rich men and women. Inequalities in income or wealth are to be explained by differences in interest or motivation. Though these beliefs are false, they do have the effect of making a capitalist society seem just or, at least, just to those who believe, as part of the Protestant ethic, that to each according to his effort is a principle of just distribution.

Ideology has often been theorized by social scientists. Many have attempted to explain why beliefs that are false are still held by almost every member of a group. According to one prominent theory of ideology, primarily due to Marx, the holding of the beliefs is to be explained functionally by the fact that the beliefs legitimate an existing social order. The Protestant ethic is widely believed, Marx would say, because it functions to legitimate a form of economic organization – namely, capitalism – that exploits the members of one economic class, the workers, for the benefit of another, the capitalists. One problem with functional explanations of ideologies is that, like other functional explanations in sociology, they offer no answer to the selection question. Marx does not tell us how beliefs that legitimate capitalism come to be held by members of the proletariat and why they are selected over beliefs that delegitimate capitalist forms of economic organization.

Not every explanation of the holding of beliefs in terms of their legitimating power is a functional explanation. Some are intentional explanations. Conspiracy theories offer intentional explanations of ideology. According to these theories, it is in the interest of members of the ruling class that the existing social order should seem to be legitimate, and the members of this class see that the Protestant ethic best serves this interest. As a result, they decide to use their power and resources to see that the Protestant ethic is widely taught and to persuade members of the working class that the ethic is true.

Intentional explanations of ideologies often employ the concept of self-deception. The intentions of the ruling class to cause members of the working class to hold false beliefs, on this view, need not be conscious or calculated. Members of the ruling class may consciously believe that the Protestant ethic is true or consciously believe that in teaching the ethic to members of the working class, they are serving the workers' interests. But it is too easy to attribute unconscious intentions, and without a rule for reasonably imputing them, they can be found everywhere and be made to explain anything.

Conspiracy theories are today's version of natural theology. The proponents see designs in the social world almost everywhere, assume that they are intentional, and conclude that a devil (not a god) created them.

Where natural theology was a preoccupation of the past, natural demon-
ology is a preoccupation of the present, and, of course, both preoccu-
pations are strong on imagination and weak on evidence. On the other
hand, intentional explanations are more plausible of a social design than
a natural design, and it is more reasonable to believe, based on the
available evidence, that there are demons in Washington or on Wall Street
than that a god in the heavens is deciding what happens in the world.

Some critics of functionalism in evolutionary biology like Lewontin
maintain that it is a form of ideology.[28] Most biologists, on the other
hand, deny that the program is ideological, because they do not believe
that it has any legitimating power. To judge that a trait is adaptive, they
reason, is not to condone or legitimate it. Therefore, when the functionalist program teaches that a trait is adaptive, it does not teach that it
is legitimate; and even if the teaching is false, it cannot be said to be
a form of ideology.

I agree that to judge that a trait is adaptive is not, thereby, to judge
that it is desirable or to condone it, but I do think that functional theories
introduce a new note of partisanship into social science; for, as I will
explain in the next section, they favor a particular stand on matters of
public policy by the way they frame the facts and draw the line between
what is fixed and what is variable.

The distinction between fixed and variable

Radcliffe-Brown looks to explain the traits of individual members of a
group – for example, the fact that they engage in certain rituals – by seeing
how the traits satisfy the needs of the group. He does not look to explain
the needs of the group by seeing how they enhance traits of the individual.
That is, he vests explanatory primacy in the group, and his functional
analysis rests on the thesis that the ritual practices of the members of
a group are explained by the structure of the group and the need to
maintain it.[29] As a result, the traits of the individual are understood as
adaptations to needs of the group, but the needs of the group are not
understood as adaptations to the traits of the individual. The needs of
the group, on his account, operate to keep the individual on a leash.

According to his primacy thesis, the needs of the group are given or
fixed, and the traits of individuals are variable or subject to change.
Whatever the needs of the group, the members, as if by an invisible hand,
adjust to serve them. Radcliffe-Brown does not say that this is desirable;
but he presents the relations between the needs and the traits as if they
were part of the natural order of things and never considers whether the

relation between the individual and the group can be otherwise. Though he says that the needs are primary and not that they ought to be, the force of his analysis is that the primacy is necessary or inevitable, and in this respect he seems to be offering a limit theory.[30] That is, his functionalism implies that changes in the relation between the individual and the group are limited by the primacy of the group's survival.

Radcliffe-Brown does not preach a conservative political philosophy any more than a liberal one. However, by teaching that, in the area of rites and rituals and other forms of symbolic action, individuals rather than groups do the adapting, he implies that the liberal ideal of citizen or consumer sovereignty – in which practices or policies of the group adapt to the interests of the members – is out of touch with the facts of social life. By not considering how changes in the rituals might better serve the interests of the individuals who practice them, he makes it seem as if the individuals are powerless to make these changes or that the changes are not subject to their wills. He does not say that the individuals must adapt to the group, but his analysis limits the space of socially possible worlds to those in which groups come first.

In evolutionary biology, the functionalist looks to explain the behavior of an individual – for example, that a man invests less time in child care than a woman – by showing that, in his environment, the traits contribute most to the transmission and survival of his genes. The biologist does not consider how, by adapting the environment, the man could invest more time in child care without reducing his fitness or how he could adapt his motivation so that his reproductive fitness has less influence on the time he devotes to child care.

Allowing only the behavior to adapt, the biologist treats the individual's environment and the influence of his genes as fixed. The reproductive fitness of the individual is primary. Like Radcliffe-Brown, the biologist is committed to a primacy thesis – namely, that the practices of the members of a species are explained by the needs of the members to successfully reproduce themselves. Whatever the needs of the genes, the individual, as if by an invisible hand, moves to serve them. The biologist does not say that this is desirable but presents it as if it were part of the natural order of things and never considers whether the relation between the individual and the genes can be otherwise.

Radcliffe-Brown's functional sociology naturalizes the conformity of the individual to the group. The functionalist program in evolutionary biology naturalizes the conformity of the individual to the gene. According to Lewontin, there are important similarities between the view of the world projected by the functionalist program in biology and the view projected by the defense of modern market society.

Liberal social theory of the last part of the nineteenth century and of the twentieth has emphasized dynamic equilibrium and optimality. Individuals may rise and fall in the social system, but the system itself is seen as stable, and as close to perfect as any system can be.[31]

The ideology of equilibrium and dynamic stability characterizes modern evolutionary theory as much as it does bourgeois economics and political theory. Whig history is mimicked by Whig biology.[32]

If the functionalist program in biology is partisan to liberal values, other functional programs are partisan to other, competing values. Few in sociology, for example, favor liberal values; for most sociologists naturalize the needs of a group. Conformity of the individual to the group is naturalized in the sense of hiding or withholding alternatives. Functionalist programs differ, but each naturalizes some traits and denaturalizes others in depicting some as changeable and others as fixed, and, as a result, each program limits the space of alternatives from which public policies may be chosen. There is nothing in the logic of functionalism that limits the space to the policies of liberal economic theory. In the hands of conservatives like Patrick Devlin, functionalism is used to promote a conservative social agenda. Though there is nothing in the logic that favors a particular conception of the good, there *is* something in the logic that assures that each program will favor some conception of the good over others, in the sense of so framing the facts that other conceptions fall outside and, as a result, seem not to be possible or feasible.

Eliminating the question of truth

There is another way in which theorizing functions draws values into social science. Among the traits that functional theories are used to explain is the holding of beliefs. As I indicated in the earlier section on ideology, some sociologists explain the fact that their subjects have a belief by showing that the belief is adaptive or functional. Often they offer such an explanation when, as they see it, the proposition believed is false and the subject's own reasons for believing the proposition to be true are, by the social scientists' standards, irrelevant, weak, or unconvincing.[33]

The subject assumes that the reasons or evidence she offers explain why she believes that the proposition is true. The sociologists assume otherwise. They replace her reasons with their own functional explanation of her belief. They ignore the content of the proposition and concentrate on the effects of her believing it.

The less the social scientists see eye to eye with their subjects and the more their own beliefs are at odds with those of their subjects, the more they discount the subjects' explanations and replace them with their own. In offering functional explanations of beliefs, the issue is no longer whether the propositions are true or whether there is evidence for believing them to be true but how holding the beliefs is adaptive or functional: how it maintains the structure of the group or enhances the transmission of a gene.

> The more deep-seated the mutual distrust, the more does the argument of the other appear so palpably implausible, even absurd, that one no longer inquires into substance or logical structure to assess its truth claims. Instead, one confronts the other's argument with an entirely different question: how does it happen to be advanced at all? Thought thus becomes altogether functionalized, interpreted only in terms of the presumed social or economic or psychological sources and functions.[34]

The practice of offering functional explanations of belief has significant moral consequences. It contributes not only to our beliefs about what is but also to our beliefs about what ought to be. First, the practice presents us with a view of the subject that is at odds with the view on which most of our moral thinking depends. The subjects of morality, as I argue in chapter 8, are so related to their own explanations of themselves that those explanations cannot be mostly mistaken. In offering functional explanations of a large body of a subject's beliefs, the social scientist implies that the subject's own explanations are mostly mistaken, and, as a result, implies that she is not a subject of morality or someone towards whom we should adopt our full array of moral attitudes or view as bearer of moral responsibility. My aim in chapter 8 is to convince you of this point. Here I can only affirm it. The subjects of functional explanation, I will argue, are not the subjects of our most prominent moral theories or of our ordinary moral point of view.

Second, in offering functional explanations of the beliefs of a subject, social scientists replace the subject's interest with their own. Whereas the subject is interested in the content of her beliefs, the scientists are interested only in the fact that the subject believes them. For example, a subject believes that the teachings of the Catholic Church on birth control are true. The scientists explain why she holds the belief by showing how it is adaptive. Their explanation does not address the teachings of the Church at all. In exchanging the subject's interest in religion for their interest in function, they make a judgment of value – namely, that their *too quick — ignores fact that "truth" is not an explanation ever for true beliefs —*

interest in the effects of her beliefs is more important than her interest in their content. Moreover, in judging that there is not a reasonable but only a functional basis for her beliefs, they deny that an interest in the truth of what she believes is of great value.

Third, when the beliefs of the subject have a moral content, social scientists, in offering a functional explanation, replace the subject's moral judgment with their own; for their reason for seeking a functional explanation is their judgment that her beliefs are false or irrational. For example, a community of women believe that heterosexuality is morally undesirable for women and explain why they believe this by arguing that, given the unequal power of the sexes, heterosexual sex is not fully voluntary. A sociologist who doesn't agree with either the belief or the women's reasons is likely to look elsewhere for an explanation, and if he sees functions where he can't see reasons, he looks for functional effects. He considers how the belief strengthens the bonds between the women or enforces the borders of their community. If the sociologist's assessment of the women's belief is based on his own moral judgment of heterosexuality, then his practice of offering a functional explanation is partisan.

Although in one respect, scientists who offer a functional explanation of a subject's belief ignore the belief's content, in another, they do not; for their reason for offering the explanation is their judgment that the belief is false and unreasonable, and among their reasons for this judgment are their own beliefs about the content. As a result, the scientists' explanation of their subject's partisan beliefs are not value-neutral but are based on their own partisanship.

wrong

Conclusion

Because functionalist theories rely on a distinction between traits that are and are not adaptable, they introduce forms of partisanship that Weber does not discuss; for he does not consider the different framing effects of the various kinds of theories employed in the social sciences. Moreover, when a theory of ideology or a functional explanation of belief is based on a judgment that the subject's beliefs are false or unreasonable, values are again brought into play, and when the beliefs are moral or political beliefs, the values are moral or political values. Though the charges that functionalist theories in sociology are inherently conservative or that functionalist theories in evolutionary biology are inherently liberal are mistaken, these theories do affect, and are affected by, the moral and political judgments that surround them, in a variety of more subtle and

— maybe partially true that social scientists tend to explain beliefs of which they disapprove, but true is not inherent in social science logic —

less obvious ways than traditional discussions of value-neutrality reveal. My point in this chapter has not been to oppose or support functional explanations in the social sciences but only to show how they oppose the ideal of neutrality.

NOTES

1   E. Durkheim, *Divisions of Labor in Society*, tr. G. Simpson (Macmillan, 1933), and A. R. Radcliffe-Brown, *Structure and Function in Primitive Society* (Free Press, 1952), pp. 133–211.
2   B. Malinowski, *The Sexual Lives of Savages in North-Western Melanesia*, 3rd ed. (Routledge and Kegan Paul, 1948).
3   K. Marx, Preface to *The Critique of Political Economy*, in *Karl Marx's Selected Writings*, ed. D. McLellan (Oxford University Press, 1977), pp. 388–90.
4   See Lewontin, "Adaptation."
5   Ibid., pp. 240–4.
6   For a discussion of the debate between holists and individualists in the social sciences, see A. Rosenberg, *Philosophy of Social Science* (Westview Press, 1988), pp. 113–40; for a discussion of the debate in biology, see E. Sober, "Holism, Individualism and the Units of Selection," in *Conceptual Issues in Evolutionary Biology*, ed. E. Sober (MIT Press, 1984), pp. 184–209.
7   J. W. N. Watkins, "Ideal Types and Historical Explanation," in *The Philosophy of Social Explanation*, ed. A. Ryan (Oxford University Press, 1973), p. 88. Watkins talks only about explanations in the social sciences; but the issues he raises are also issues in the philosophy of biology, for there is a debate between individualists and holists within evolutionary biology that parallels the debate in the social sciences. For a discussion of the parallels see Sober, "Holism."
8   See, e.g., R. Dawkins, *The Selfish Gene* (Oxford University Press, 1976).
9   For a discussion of this issue, see S. J. Gould, "Caring Groups and Selfish Genes," in *Conceptual Issues in Evolutionary Biology*, ed. E. Sober (MIT Press, 1984), pp. 119–24.
10 Ibid., p. 123.
11 For more on the issue of individualism in the social sciences, see chapter 5 and the discussion of micro and macro explanations in economics.
12 See C. G. Hempel, *The Philosophy of Natural Science* (Prentice-Hall, 1966), pp. 47–9.
13 The methodological individualist's requirement that the facts be deducible from principles relies on a more general requirement for scientific explanation endorsed by philosophers of the natural sciences. The requirement is that the explanatory information adduced by the explanation affords good grounds for believing that the phenomenon to be explained did occur. See ibid., p. 48. Functional explanations do not seem to satisfy this relevance requirement, for the fact that a trait is functional does not afford good grounds for believing that it is present, given the facts of adaptive failure.
14 The requirement that the statements constituting an explanation be testable is,

along with the relevance requirement, one of two basic conditions of adequacy for explanations in the sciences, according to most philosophers of the natural sciences. See ibid., p. 49. The failure of functional explanations to meet these requirements leads these philosophers to conclude that they are not scientific explanations. An alternative view is that these requirements are too strict and that scientific explanations are more variable. For alternative views, see A. Garfinkel, *Forms of Explanation* (Yale University Press, 1981), and B. van Fraassen, *The Scientific Image* (Oxford University Press, 1980).

15   Lewontin, "Adaptation," p. 244.

16   Radcliffe-Brown, *Structure*, p. 151.

17   Ibid., p. 143.

18   The biologist, of course, can't appeal to God's intentions, because, as I explained earlier, biology, with the discovery of natural selection, divorced itself from natural theology.

19   J. C. Harsanyi, "Individualistic and Functionalistic Explanations in the Light of Game Theory: The Example of Social Status," in *Problems in Philosophy of Science*, ed. I. Lakatos and A. Musgrave (North-Holland Publishing Co., 1968), p. 307; emphasis original.

20   For a discussion of this issue, see J. Elster, *Ulysses and the Sirens: Studies in Rationality and Irrationality* (Cambridge University Press, 1979), pp. 28–35.

21   Some social scientists, however, have theorized a mechanism of cultural selection with gene-like entities that transmit the cultural traits and selection pressures that operate on them. See, e.g., W. H. Durham, "Toward a Coevolutionary Theory of Human Biology and Culture," in *Evolutionary Biology and Human Social Behavior: An Anthropological Perspective*, ed. N. A. Chagnon and W. Irons (Duxbury Press, 1979), pp. 39–58.

22   See C. Geertz, *The Interpretation of Cultures* (Basic Books, 1973), for a discussion of the idea of thick and thin descriptions of a culture.

23   See D. Gregg and E. Williams, "The Dismal Science of Functionalism," *American Anthropologist*, 50 (1948), pp. 320–3.

24   Lewontin, "Adaptation."

25   P. Devlin, *The Enforcement of Morals* (Oxford University Press, 1965).

26   See G. A. Cohen, *Marx's Theory of History: A Defense* (Princeton University Press, 1978), pp. 278–96, for an interesting presentation of this view.

27   The term "ideology" has many different meanings, but the one that interests me can be found in Marx's writings – e.g., *The Economic and Philosophical Manuscripts* and *The German Ideology* – and, as I explain in chapter 10, is central to the idea of a critical theory. For a survey of the different meanings and the importance of the term in political philosophy, see T. Eagleton, *Ideology: An Introduction* (Verso, 1991); and for an account of the relation between the idea of ideology and functional analysis, see Cohen, *Marx's Theory of History*, pp. 289–96.

28   Lewontin, "Adaptation," pp. 249–51.

29   See Cohen, *Marx's Theory of History*, pp. 134–74, for a discussion of the primacy thesis that Marx assumes in offering his own functional analysis of history.

30 See chapter 3 for a discussion of limit theories.

31 Lewontin, "Adaptation," p. 250.

32 Ibid.

33 The assumption is that true or reasonable beliefs are not in need of a so-
    cial scientific explanation but that false or unreasonable beliefs are. See R. Keat
    and J. Urry, *Social Theory as Science* (Routledge and Kegan Paul, 1975),
    pp. 204–12, for a discussion of the assumption. My point is not that the as-
    sumption is appropriate or reasonable but that to the extent that social scien-
    tists rely on it in offering functional explanations of moral or political belief,
    they are making judgments of moral or political value.

34 R. K. Merton, *The Sociology of Science* (University of Chicago Press, 1973),
    p. 100.

but this assumption is wrong

— agreed, but shouldn't do this critique on the bases of bad social science —

5

Rational choice theories in positive and normative economics

My point in the last two chapters was that Weber's map of values in the social sciences leaves much of the territory uncharted and ignores many social influences on the theoretical work of the social sciences. The account reveals too little about values in theorizing in psychology and comparative political theory, as I explained in chapter 3, and too little about values in theorizing in sociology and behavioral biology, as I explained in chapter 4. In this chapter, I turn to theorizing in neoclassical economics – the most liberal of all the liberal social sciences – and explain how values are drawn into the practice of theorizing, predicting, and assessing economic choices. First, however, I describe the aims and methods of positive and normative economics and explain how they rely on rational choice theory. Next, I consider the role of idealization in economics and how it bears on the issue of partisanship.

The aims of an economic science

Weber maintained that economics is a science of means and not ends, because when it comes to ends, no science is possible. Many economists accept Weber's view. The only science of economics, they maintain, is a science of predictive or positive economics. The aim of the science is to predict but not to appraise the results of economic policy. Some economists, however, believe that economics should appraise the results as well as predict them. The science of economics, they maintain, should include normative economics, and the aim should be to develop measures for policymakers to use to determine whether an economic outcome or end is desirable. Unlike positive economics, normative economics aims to be a science of both means and ends.

The difference in aim between normative and positive economics can be illustrated by what is called "the policy syllogism." The syllogism has the following form:

> 1 A causes B.
> 2 B is desirable.
> 3 Do A.

The conclusion of the syllogism is a direction for action, which is what policymakers are looking for. The first premise is a statement of means. It tells the policymaker that A causes B and, as a result, that A is a means to B. The second premise is a statement of ends, which tells the policymaker that B is a good or valuable end. From premises 1 and 2, the policymaker can decide what to do.

The aim of positive economics is to supply policymakers with the first premise of the syllogism, whereas the aim of normative economics is to supply them with premise 1 and criteria by which to assess premises like 2. Positive economics, for example, may supply policymakers with a premise about the relation between the minimum wage, A, and unemployment, B, with which to predict the effect of changes in the minimum wage on unemployment. But positive economics will be silent on the value of unemployment and, as a result, silent on whether changes in the minimum wage are desirable.

The aim of normative economics, on the other hand, is to provide policymakers with standards for measuring human welfare or well-being and determining whether an increase in unemployment or the minimum wage is desirable. Though neither positive nor normative economics is meant to yield value judgments like 2, the aim of normative economics is to provide policymakers with a means to appraise or evaluate such judgments of value.

Premises like 1, on Weber's view, are value-free. They do not involve any appraisal or evaluation of A or B but merely describe the relationship between them. The statement that increases in the minimum wage cause increases in unemployment, for example, does not imply that a change in the minimum wage or in the level of unemployment is desirable; so, on Weber's view, it is free of moral and political value. Premises like 2, according to Weber, are value-laden. They express "the desirability or undesirability of social facts from an ethical or cultural point of view."[1] A theory that includes premises of this form would not qualify as a science, for some disputes over whether to accept such a theory could not be resolved by the methods of science. If economics is to be a science, then, it can offer the policymaker only the first premise of the policy syllogism. Though positive economics can contribute to reasoning about public policy, its contributions are not decisive, for they are silent on whether a premise like 2 is true and even on how the truth of 2 should be decided.

Positive economists are usually more attracted to the market as a mechanism for making allocation decisions than to any use of the policy syllogism; for the market, on their view, is a means of directing the flow of resources that avoids public policy and the need to make judgments of collective or social value altogether. With the market, no political process is required to choose between alternative allocations or the ends that each is expected to serve; for the choice of allocations results from the market choices of every individual who buys or sells in the market. According to these economists, the market advances value-neutrality in a major way, for as long as it is kept free of government regulation and the political process, the only values that enter into economic decision making are those of each of the participants, and the market itself remains neutral and does not favor the values of any one participant over another.

Positive economics

The positive theories of economics are rational choice theories. Behavior is theorized as the outcome of a rational choice, and a choice is rational, according to this approach, if and only if it maximizes some notional function like utility or some accounting magnitude like profit. For example, according to the economic theory of the household or the firm, a choice to consume or produce a unit of some good is rational if and only if the marginal benefit to the household or the firm exceeds the marginal cost. Rational choice theories are based on the assumption that a subject's choices are always rational. Economists believe that the assumption yields true predictions of the behavior of households and firms in free market economies like those of western Europe or North America.

Theories of the firm and the household in economics, like the functional theories of sociology and behavioral biology, are based on the notion of optimality. The subjects of each theory are assumed by the theory to choose from the alternatives the one(s) that, according to the theory, is (are) optimal. The theories differ in how they define the optimum or identify the function that their subjects are assumed to maximize. According to the theory of the firm, firms maximize profit, growth of output, or market share. According to functional theories in behavioral biology, organisms maximize some biological measure like the number of mates or offspring or the share of the available food supply. According to functional theories in sociology, members of groups maximize some social measure like the bonds between members or conformity to the group's rules or traditions.

Rational choice theory is used to establish premise 1 of the policy syllogism. From the theory, economists deduce propositions (represented graphically as a set of supply and demand curves) relating an agent's choices and their cost (price). With households, they relate the price and the quantity of a good consumed, while with firms, they relate the price and the quantity produced. Thus, from the theory that firms maximize profits and a few background assumptions, economists conclude that the demand for labor is downward sloping, and, from the downward-sloping curve, they reason that if the minimum wage decreases and lowers the price of labor, firms will increase the size of their work force and decrease unemployment. The curve supplies economists with a method of predicting changes in employment and a method for finding a means to the end of increasing employment. Policymakers who judge that increases in employment are desirable, premise 2, can reason that they ought to raise the minimum wage, 3, if they learn the truth of premise 1 from predictive economics.

The nature of rational choice

The rational choice theories offered by economists can be understood in a number of different ways. According to one understanding, the subjects know the optimal choice, while according to another, they only act as if they do. The distinction I am drawing is the same one as Herbert Simon drew between procedural and substantive or as-if rationality.[2] Simon's idea is that psychology and economics have adopted different views of rationality, economics a substantive view and psychology a procedural one.

Psychologists are interested in the actual process, the reasoning, that leads to the selection of an alternative; whereas economists are interested only in the result – namely, whether the selection maximizes utility or profit. They treat the household or firm as a black box. They are not interested in why the firm acts as if it were attempting to maximize profit but only in the fact that the firm does act this way. From the fact that it does, economists can make predictions about how firms will behave under changing market conditions, and on the basis of the as-if or substantive rationality of firms, they can theorize what and how much gets produced and with what resources and supply the first premise of a policy syllogism.

Simon argues that many households and firms are not rational in the procedural or substantive sense and, as a result, that economists cannot predict from the fact that a certain consumption or production decision is optimal that a household or firm will make it. This is a reason, he believes, to give up optimality in theorizing the behavior of households and firms. However, on the view of other economists, even if Simon is correct and households and firms don't optimize, economics should retain optimality as its central or core theoretical concept, for it doesn't matter whether individual households or firms act as if they were attempting to maximize profit or utility. It matters only how they act in the aggregate or on average. If, in the aggregate, deviations from the optimality assumption cancel out, it doesn't matter that each or even most individual households or firms are not rational in either sense. As John Hicks writes: "But economics is not in the end most interested in the behaviour of individuals, it is concerned with the behaviour of groups."[3] Hicks offers a third interpretation of rational choice theory in economics.

On the third interpretation, it is not necessary that each firm act as if it were attempting to maximize profit but only that the aggregate effect of the behavior of firms is equal to what it would have been had each firm acted as if it were substantively rational. Firms do not need to be rational in either the procedural or the substantive (as-if) sense, on Hicks's view. All that is necessary is that they be rational in what might be called the "doubly as-if sense"; that is, it is as if firms acted as if they were attempting to maximize profit (as if they were rational in the as-if or substantive sense). On this view, the aim of theories in economics is not to yield true predictions of microeconomic events like the production decisions of an individual firm but only true predictions of macroeconomic events like the effect of changes in the price of labor on aggregate employment. The test of the rationality postulate is the behavior not of a firm but of a market, an industry, or the entire economy.

Explanations based on the doubly as-if sense of rationality are not favored by methodological individualists, for they rely on a characteristic of a group – namely, doubly as-if rationality – rather than characteristics of individuals. The debate between methodological individualists and holists in economics is over macro and micro explanations of the behavior of firms, between explanations at the level of aggregates or groups of firms and explanations at the level of individual firms. But the debate is not settled by the fact that firms are, in a metaphysical sense, more basic, but by assessing the theoretical support for the doubly as-if conception of rationality or the predictive success of theories that employ this conception of rationality.[4]

Rationality and the selection question

Neither as-if nor doubly as-if rationality offers any answer to the selection question.[5] Neither tells us how it comes to pass that a household or firm selects the optimum from all possible or feasible alternatives. Procedural rationality, however, does offer an answer. Of all the alternatives, the reason why the household or firm selected the optimum is that its being optimal is a reason for it to do so. On this view, the household or firm engages in a process of practical reasoning, and the choice of the optimal alternative is the conclusion. Procedural rationality provides intentional explanations of the firm's choices, while substantive and doubly as-if rationality do not.

A social scientist who attributes substantive rationality to a subject or doubly as-if rationality to a group of subjects has to look elsewhere for an answer to the selection question. Some economists have theorized a mechanism that resembles natural selection.[6] They reason that in a competitive economy firms that have the trait of substantive rationality are more fit than firms that lack it. Firms that are rational in the substantive sense acquire resources and prosper, whereas those that are not lose resources and close. As a result, the market evolves through time in such a way that the proportion of firms with the trait increases. Competition resembles a Darwinian selection mechanism and produces the same results as would have been produced had all the firms in the market been rational in the procedural sense. As if by an invisible hand, firms act as if they were procedurally rational – that is, planned to maximize profits – because selection pressures – namely, competition for land, labor, and capital – drive those firms that don't maximize profit from the market.

However, evolutionary theories of market competition do not offer an answer to the selection question in economics, for competition between firms does not explain why any given firm selects the most profitable alternative. Competition between firms at most explains why the proportion of profitable to unprofitable firms in a market increases over time. The forces of market competition do not explain the presence of substantive rationality in some firms and its absence in others, for they do not explain what causes any firm to choose the optimum. That is, there is nothing in the theory of market competition that plays the role that the gene plays in the theory of evolution by natural selection, no mechanism that causes a trait to arise in an individual.

As economists theorize the behavior of the firm, there is nothing in the theory that reveals anything inside the firm. The theory of evolution by natural selection, on the other hand, theorizes a structure inside the organism – namely, the genes – that explains the disposition of the organism to optimize and thereby answers the question of how the organism comes to "select" alternatives that contribute most to fitness. In theorizing evolution, biologists can cite the gene to explain how the subject selects the optimal over a suboptimal alternative. Because there is nothing corresponding to the gene in theorizing evolution in economics, there is nothing that explains how the firm comes to "select" alternatives that contribute most to profits over those that contribute less.

Whatever power the theory of evolution by natural selection has to explain the behavior of an individual organism it has by theorizing that something inside the organism expresses itself through the organism's behavior. Without theorizing that anything within the firm – for example, management – expresses itself through the firm's behavior, the economist's theory of market competition has no power to explain the behavior. Given the way in which economists theorize rationality, by contrast with the way that behavioral biologists theorize evolution, rational choice theories in economics – that is, substantive and doubly as-if rationality – do not explain rational choice.

Most economists are unconcerned that their theories do not explain choice. The goal of economics as a science, as they see it, is not to explain choices but only to predict them. As Milton Friedman writes: "The ultimate goal of a positive science is the development of a 'theory' or 'hypothesis' that yields valid and meaningful (i.e., not truistic) predictions about phenomena not yet observed."[7] If the hypothesis that firms are substantively rational yields valid predictions of the supply of a good by a firm or group of firms, then, as Friedman sees it, the goal of economics has been met, whether or not the hypothesis yields an explanation of how any firm selects or decides how much of a good to supply. According to his view, the selection question is not an economic question, and theorizing in economics should not be expected to provide an answer to it.

Friedman assumes that economists have a reason to trust the predictions yielded by their rational choice theory, even though their theory is silent on the question of causes. They have good reason to assume, on his view, that a firm will choose the most profitable alternative, even though they know nothing about the process of decision making within the firm that leads to its choices. The fact that the firm has acted profitably in the past, he seems to think, is reason enough to believe that it will act profitably in the future.

Friedman's critics have argued that there is no prediction of choices in economics without an explanation of how the choices are made. As one critic, Harvey Leibenstein, writes:

> Predictive capacity without explanatory capacity is worthless. Mere clairvoyance, irrespective of its sharpness, does not itself have scientific

standing. Only predictive capacity that arises out of having coherent and communicable explanations has scientific standing. The power to predict is subsidiary to the power to explain. Explanation without prediction is sufficient, but prediction without explanation is of no consequence from a scientific standpoint.[8]

A firm's past is a basis for predicting its future only on the assumption that circumstances inside the firm remain unchanged. A theory that explains why the firm was profitable in the past must describe how the firm was managed. According to Leibenstein, a theory that yields reasonable predictions of its profitability in the future must also describe how the firm is managed.

Most economists maintain that functional theories like those offered by sociologists do not predict or explain the choices of individuals within a group because the theories do not supply an answer to what I have been calling "the selection question."[9] On their view, functional theories are unsatisfactory – they have no real predictive or explanatory power – because they do not offer a social mechanism by which the salutary social effects, the social optimum, gives rise to the actions – for example, ritual behavior – that produce these effects. A functional theory, on their view, has no predictive or explanatory power unless it includes a causal feedback loop between the effects and the actions that maintain them, and hence an answer to the selection question. But few if any functional theories include any causal mechanism at all. Therefore, few if any have any predictive or explanatory power.[10]

Many economists contrast the functional approaches of sociology, which assume that social institutions and behavior can be predicted or explained by their social functions, with the rationalistic approaches of economics, which assume that behavior can be predicted or explained as a rational pursuit of various personal objectives or interests. They argue that the rationalistic approaches have the predictive or explanatory power that the functional approaches lack.[11] But to the extent that the rationalistic approaches of economics are based on a substantive rather than a procedural concept of rationality, they have little explanatory power, and, lacking explanatory power, they yield predictions that have little power as well. That is, the same objection can be raised against the rationalist approach of economics as economists raise against the functionalist approach of sociology – namely, that there is no description of how anything happens. The economists' rational choice theory is unsatisfactory, has no real predictive power, because it does not describe the procedure by which the salutary economic effects, the satisfaction of personal objectives or interests, give rise to the behavior that satisfies the objectives or interests. Without a description of the procedure, the predictions yielded by the theory have no scientific standing, for the theory offers no reason to believe that in future a household or firm will choose the alternative whose economic effects are most salutary, no matter what it did in the past.

Independent utility functions

Most economists' conceptions of rationality are narrow. The preferences that they attribute to their subjects are limited by the axioms of a precise but too simple choice theory. According to the axioms, every subject acts in unsympathetic isolation from every other: "The first principle of Economics," the nineteenth-century economist Frank Edgeworth writes, "is that every agent is actuated by self-interest."[12] The preferences of each household or firm (that is, their "utility functions"), according to this principle, are independent of the preferences of every other, and, as a result, the value that one subject places on some good or service is unaffected by the values placed on it by another. No households or firms, according to this narrow conception of rationality, are beneficent, altruistic, envious, or spiteful. The preferences of households, according to Edgeworth's principle, do not include a preference for status or positional goods or a preference for the well-being of others.[13]

Since the moral or political values of a subject are expressed in an interest in the interests of others, economists, by excluding these interests, exclude the moral and political values of their subjects from their theorizing. They try to predict the choices of their subjects on the assumption that these choices are unaffected by the subject's own moral or political values. In so doing, they go beyond value-freedom. Weber discouraged social scientists from including their own moral or political values in their science; he called on them to exclude their own sympathies. But he encouraged social scientists to include their subjects' sympathies and to describe their moral and political values.

A judgment by an economist that a consumer prefers whatever market-basket her children prefer is a description of the consumer's, not the economist's, values; but, on the view of many economists, a description, no more than a prescription of sympathy, has no place in the economists' theorizing. Economics for them is an amoral study of amoral agents in a market. The economist tries to be silent, and her subjects are treated as if they *were* silent, on matters of moral value. In short, the economist's aversion to judgments of ethical value leads her away from the second premise of the policy syllogism, away from the policy syllogism, and away from morally conditioned market choices to the ideal of market transactions between rational economic men.

Most economists admit that it is unrealistic to assume that their subjects are purely self-interested or act in unsympathetic isolation. They allow that consumers and firms do sometimes measure costs and benefits to self on the basis of costs or benefits to others; but they believe that the assumption that each individual's utility function is independent of every other's greatly simplifies their theory without substantially reducing its predictive power. Their narrow conception of rationality, they believe, yields true or approximately true predictions with a minimum of theoretical labor. Their rational man is an ideal-type (in Weber's sense), and the validity of the type, they maintain (following Friedman), depends on how well it predicts the choices of firms, households, or industries and not how well it matches any actual, internal psychology.

As I have already noted, not every economist adopts Edgeworth's narrow conception of rationality. Some do not agree that it yields true predictions and look for a broader notion of rationality on which to construct their choice theory.[14] According to the narrow view, no one will contribute to a good unless there are private benefits, but many people do contribute in the absence of private benefits. A viewer of public television, for example, will not contribute to its support, according to the narrow conception, if the programs are available to contributor and noncontributor alike. If the pleasures of viewing are open to all, the theory predicts that no one will contribute unless there are side benefits or private inducements whose benefit to the viewer exceeds the costs of her contribution. But many viewers contribute when there are no private benefits. Theories based on the narrow notion yield the prediction that every viewer will choose to ride free on the contributions of other viewers, whereas in fact, many viewers do not do so but, instead, pay their own way.[15]

Edgeworth did not believe that selfishness prevails in all areas of human life but only in war and trade. The theory of the rational economic man yields true predictions, he thought, as long as it limits itself to war and trade and ventures no predictions about other areas of life.

> Admitting that there exists in the higher parts of human nature a tendency towards and feeling after utilitarian institutions, could we seriously suppose that these moral considerations were relevant to war and trade; could eradicate the controlless core of human selfishness, or exercise an appreciable force in comparison with the impulse of self-interest.[16]

But even if the theory is limited to war and trade, it yields false predictions, for, as Kenneth Arrow points out, trade depends on trust, and trust does not result when parties act only from unsympathetic self-interest.

Trust is an important lubricant of a social system. It is extremely efficient; it saves a lot of trouble to have a fair degree of reliance on other people's word. Unfortunately this is not a commodity which can be bought very easily. If you have to buy it, you already have some doubts about what you've bought. Trust and similar values, loyalty or truth-telling, are examples of what the economists would call "externalities." They are goods, they are commodities; they have real, practical economic value; they increase the efficiency of the system, enable you to produce more goods or more of whatever values you hold in high esteem. But they are not commodities for which trade on the open market is technically possible or even meaningful.[17]

The theory of the rational economic man yields false predictions about trade, because it predicts that the parties in a trade will not have a fair degree of reliance on each other's word and, as a result, will not engage when, in fact, they do engage in trades.

Moral motivation is a source of order in actual markets, but it is not a source in a market of rational economic men; the only source of order in this market is unsympathetic self-interest, but unsympathetic self-interest does not ensure a stable market. In a market of rational economic men, each will calculate whether he will serve his interests more by breaking his agreements than by keeping them and knows that every other man will do so as well. No man has a reason to trade with another unless he knows that the costs to the other of not honoring the terms of the trade are greater at the margin than the benefits. But often one party does not know the costs to another of not honoring the terms of the trade, and, as a result, according to the theory, will not undertake what might be a mutually beneficial trade.

If moral motivation is required to assure stable or efficient markets, economists ought to favor research that gives prominence to moral motivation. Instead, they favor research that excludes it. To the extent that real households or firms view the ideal-type of the rational economic man as a norm, the economists' research motivates them to act in ways that decrease, rather than increase, the stability of a market. Nevertheless, the presence of a stable or efficient market is evidence against the theory of the rational economic man, for the theory predicts a market failure whenever it does not serve the man's unsympathetic self-interest to keep his agreements, and the fact that markets often don't fail in such circumstances shows that even within trade and war the theory's predictive power is weak.

The fact that economists ignore the moral concerns of their subjects does not mean that their research is value-neutral. Economists could include the moral concerns of their subjects in their research without being partisan – that is, without favoring one conception of the good over another. Economists do not purchase more neutrality for their science by discounting the morality of their subjects. Moreover, by ignoring the moral values of their subjects, they do not increase the explanatory or predictive power but only the simplicity of their theories.

Values in positive economics

Theories in positive economics, if simple, are not neutral, but, in a number of ways, favor some values over others. First, they include the judgment that firms and households are substantively rational, and this judgment is partisan. The judgment does not describe what is, for the terms "firm" and "household" are ideal-types and do not describe any actual firm or household. Yet, the judgment is not a judgment of what ought to be, for, in judging that a firm acts as if trying to maximize profits, the economist is not judging how the firm ought to act or that acting to maximize profit is desirable.

The judgment is practical. Though most firms, in truth, do not maximize profits, economists say they do in order to achieve an end that many economists value. Consequently, the judgment that firms maximize profits favors that end and is not neutral on whether it is valuable. For most economists, the valuable end is prediction. Theories, they think, should favor the theoretical virtue of accurate prediction. However, since predictive power is a scientific rather than a moral or political value, they do not think that their use of the ideal-type favors one conception of the good over another, and would deny that their theory of the household or the firm is partisan.

In practice, however, their theory has little predictive power; yet still the economists employ their ideal-type.[18] If the only virtue of the neo-classical theory of the firm were the accuracy of its predictions, it would have little virtue at all.[19] But the theory has other virtues and serves other values better than the value of prediction. These are not scientific values like prediction, explanation, or any of the theoretical virtues, but more clearly political values. Though the economists' theory does not have much predictive power, it does have substantial political power, for it favors a conception of the good in which the best solution to a private or public problem is a free market solution and favors a conception of human perfection in which the agents are economically self-interested. One real virtue of the economists' theory of the firm is that it favors the politics of pursuing a policy objective – for example, an increase in employment – by coupling the objective with an increase in the profits of a firm – for example, through a cut in the minimum wage.

Economists might not choose their theories or ideal-types with a political end in mind, but the fact that they cling to theories with few theoretical virtues needs explanation. One type of explanation would be an intentional explanation; but even if the political benefits of the choice were unintended, they could be cited to explain them – for example, as part of a functional or invisible-hand explanation of the economists' theory choices. In any case, merely showing that the choices offer political benefits makes the point that the theory is partisan, for it shows that the theory favors a conception of the good in virtue of which the effects of the economists' choices are benefits.

One reason to favor the neoclassical theory, despite its predictive failures, is that the theory is both a description and a norm. Economists have a reason not to improve the theory as a descriptive model of the behavior of firms if they want to retain its status as a normative model of the firm.[20] But if that is the reason for choosing the theory, the choice favors whatever values are favored by the norm, and the theory is partisan to the value behind the norm that firms ought to maximize profits.

Positive economics is partisan in a second way. Economists cannot be neutral on all questions of ends, for they cannot pursue every economic question or attempt to establish the relation between every pair of economic variables. They must choose the ends for which to supply a means, and their choice must rely on their own judgment of what ends are desirable. Value-relevance in economics requires that economists rely on a premise like premise 2 of the policy syllogism, in order to choose which premise like 1 to study. The logic of discovery in economics, as in any other science, is a matter of practical reason and is itself based on a premise like 2.

For example, some economists in the USA are guided in their choice of questions to ask or problems to study by a preference for private rather than public ownership of assets. The direction they take in their work is rationalized by their preference. They theorize the results of transferring public services like the post office or the jails to profit-oriented contractors but not the results of transferring weapons production or pollution control from profit-oriented contractors to government. The choice to study privatization over nationalization serves a preference for a smaller rather than a larger public sector. Further, when they study privatization, these economists often focus on the monetary costs and benefits and overlook the moral and political costs of private contracting – for example, an increase in inequality of wealth or income or an increase in the influence of private contractors on issues of public policy. Some economists limit their study to monetary costs and benefits because they favor private over public ownership; others limit their study for methodological rather than political reasons, maintaining that value-freedom forbids a judgment of the moral and political costs or benefits of increasing private ownership. In either case, the effect of limiting the costs or benefits favors private over public solutions to problems of public policy.

Weber drew a distinction between value-relevance and value-freedom. Economics should be value-relevant, he thought, but it should not be value-laden. For economists to choose to study privatization on the basis of a preference for private ownership makes the study value-relevant; but for them to include in their study the judgment that private is preferable to public ownership makes the study value-laden. In making their study value-relevant, the economists go beyond the first premise of the policy syllogism and adopt a premise like the second. In trying to keep the study value-free, they do not recommend to the policymaker private ownership or advise against public ownership. Nevertheless, the economists' preference for private ownership is <u>included</u> in their studies of private contracting; for the means they have to offer the policymaker are <u>constrained</u> by the problems they have chosen to study, and their choice of problems is constrained by their preference for private over public ownership.

Positive economics is partisan in a third way. Economists do not spell out all the conditions that are necessary or sufficient for the occurrence of an event or the achievement of an end B. What they cite as a cause is only necessary or sufficient for B, given other events or conditions that influence B. An economist who says that increases in the minimum wage cause increases in unemployment means that if the minimum wage goes up, then unemployment goes up, *ceteris paribus*. Were consumer demand to increase, then employment could increase rather than decrease in spite of an increase in the minimum wage. However, the economist cannot replace the *ceteris paribus* clause with a description of all the conditions necessary before an increase in employment will follow an increase in the minimum wage, so the first premise of the policy syllogism must include a *ceteris paribus* clause.

The economist must decide which factors influencing employment to cite as causes and which to cite as *ceteris paribus* conditions. Most economists would cite a rise in the minimum wage, for example, but not the indifference of employers to unemployment, as a cause of unemployment. Yet, were employers not indifferent, wages could rise without a rise in unemployment. Why, then, does the economist cite the rise in wages and not the indifference as a cause, and why the indifference but not the rise in wages as a *ceteris paribus* condition?

As the distinction between cause and *ceteris paribus* conditions is drawn in economics, the distinction does not reflect the economists' facts so much as their interests. Often, the conditions they cite as causes are those they are interested in varying, while those they cite as *ceteris paribus* conditions are those they are interested in fixing. They fix the indifference of employers, for example, but are eager to vary the minimum wage. The contrast between the fixed and the variable is imposed *by*, rather than imposed *on*, the economist. Neither the indifference of employers nor the minimum wage is part of human nature or a matter of social necessity. Both can be influenced by public policy. The indifference, rather than the minimum wage, is fixed not because nature has fixed it but because the economist has decided to theorize firms as narrowly rational: as unsympathetic and as self-interested in all decisions, including those on employment.

The standard model of the firm excludes considerations of fairness and loyalty. It assumes that firms realize a single, well-defined objective – namely, profits – within budgetary and legal constraints. As a result, firms, by definition, have no interest in being treated fairly or in treating others fairly. The condition of indifference is taken for granted in studying the relationship between unemployment and wages, not because there is empirical evidence that firms are indifferent to the interests of their employees but because the logic of the model of the firm requires it.[21] The reason why indifference to employees is a background condition in the wage laws rather than a cause is not empirical but methodological; that is, the indifference is a consequence of the economists' choice of idealization of the firm. To the extent that their choice of idealization or ideal-type is partisan, their choice to make indifference a background condition is as well.

Whatever the economists' reasons for choosing one idealization over another, their choice influences their discussion of causes and economic laws and, in turn, limits public policy. In treating the minimum wage, rather than the indifference of employers, as causing unemployment, for example, economists are limiting the means of the policymakers to achieve their desired ends. Policymakers decide that increasing employment is desirable, premise 2 of the policy syllogism. They turn to the economists to learn how to increase it, premise 1 of the policy syllogism; but what the economists have to teach is limited by their commitment to narrow rationality. Because the economists theorize firms and households as narrowly rational, they cannot advise the policymakers that lessening the indifference lessens unemployment and is a means to the policymakers' end.

In short, the capture of research on employment by economists who favor a narrow conception of rationality has confined the debate about unemployment to a certain set of policy alternatives and has favored the politics of *laissez-faire*-capitalism, whatever the intention of the economists. As Stephen Jay Gould explains in his history of efforts to measure human intelligence, "many questions are formulated by scientists in such a restricted way that any legitimate answer can only validate a social preference."[22] Economists have formulated questions about employment in just such a restricted way. As they have formulated these questions, any legitimate answer can only validate a social preference for narrow rationality and a free market economy.

Values enter into the first premise of the policy syllogism in another, fourth way. The economist must distinguish causal or lawlike relations between economic variables and accidental generalizations or mere correlations. The common way of drawing the distinction is in terms of counterfactuals: causal or lawlike relations hold in counterfactual situations, whereas mere correlations do not. If there is a causal relation between A and B, then the correlation between them will remain under certain changes or transformations of the actual economic world. If increases in the price of labor, for example, cause decreases in the demand for labor, then demand varies inversely with price in the actual economic world and in certain possible economic worlds, W, as well.

Whether the relation between economic variables is causal depends on which economic worlds other than the actual one the economist includes in W. If W includes the world in which business tax rates are pegged to employment, there is a social contract between capital and labor, firms are worker-owned or controlled or are constrained by considerations of fairness or loyalty, then, in these worlds, the demand curve for labor is not downward sloping, and any relation between lower wages and higher employment in the actual world is coincidental rather than lawlike. On the other hand, if W includes only worlds in which firms are substantively rational, in which public policy does not favor full employment, or in which the interests of capital are opposed to those of labor, then the relation between changes in the price and demand for labor in the actual world is lawlike.

The difficulty for economics is to say in what range of possible economic worlds a relation between economic variables must hold before the relation in the actual world can be treated as lawlike. Obviously it cannot be all logically possible worlds, for then the causal relation would not be empirically contingent but logically necessary, and it cannot be all physically possible worlds, for then the relation would be physical rather than economic or social. Economists work with a system of worlds that is narrower than that theorized by natural scientists but broader than the world of their own present economy.

The question of what worlds to include in W is a practical question. Economists limit the system of economic worlds they consider to those that seem to them to be practically possible.[23] However, their judgments of what social worlds are practically possible are based on their own political values. The set of worlds W is limited to economies that serve ends that economists find desirable or can be reached from the actual or present world by steps they find acceptable. The world in which labor owns or controls the means of production is not included in W. Though there are economies in which the means of production are owned or controlled by labor, they are ignored, and W is limited to free and mostly unregulated market economies.

Weber might say that the choice of worlds to include in W is simply a matter of value-relevance, but Weber's notion of value-relevance, as I explained in chapter 2, is very broad and includes more than current proponents of value-neutrality allow. In any case, the values that influence the choice influence the economists' laws, for they are part of their reason for judging that the relation between two economic variables A and B is lawlike or causal rather than accidental or merely correlational. As a result, the first premise of the policy syllogism is not neutral but partisan.

misses the whole above away for "laws" several science at all

Values in normative economics

The aim of normative economics is to help policymakers construct or articulate a concept of human welfare or well-being. To pursue the aim, economists go beyond the first premise of the policy syllogism to formulate welfare criteria for policymakers to use to appraise alternative ends or consequences and defend the second premise of the syllogism. Yet, like positive economics, normative economics tries to be a science, and most normative economists share Weber's view that judgments of moral and political value are not scientific. Consequently, normative economists would like a standard for assessing welfare that does not require them to rely on their own judgments of moral or political value. However, most recognize that value-freedom is not possible in normative economics and instead aim to develop a science of welfare with a minimum of ethical postulates.

The oldest form of normative economics is utilitarianism. There are a number of versions of utilitarianism, which differ in how they identify well-being or welfare. In one version, a subject's welfare is identified with the satisfaction of her actual desires. That is, her desires are the standard by which the economist is to judge her well-being, and the measure of her well-being is the degree to which the desires are satisfied. In another version, a distinction is drawn between what the subject desires and what is desirable, and a subject's welfare is identified with achieving what is desirable. In the second version, economists substitute their own judgments of what is desirable for the desires of their subjects and thereby introduce their own values into the welfare criterion. As a result, all economists agree that in the second version, utilitarianism is not value-free in Weber's sense but value-laden.

Most economists, following Lionel Robbins, maintain that even if a subject's actual desires are the standard by which her well-being is judged, utilitarianism is laden with the economists' own judgments of value; for utilitarians must add together a measure of the welfare of each subject and obtain a measure of welfare for all. To obtain such a measure, the economist must compare the well-being of one subject with the well-being of another. Robbins maintains that there is no empirical basis on which the well-being of two subjects can be compared and that any interpersonal comparisons of well-being must be ethical (based on the values of whoever is making the comparison). He concludes that economics should be free of such comparisons, for he shares Weber's view that judgments of ultimate ethical value are unscientific.

> It is one thing to assume that scales can be drawn up showing the order in which an individual will prefer a series of alternatives, and to compare the arrangement of one such individual scale with another. It is quite a different thing to assume that behind such arrangements lie magnitudes which themselves can be compared.[24]

> To state that A's preference stands above B's in order of importance is entirely different from stating that A prefers n to m and B prefers n to m in a different order. It involves an element of conventional valuation. Hence it is essentially normative. It has no place in pure science.[25]

Because each interpersonal comparison includes an element of conventional valuation, the standard of assessment that utilitarianism offers normative economics cannot be value-free but must be value-laden and must rely on a series of disputable postulates.

So long as it adopts the standard of welfare of utilitarianism, normative economics, most economists conclude, cannot be a science and is more properly an area of ethics rather than economics. But some economists believe that there is a standard of welfare that, unlike the standard of utilitarianism, does not rely on the economists' own valuations or any strong or controversial ethical postulates. The standard is due to Vilfredo Pareto, and it provides a measure of collective or social well-being without the need to compare or assess the judgments of value of individuals. According to Pareto's standard, we can legitimately speak of a welfare improvement if a change in the world makes at least one person better off without making another worse off. In other words, human welfare is increased by an arrangement or state of affairs A if and only if at least one subject favors A and no subject opposes it. A is the welfare optimum if and only if there is no other arrangement B that one subject favors more than A and no subject favors less than A.

Using this standard, some economists believe that they can assess ends as well as means without making any welfare judgments of their own. With the Pareto standard it seems possible for economists to theorize welfare without ladening their theory with their own moral values; for to show that A is Pareto-optimal assumes no more than that scales can be drawn showing the order of each subject's preferences. The Pareto standard does not require that the measure of the preferences of one subject be compared with that of another and does not assume an objective welfare function that sums the welfare of individuals. With the Pareto standard no interpersonal comparison of well-being is necessary. As a result, the standard does not seem to involve the element of conventional valuation that, on Robbins's view, makes utilitarianism unscientific and partisan.

But even if it does not involve interpersonal comparisons, the Pareto standard does involve an element of conventional valuation, for, as A. K. Sen has argued, without an evaluation of a subject's preference for A there is no reason to think that A increases rather than decreases her welfare.[26] The fact that someone prefers A to B and no one prefers B to A does not make A morally superior unless the subject's preference for A has moral merit. If the preferences are short-sighted, uninformed, or unfair, then there is no reason to believe that A will increase welfare more than B, even though A, according to Pareto's standard, is better than B.

The Pareto standard is not a standard of welfare unless it includes some moral evaluation of a subject's preferences. Such an evaluation, however, is a judgment of moral value; so to use the Pareto standard to theorize welfare requires that economists rely on their own judgments of moral value. The Pareto standard looks attractive to economists because it seems to offer a standard of welfare that does not require them to offer their own evaluations. But without their evaluations of their subjects' preferences, the Pareto standard is no more a standard of human well-being than a standard of human misery.

A central theme in economics since Adam Smith is that a market economy is the best means to achieve human well-being. This idea rests on two assumptions: first, that every perfectly competitive equilibrium is Pareto-optimal; and second, that Pareto optimality is a measure of well-being. Critics of Smith's idea question both assumptions, for in markets with externalities, every perfectly competitive equilibrium is not Pareto-optimal, and in markets in which every satisfied desire does not contribute to the good, Pareto optimality is not a measure of well-being.

Economists often defend free markets by maintaining that in free markets consumers are sovereign: what they get is what they want. Free markets are good, according to these economists, because they supply means to the consumer's rather than the economist's or policymaker's ends or preferences. But free markets and consumer sovereignty are no better than the preferences that are satisfied in the markets. The satisfaction of a consumer's preference is not a good if the preference is the effect of causes – for example, false or deceptive advertising – that are not themselves good. The ideal of value-freedom prohibits economists from judging whether a cause is good or bad; but then it prohibits them from judging whether free markets and consumer sovereignty are good or bad as well.

The same can be said about the economists' use of the Pareto standard. The satisfaction of a subject's preference is not a good if the preference is the effect of causes – for example, misinformation – that are not themselves good. The ideal of value-freedom prohibits economists from judging whether a cause is good or bad; but then it prohibits them from judging whether a Pareto optimum is good or bad as well. However, only if economists judge that it is good can they use or recommend the Pareto standard as a measure of human welfare or well-being.

Some economists who equate the Pareto standard or consumer sovereignty with human well-being assume that the satisfaction of any preference is a moral good. This assumption is itself a judgment of moral value, for the economist is judging that it is always morally desirable that a subject's desires be satisfied. As a result, the Pareto standard is laden with the economists' values, even if the economists measure well-being by the preferences of their subjects and without any attention to how those preferences are formed. Most economists simply assume that their subjects are the best judges of their own welfare – that is, that what they prefer is what is better for them – but this assumption is as much a conventional valuation and as controversial as any interpersonal comparison of values. In short, Pareto's welfare standard is no freer of value-commitments or controversial value-commitments than the utilitarian standard.

The usual criticism of the Pareto standard as a standard of welfare is that it offers too little. It does not allow welfare comparisons between alternatives A and B when one subject prefers A to B and another B to

A. Since conflicts like this are the rule, the standard does not offer a means of assessing the effects of different or competing public policies in the actual world. But, as a few critics have pointed out, the Pareto standard offers less than too little.[27] For only if the economist judges that a subject's preferences have moral merit is the standard a welfare standard; if the economist judges the moral merit of her subject's preferences, the standard is no better than utilitarianism, for it too relies on an element of conventional valuation.

Normative economists face a dilemma. If their standard of welfare can be used to assess premises like 2, then, since 2 is clearly a judgment of moral value, the standard is laden with value. If the standard cannot be used to assess 2, then in recommending the standard, economists are not pursuing the aim of normative economics – namely, to offer policymakers standards with which to measure human well-being. Economists can describe the preferences of each of their subjects without invoking their own values, but their description by itself tells the policymaker nothing about premise 2 and nothing about whether an action or policy is desirable.

The Pareto criterion relies on other value assumptions, which oppose the economists' quest for value-neutrality. According to the Pareto criterion, social welfare – the well-being of a collective or a community – is exclusively a function of the well-being of each of the individual members. For example, by the Pareto criterion, the harm that a policy does to a tradition or to the values or ideals that bind a community of people together or provide the ground for their preferences does not diminish the welfare of the community unless at least one member feels harmed by the policy. The possibility that the community is made worse off but no member suffers is excluded by the criterion.

The Pareto criterion, like most of the other welfare criteria proposed by economists, is individualistic and reflects the liberalism behind positive and normative economic theory.

It should be noted in what the word "welfare" is being used in the context of liberal political economy: it is the private, incommunicable experiences of each individual taken separately, and indeed "isolated" from his community, that are the relevant criteria of well-being. Even though the doctrine does not preclude collective provision of (carefully specified) goods and services, the rationale for it lies in the claim that only in such a form can certain individual satisfaction be achieved. It is no accident, then, that the word "efficiency" is often used as a synonym for welfare in liberal individualism, for this is defined precisely as the satisfaction of necessarily subjective desires. In the tradition of methodological individualism, it is maintained that there is no such thing as a collective social welfare function which is not logically reducible to statements about individuals.[28]

Economics shares with liberal political theories the view that the only measure of the virtue of a social institution or practice is how the members fare within it. According to the liberal view, only individuals have any moral status, rights, obligations, duties, or well-being that can be respected, protected, perfected, enforced, or improved. On the liberal view, there is no politics of the common good but only a politics of many different individuals each with her own good or conception of the good. Whatever the merits of the liberal view, it hardly rests on weak or non-controversial ethical postulates.

The Pareto criterion also assumes that any veto of a move from the status quo, no matter what the distribution of resources within the status quo, shows that the move is not a welfare improvement. In other words, the criterion is entirely ahistorical, for it ignores the welfare properties of the initial distribution as well as the source or motivation of any veto. Abolition of slavery, for example, was not welfare-enhancing according to the Pareto criterion, despite the inequities of slavery and the benefits to the freed slaves, because at least one slave-owner was less well off after the change in the economy. In assessing abolition, the criterion is neutral on the welfare properties of slavery but not on the value of the slave-owner's veto.

The problem with the Pareto approach, like others that try to limit the role of ethics in the assessment of individual or collective well-being, is that it requires silence on all those questions of distribution that lie at the heart of any serious and real debate about welfare, but uncritically operates within – and at least tacitly endorses – many of the ethical assumptions that frame those debates – for example, that an allocation of resources that perfectly matches the provision of goods and services with the subjective choices of individuals has some moral value. In aspiring to value-neutrality, normative economics avoids some ethical judgments but relies on others. However, the overall result is not a value-neutral but an ethically lame science.

Conclusion

The ideal of value-neutrality is central to positive economics if not to normative economics. However, because positive economics relies on idealizations that do not purchase predictive or explanatory power but severely limit the space of possible policy decisions, they are partisan. The justification of the economists' narrow conception of rationality and the neoclassical theory of the household and firm is not any theoretical virtue but the political virtue of competitive markets and libertarian governmental restraint.

Values also shape the economists' judgments of economic causes and lawlike relationships, for in calling only some of the conditions that influence an economic event "causes" and in limiting the possible worlds in which economic relationships must hold for them to be lawlike, economists also rely on their personal or political values. In short, though no theories in the social sciences are or can be value-neutral in ways that most social scientists dream or imagine, theorizing in economics relies upon the value-judgments of the economists in ways that set economics apart from the other social sciences, despite the fact that economics presents itself and is often seen as the most scientific of the social sciences and the one most concerned to be value-neutral.

NOTES

1   Weber, *Methodology*, p. 56.
2   H. Simon, "From Substantive to Procedural Rationality," in *Philosophy and Economic Theory*, ed. F. Hahn and M. Hollis (Oxford University Press, 1979), pp. 65–86.
3   J. Hicks, *Value and Capital* (Oxford University Press, 1939), p. 34.
4   For a discussion of the principle of methodological individualism, see chapter 4.
5   For a discussion of the selection question, see chapter 4.
6   See, e.g., A. Alchian, "Uncertainty, Evolution and Economic Theory," *Journal of Political Economy*, 58 (1950), pp. 211–22.
7   M. Friedman, "Methodology," p. 213.
8   H. Leibenstein, *Beyond Economic Man* (Harvard University Press, 1980), p. 13.
9   Harsanyi, "Individualistic and Functionalistic Explanations," pp. 305–21. See the quote from Harsanyi in chapter 4 of this book.
10 See Elster, *Ulysses*, pp. 28–35, for a discussion of this point.
11 Harsanyi, "Individualistic and Functionalistic Explanations," p. 305.
12 F. Y. Edgeworth, *Mathematical Physics: An Essay on the Application of Mathematics to the Moral Sciences* (London School of Economics and Political Science, 1932), p. 16.
13 Some economists have proposed axioms of choice that do not include the independence axiom. See, e.g., D. Collard, *Altruism and Economy: A Study in Non-Selfish Economics* (Oxford University Press, 1978), for a survey. But the broader conceptions of rational choice have not been adopted by working

economists or included in the reasoning used to arrive at premise 1 of the policy syllogism.

14 See, e.g., A. K. Sen, "Rational Fools: A Critique of the Behavioral Foundations of Economic Theory," in *Philosophy and Economic Theory*, ed. Hahn and M. Hollic (Oxford University Press, 1979), pp. 87–109.

15 See D. Kahneman, J. L. Knetsch, and R. H. Thaler, "Fairness and the Assumptions of Economics," *Journal of Business*, 59 (1986), pp. 285–300, for a discussion of how the standard microeconomic model fails to provide an adequate foundation for a descriptive theory of decision making for households or firms.

16 Edgeworth, *Mathematical Physics*, p. 52.

17 K. Arrow, *The Limits of Organization* (Norton, 1974), p. 23.

18 Simon, "From Substantive to Procedural Rationality."

19 Defenders of the narrow economic model would say that no other present model matches it in scope, power, and simplicity; but, if true, part of the reason is the reluctance of economists to countenance any but the narrow model.

20 See A. Tversky and D. Kahneman, "Rational Choices and the Framing of Decisions," *Journal of Business*, 59 (1986), pp. 251–78, for a similar diagnosis of the continuing appeal of expected utility theory in the face of the many deviations of actual behavior from the theory.

21 See Kahneman, et al., "Fairness," p. 286. The authors challenge the descriptive adequacy of nonfairness as a tenet of the theory of the firm. There is much evidence, they maintain, that firms forgo legal opportunities for profits to avoid acting unfairly. They propose to expand the model by including more realistic assumptions, including the assumption that firms operate within fairness as well as legal and budgetary constraints, and maintain that many economic phenomena can be predicted on the basis of the additional assumptions that are anomalies in the standard model. My point is that the *ceteris paribus* condition is justified not by the facts of economic behavior but only by the interests of the economist; their point is that the facts of behavior actually oppose the condition.

22 Gould, *Mismeasure*, pp. 22–3.

23 See Garfinkel, *Forms of Social Explanation*, p. 151, for a discussion of this point in terms of the natural sciences.

24 Robbins, *Essay*, p. 138.

25 Ibid., p. 139.

26 A. K. Sen, *On Ethics and Economics* (Basil Blackwell, 1987).

27 Ibid.

28 N. Barry, *Welfare* (University of Minnesota Press, 1990), pp. 50–1.

6

Collecting data in the
social sciences

In the preceding chapters, I looked at one important part of the practice of the liberal sciences, theorizing. In chapter 2, I looked at the practice of formulating and validating theories containing simple class-terms, as well as theories containing ideal-types, and in chapters 3–5 at the practice of formulating and validating developmental theories in psychology and political science, functional theories in sociology, and rational choice theories in economics. In this chapter, I look at another important part of the practice of liberal science: gathering the facts and collecting the data. My aim is to describe the influence of values on the scientist's choice of what data to collect and how to collect them and the influence of the gathering of data on the values of the surrounding community. I also explain how the ideal of value-neutrality influences the way interviews and experiments in the social sciences are conducted and how the interviews and experiments favor one conception of the good over others.

In addition, this chapter offers an account of the methods used to collect data in the social sciences and the conceptions of reliability and validity that frame those methods. Most social scientists believe that the methods must be value-neutral for the data to be reliable or valid; but, as I explain, given the conception of validity employed in the social sciences, the data are valid only if the methods are not neutral but partisan. Further, the data can be reliable and partisan as long as the values favored by the data are shared by everyone who collects them.

The reliability and validity of data

Social scientists collect their data in different ways – through structured and unstructured interviews, naturalistic and experimental observation, field experiments and laboratory experiments, self-reports, archival records, questionnaires, psychological testing, and archeological retrieval – by following some guidelines or protocols – protocols for conducting interviews, designing and conducting experiments, writing questionnaires, selecting samples, constructing psychological tests, searching an archive, deciphering a record, and excavating a burial ground. These protocols tell the social scientist how, where, and when to obtain her data, and they guide her in observing and measuring the individuals, artifacts, institutions, or events which, when properly observed and measured, supply her with facts or evidence against which to test her theories or hypotheses. Guidelines or protocols for interviewing, for example, contain statements like:

The use of follow-up questions or probes is advisable at many points in the ordinary interview, especially in connection with free responses. The questionnaire should anticipate where these are required and should provide the appropriate wording.[1]

To determine whether individual questions and their sequence have the same meaning for all respondents and are clearly understood, it is generally recommended that, after the schedule has been developed through pilot interviewing, a pretest be conducted on a random sample of the respondents.[2]

Guidelines for naturalistic and experimental observation include:

Reliability precedes questions of validity. Consequently, interobserver agreement must always be obtained and reported.[3]

These guidelines are intended to eliminate or neutralize differences in how researchers observe, interview, survey, or describe their subjects, and to help them offer data free of the values of whoever collects them.

Because interviewers are human beings, such biasing factors can never be overcome completely, but their effects can be reduced by standardizing the interview, so that the interviewer has as little free choice as possible. Thus, the use of standard wording in survey questions aims to prevent the bias that would result if each interviewer worded the question in his or her own fashion. Similarly, if interviewers are given standard instructions on probing procedure, on the classification of doubtful answers, and so on, their biases will have less chance to operate.[4]

Only observations or data collected in accordance with these guidelines are treated as facts, used to test theories, presented in published research, and considered to be good scientific data.

On the liberal view, data are good only if value-neutral and are value-neutral if reliable and valid.[5] Data are reliable if they are repeatable and consistent. Reliability is measured by inter-observer agreement, for if there is agreement between observers, then the observations of each should be free of personal partisanship. But partisanship can survive inter-observer agreement. Political interests that are shared by every observer or are woven into the protocols can influence the observations of all. Reliable data reflect the world as seen by every observer, but the image of the world of all can still be culturally or politically partisan.

Good data, according to the liberal view, should be free of shared as well as personal politics; they should have what the liberal sciences call internal and external validity. Internal validity means that the data are true of the participant subjects or those from whom the data are collected. They record the way the subjects of the interviews, surveys, experiments, records, tests, or observations are and not how the observers think they are or ought to be. Externally valid data are true of the participant subjects (those in the sample) and of unobserved subjects (those in the larger population) as well. They are true of the individuals or groups over whom the variables of the theory range – the theoretical subjects – and not merely those from whom the data are collected.

Techniques for evaluating the validity of data vary with the instruments or methods used to collect them. The internal validity of interview data is checked by examining the questionnaires, seeing how the interviews are conducted, and comparing the responses of different subjects to various questions. The external validity of the data is checked by an assessment of the representativeness of the respondents chosen for the interviews and by comparing their responses with other information about the theoretical subjects.[6] The external validity of data collected through testing is measured by evaluating the test, and the test is evaluated by its ability to distinguish between subjects already judged to be different or by comparing the test results with the results of other tests believed to measure the same characteristics of the subject.[7]

However, none of these techniques assures that reliable and valid data are value-neutral. They assure agreement but not neutrality; for they do not eliminate values common to the instruments of observation, the different test results, the different ways of measuring or coding the responses, or the beliefs about the subjects previously accepted or assumed in the ways the tests or surveys are validated.

Consider test data. Scholastic aptitude tests are used to measure the cognitive abilities of some population of subjects. The data they collect are the subjects' scores on the tests, and the validity of these data is measured by content and predictive validity – by the approval of the test items by experts and by how well the test scores predict the performances of the subjects on some range of other tasks which prominent members of the surrounding community already agree are measures of scholastic aptitude. That is, according to the standard methods of psychological measurement, the test data are accurate measures of the scholastic abilities of the test subjects in proportion to their predictive power and, in particular, their power to predict the scholastic performance of these subjects.

One particularly prominent scholastic aptitude test is the GRE General Test developed by the Educational Testing Service to measure the general verbal, quantitative, and analytical abilities related to successful performance in graduate school.[8] According to the ETS, the test measures skills acquired over a long period of time and not related to any specific field of study.[9] The ETS maintains that the data collected with the test – that is, the scores on the test – are valid, basing their claim on research indicating that the scores are good predictors of success in the first year of graduate school. In principle, the validity of the test is the extent to which it measures the intellectual abilities of the subjects; but, in practice, the validity is a matter of how well the overall test measures success in a representative sample of the nation's graduate schools (the predictive validity of the test) and how well the individual items on the test measure what some representative specialists judge to be the skills required for success in graduate study (the content validity of the test).[10]

Once we look at how, in practice, the validity of the test data are determined, we see that valid test data need not be value-neutral. In fact, if there is partisanship in the criterion of success used to determine the predictive validity of the test or in the judgments of the specialists used to judge the content validity, it will pass through to the test and the test data. The test and the data will be partisan not in any overt or intentional sense, but in the institutional sense discussed in chapter 1. If there is partisanship in the grading of first-year graduate students in the representative sample of schools, then predictive validity will not free the test of that partisanship but will require that the test include it.

The Educational Testing Service recently defended its GRE exams against charges of racial bias by showing that the scores predicted the success in graduate school of racial minorities as well as they predicted the success of white students. That is, the ETS showed that the correlation coefficient – that is, the degree of correlation between test scores and graduate school grades – is the same for students of different races. However, this does not show that the exams, grades, or data are value-neutral – for example, that they do not favor the cultural values of one group of test subjects over those of another – but only that any partisanship is matched on the different rungs of the educational ladder, the partisanship passing up and down the ladder from the schools to the testing service.

What the predictive validity of the GRE test assures is that the cultural biases in the measures of success employed by graduate departments or graduate schools are included in the data collected by the test. Graduate programs in history, philosophy, literature, sociology, and art history favor one among many conceptions of good reasoning, analysis, exposition, interpretation, criticism, and writing, and the achievements of first-year graduate students in these programs are measured in relation to these conceptions. For the coefficient of correlation between test scores and success in graduate school to be high, the test must favor the conceptions of good disciplinary practice that the graduate programs favor; and if these conceptions are partisan, the ETS must pass the partisanship through to its aptitude test.

In the case of institutional discrimination against black Americans in schooling, students are assigned to schools not on the basis of their race but on the basis of their place of residence, but the influence of race on residence is passed through to the schools. With aptitude testing, the racial partisanship favoring one dialect, vocabulary, grammar, literature, or body of experience over another is passed from the schools – the discipline of the classroom and the curriculum – to the test data. The ETS believes that its data are racially neutral because they are valid, but the ETS is mistaken. Because its data are valid, they are not racially neutral, because the schools are not neutral.

Most of the data in child psychology, to cite another example, come from experimental or naturalistic observation. The observations are guided by protocols meant to insure that the data are reliable and valid. However, the protocols insure only that the data cohere with similar data and some accepted or common beliefs about the experimental subjects. As I explain in chapter 7, the very practice of sorting some subjects by their stages in life and including childhood as a life-stage is partisan. As a result, data about children, no matter how they are collected, reflect the values behind the choice of life-stages. The data may be true of the children, but the subjects are counted as children because of the values of those who sort the subjects this way. The data are not mirror images of the subjects but portraits drawn to fit or reflect an interest – namely, the interest behind treating subjects between the ages of 4 and 12 as forming a kind.

The methods of observing the subjects pass through to the data the conception of human perfection or the good life that leads the community to distinguish adults from children. The data would not be valid were they collected from adults rather than children; but childhood is a stage of life, and stages of life are not natural facts but reflections of a community's values. Since the distinction between adults and children is based on values, the data of childhood collected by the psychologists assume those values. Their data are partisan, but the partisanship is not overt or intentional. The psychologists do not allow their own thoughts about children to color their data, but the very fact that they count their data as the data of childhood means that values have trickled down from the community to their own practice of data collection and to the reliable and valid data they collect.

My general point is that the methods for collecting data in the social sciences eliminate overt, intentional forms of partisanship but not institutional partisanship – perfectionist ideals shared by the surrounding community. In fact, the ideal of validity requires that the surrounding partisanship be passed on to the data. In passing the partisanship on from the schools, churches, clinics, and courts to their data, the social scientists are unable to live up to their own ideal of value-neutral data; but unless they pass the partisanship on, they are unable to live up to their own ideals of valid data.

Valid data and codes of ethics

The methods or protocols for interviewing, sampling, psychological testing, and naturalistic or experimental observation are not intended to describe the social scientists' practice but to prescribe it. They don't tell the social scientist what she does but what she ought to do. So, in Weber's terms, they are not value-free but value-laden; they contain a norm or ideal from which directives for immediate practical activity can be derived.[11] However, the values with which the protocols are laden, the liberal would say, are scientific values, for the practical activity they direct is the collection of scientific data.

On the liberal view, a protocol or method for practicing a liberal science should be prescriptive but not morally or politically prescriptive and should direct against bad science but not bad conduct. As long as they are reliable and valid, the data are good, even if the methods used to collect them are morally objectionable. The American Anthropological Association writes, for example:

> Constraint, deception and secrecy have no place in science. Actions which compromise the intellectual integrity and autonomy of

research scholars and institutions not only weaken those international understandings essential to our discipline, but in so doing they also threaten any contribution anthropology might make in our own society and to the general interests of human welfare.[12]

It does not say that data collected using constraint, deception, and secrecy are not good as data or that the research is not good as anthropological research. It says that anthropology is less respected and useful when such methods are used, not that a measure of the quality of data in anthropology is how well the methods for collecting the data conform to a code of ethics.

Given the liberal ideal of value-neutrality, ethical codes must be located outside, rather than within, the codes of good science. The separation between good science and good conduct is central to the ideal of a value-neutral science; for if the protocols of good science included an ethical code, the science would favor whatever conception of the good was favored by the code. The separation of ethical values from the value of good data collection is a feature that the liberal sciences share with the natural sciences.

The separation is clear, for example, in biomedical research. Consider the debate over the use of the biological data collected during so-called medical experiments carried out on the inmates of the Nazi death camps by camp physicians. Both the opponents and the proponents of the use of the data agree that the methods used to collect them were ethically unacceptable; they agree that the fact that the experiments or interviews were unethical does not itself preclude the data's being either reliable or valid. Until recently, they also agreed that some of the data – for example, the data from the Dachau hypothermia experiments – were collected while adhering to scientific principles. They maintained that though many of the experiments were not properly designed – for example, they lacked control groups – a few *were* properly designed and conformed to all the experimental protocols of biomedical science.[13]

Before their validity was called into question, the debate over these experiments centered on whether it is morally permissible to use reliable and valid data gathered in the past in an inhumane or morally impermissible manner. The general moral question posed by the Nazi case, on everyone's view, was whether it is ever morally permissible to use reliable and valid data collected in unethical experiments or interviews, not whether data collected in unethical experiments or interviews could ever be reliable or valid. The practice of science by the Nazis violated the Nuremberg code on human experimentation, but few critics suggest that the practices ought not to be called science simply because they violated the code.[14] So long as the practices do not violate the norms of "neutral" science, they are scientific, even if evil or unethical.

According to the liberal view of the relation between science and ethics, moral education should supplement, but is not part of, an education in the sciences. Some codes of ethics, for example, require experimenters to seek consent from their subjects; but the experimenters do not lose their claims to be doing science for failing to do so, for obtaining informed consent, on the liberal view, is not itself a part of science, since codes of ethics and science are thought to be absolutely heterogeneous. As Weber writes in "Science as a Vocation":

> Now one cannot demonstrate scientifically what the duty of an academic teacher is. One can only demand of the teacher that he have the intellectual integrity to see that it is one thing to state facts, to determine mathematical or logical relations or the internal structure of cultural values, while it is another thing to answer questions of the value of culture and its individual contents and the question of how one should act in the cultural community and in political associations. These are quite heterogeneous problems.[15]

Scientists believed that the hypothermia experiments had some scientific validity because they upheld Weber's concept of the heterogeneity of science and ethics. Of course, science does not condone the Nazis' experiments or any other ethically questionable practice, for as science, it neither condones nor condemns any violation of any code of ethics.

The relation between science and ethics is seen by those in science in the same way as the relation between business and ethics is seen by those in business. There is faith that what is good for business is good for the general public and hope that an invisible hand will steer corporate profit and public welfare always in the same direction. But faith and hope are not enough. Individuals or firms by pursuing their own gain do sometimes advance the public interest; but markets are not magic, and often profits do not trickle down, and the consequences of private gain are not the public good.

Business and ethics, like science and ethics, are treated as separate spheres, each with its own values and norms. In the sphere of business the value is individual return on investment, and in the sphere of ethics the value is respecting the rights of individuals or increasing the public welfare. Even when ethical values affect a business decision – when, for the moment, good ethics is good business – the relationship between good ethics and good business is only contingent and coincidental, for the standards of goodness in business and ethics are entirely heterogeneous.

Similarly, there is faith that what is good for science is good for its subjects, but no invisible hand can be expected to steer reliable and valid data in the sciences always in the direction of the well-being of the theoretical or participant subjects of science. Sociologists, by pursuing reliable or valid data, may advance the interests of their respondents; but, as a rule, the benefits of good interview data do not trickle down to the respondents, and reliability and validity do not emerge as a moral good. As long as the ideals of science and business are liberal, there is no assurance that by living up to its ideals, science or business will improve the prospects or fortunes of the public. In particular, in any given area of research in the liberal sciences, the relationship between collecting good data and doing good will be only contingent and coincidental.

My point here is not that the pursuit of good data or profit requires a scientist or business firm to act unethically or in opposition to the public good, but only that it permits it; for there is no assurance that good data or profits are achieved better by doing the morally right rather than the morally wrong thing. Unless good science or business is measured by the yardstick of what morally ought to be, neither can promise less moral harm than moral good; but if good science *is* measured by what morally ought to be, science cannot be what liberals think it ought to be: free of moral, cultural, and political value.

The separation of science and ethics is the liberal ideal, but teaching and research in the social sciences, I have been arguing, are unavoidably partisan. A science can be free of values in the form of an ethical code, but not free of values. Ethical codes are manifest forms of partisanship; but partisanship in the liberal sciences is seldom manifest but usually latent or, as I suggested, in chapter 1, seldom *de jure* but often *de facto*. But manifest forms of partisanship have an advantage over latent or *de facto* forms, since they are usually the subject of discussion and debate. The decision to adopt a code of ethics or to include a code in one's science invites doubts, objections, resistance, or alternatives. When the values in the science are not in the form of a code but in the design of experiments, tests, or interviews or in the categories into which the data are sorted (part of the temple rather than the service), neither the researchers nor their subjects are able to see, let alone debate, them. In short, the question isn't whether the data should or should not be partisan, but how and where the partisanship should be placed.

Research requiring harm

Some protocols designed to provide social scientists with reliable and valid data do not merely permit, but require, harm to be done to the participant subjects, for they call for discomfort, stress, or deception, or they prohibit social scientists from obtaining the informed consent of their subjects. "The use of deception has become more and more extensive, and is now a commonplace and almost standard feature of social psychological experiments. Deception has been turned into a game, often played with great skill and virtuosity."[16] The goal of collecting reliable and valid data in psychology, according to many psychologists, requires concealment or deception and, as a result, research on human subjects without their informed consent. Informed consent, on their view, reduces the quality of the data and calls the results of the psychological research into question.

> Informing subjects about the purpose and procedures of a study has been found to alter subject's data by reducing the spontaneity and naivete in the responses to manipulated variables in a controlled setting. Gardner [G. T. Gardner, "Effects of Federal Human Subjects Regulations on Data Obtained in Environmental Stressor Research," *Journal of Personality Social Psychology*," 36, pp. 628–34] conducted an experiment to test the effects of Federal informed consent regulations on the results of environmental noise research. In brief, his study focused on negative performance aftereffects of noise by comparing a group of subjects that gave informed consent with a group of subjects that had not. The findings revealed that only subjects from whom informed consent was obtained failed to show the expected negative performance aftereffects.[17]

Concealment or deception is necessary if the researcher is to establish the reliability or validity of her data, because informing the subjects could bias their responses to the experiment or interview.[18]

Good sociology may also require concealment and deception. Sociologists maintain that there are circumstances in which it is impossible to recruit respondents and obtain good interview data without concealing facts from potential respondents or misleading them about the interview.

> There are some situations ... in which the characteristics of the respondent set, the interview demands, and the interviewer combine to make the likelihood of participation so remote that the interviewer is led to consider the possibility of covert interviewing – that is, concealing his true role and collecting information by playing a role other than that of interviewer. He may, for example, try to obtain membership in the group that he is studying, or he may

attempt to become an inconspicuous and innocuous part of the environment of the respondent set.[19]

The sociologist is in a bind when she needs to deceive or mislead her subjects in order to collect good data, since acts of deception and concealment violate her own code of ethics. She faces a conflict: either she conforms to her ethical code or she impairs the effectiveness of the interviews and lowers the quality of her data. One solution, popular among sociologists and social psychologists, is to fashion or tailor a code of ethics that permits deception and concealment, or, in other words, to cut the morality to fit the science.

The codes of ethics adopted by professional associations like the American Psychological Association and the American Sociological Association have been well tailored. They permit the use of deception and concealment whenever the harm to the subject is slight and is offset by expected benefits to others.[20] These codes of ethics are based on the ethics of cost-benefit analysis. Minor harms to the subject can be balanced by expected benefits to society. However, since knowledge is seen as good for its own sake, little evidence of benefits is necessary.[21] What is lacking in the codes is the idea that the participants have rights that override the expected benefits of the research. In particular, subjects are not seen as having rights to the truth about the experiment or interview, truth that could be used to decide whether or not to participate.[22]

In this respect, codes of ethics in the social sciences are much more permissive than the Nuremberg code governing permissible medical experiments or the World Medical Association Declaration of Helsinki on biomedical research involving human subjects. The first basic principle of the Nuremberg code is that informed or voluntary consent is absolutely essential in any experiments with human subjects, and, according to the code:

> [Voluntary consent] requires that before the acceptance of an affirmative decision by the experimental subject there should be made known to him the nature, duration, and purpose of the experiment; the method and means by which it is to be conducted; all inconveniences and hazards reasonably to be expected; and the effects upon his health or person which may possibly come from his participation in the experiment.[23]

Informed consent precludes the kind of concealment and deception commonly employed in psychological and sociological experiments. Social scientists are aware of this, of course; but they maintain that informed consent is less important in social science than in biomedical research because of the differences in risk to the subjects.[24] However, if risks are different, personal autonomy is the same. No differences between biomedical and social science research make autonomy a less appropriate ideal for one than the other, and the point of the doctrine of informed consent is to protect the autonomy, not merely the welfare or well-being, of the subject.

Pure research in the social sciences is intended to increase social well-being by increasing knowledge and is not designed to protect the rights of the participant subjects or even to give their well-being special prominence. The research is merely permitted to show concern for them when necessary to secure or maintain their participation.

If, by restricting the respondent too sharply to information relevant to the substantive goals of the research, the interviewer ignores the respondent's interests, concerns and feelings, the interviewer may reduce, or even lose, the respondent's participation. On the other hand, if, through excessive concern with participation, the interviewer allows the respondent's interests to govern the content of the response, the resulting material may have little or no relevance to the subject matter of the research.[25]

Concern for the subject is inappropriate whenever it would decrease the likelihood that the data collected will be reliable or valid. As a result, good data in the social sciences is seldom good for those from whom the data have been collected.

The conduct of interviews

Good psychology and sociology can require more than the deception of participant subjects; they can require their subordination. Much of the interviewing to collect data for research in the social sciences is directive rather than nondirective. In directive interviewing, interviewers move the respondent through predetermined topics and limit their participation to answering questions.[26] They determine both the topics of the interview and what the respondent is to say about them.

Directive interviewing prescribes a unilateral relationship in which the interviewer elicits but does not give information.[27] Interviewers may interrogate respondents on details of their lives but are required to reveal as little about themselves as possible.

In a social relationship, it is customary for both parties to develop a mutually satisfactory balance between giving and receiving information. . . . Although one of the parties may emerge as more influential in determining the choice of subject matter and the direction and duration of the conversation, such leadership may shift back and forth so that, in the long run, both parties have a sense of mutuality. In interviewing, on the other hand, the task of gathering information calls for a largely unilateral relationship, the interviewer taking the leadership role in questioning the respondent or in guiding him in the shaping of his answers. If the interviewer, either because of his personal needs or because of needs he perceives in the respondent, drops his role of questioner and launches into personal anecdotes, an exchange of view, or other personal matters, or if he permits the respondent to assume the role of questioner, he will inevitably prolong the interview beyond the point of maximal usefulness; moreover, he will risk biasing the responses through the disclosure of his own views and values.[28]

In a relationship in which power is shared, each party is expected to answer and not always parry the other's questions; in directive interviewing, the interviewer is obliged to always parry them. Only if she parries can the interviewer be sure that she is not biasing her subject's responses; only if she refuses to share her own sentiments or opinions with her subjects can she be sure that their responses would have been the same had the interviewer been different and that the data she gathers are reliable.[29]

The interview protocols define the roles of the parties to the interview, and the role they assign to the respondents is that of deferring to the interests and requests of the interviewers. "The person doing the interviewing must actively and continually construct the respondent as passive."[30] They must answer rather than ask questions, serve rather than be served, defer rather than resist, agree rather than disagree, and please rather than displease. "It is not enough for the scientist to understand the world of meaning of his informants; if he is to secure valid data via the structured interview, respondents must be socialized into answering questions in proper fashion."[31] The protocols require the interviewers to be impersonal, detached, and silent about their own thoughts and feelings and require the respondents to be open, obliging, and personal about theirs.[32]

The relationship between interviewer and respondent reproduces traditional sex roles, for the interviewer, at least in direct interviewing, always wears the trousers.[33] "It is no accident that the methodology textbooks (with one notable exception – Moser, 1958) refer to the interviewer as male. Although no interviewees are referred to as females, there are a number of references to 'housewives' as the kind of people interviewers are most likely to meet in the course of their work."[34] Though the research may be intended to increase our understanding of social equality or personal autonomy, the methods of interviewing work against these values. "Interviewers define the role of interviewees as subordinates; extracting information is more to be valued than yielding it; the convention of interviewer–interviewee hierarchy is a rationalization of inequality; what is good for interviewers is not necessarily good for interviewees."[35] The protocols do not merely prevent the interviewer from increasing the status of the respondents or promoting their interests but require her to lessen their status by subordinating their interests to her own. The protocols are recipes for preparing participant subjects to meet the requirements of a science diet. The participants are squeezed, pressed, and rolled until their reluctance, concerns, and curiosity are kneaded out and they fit neatly into the scientist's measuring cup.

Ann Oakley recommends that sociologists interested in women's empowerment give up textbook methods for collecting reliable and valid data and make their practice as sociologists more directly relevant to feminist values. Instead of aiming at knowledge that others might use to increase the power or prospects of women as theoretical subjects, feminist sociologists should aim at increasing the power or prospects of the women who are their participant subjects. To this end, their interviews should give their female respondents an opportunity to tell their own stories in their own words.[36]

Proponents of liberalism in the social sciences would say that feminists like Oakley are recommending that sociologists give up science for social activism. The practice of friendly conversations with women is nice, but what does it have to do with the practice of science? To do good for women, they would say, we have to know the truth about women; this truth comes through reliable and valid data; and reliable and valid data come through the standard protocols.

In reply, Oakley maintains that feminist methods are more suitable than the standard methods when doing repeated or longitudinal interviewing and so should be adopted when doing such interviewing.[37] But her defense of her approach seems like a retreat to the textbooks; for she defends her efforts on behalf of her female subjects as a means of winning their confidence and loyalty and of persuading them to continue to participate in her interviews rather than as a response to their own expressed needs. She cites research by Laslett and Rapoport to show that by being responsive to the respondent, interviewers can collect more information in greater depth than they could were they to follow the protocols of directive interviewing.[38] She maintains that her alternative to a masculine model of sociology enables her to collect more or better data, for her alternative promotes the trust on which a continuing interview relationship depends. "It becomes clear that, in most cases, the goal of finding out about people through interviewing is best achieved when the relationship of interviewer and interviewee is non-hierarchical and when the interviewer is prepared to invest his or her own personal identity in the relationship."[39]

If Oakley's aim is to collect reliable and valid data and her responsiveness to her subjects is merely a means, then the changes she is recommending in interviewing women seem to be more for the sake of liberal science than for women. To convince her more liberal colleagues of the soundness of her methods, she makes them sound more familiar than feminist – a more enlightened way of using women to collect data for theorizing in sociology, but a way of using them nonetheless.

The issue is whether the data are better in a sense that the liberal sociologist would accept – more reliable or valid and better for theorizing (where theorizing is thought of in a traditional way as representing an underlying reality) – or better because they are more responsive to the interests of women. Oakley suggests that her goal is to have her respondents find out about themselves through interviewing; but she also suggests that it is to have the interviewer find out about them through interviewing. She leaves it unclear whether her aim is more willing women for sociology or a more willing sociology for women.

Oakley is caught between two opposing approaches to research in the social sciences. On one approach, the traditional, nonpartisan, or liberal approach, the participant subject has no role but to provide the researcher with good data. The participant subject does not influence how the research is conducted, and the research is not designed to be good for her. She is merely the means by which the researcher attempts to acquire the data. On another approach, a perfectionist approach, which I discuss in chapter 10, the research is designed for the good of the participant subject, according to her own conception of the good, and the data are not good unless the subjects find the practice of gathering them unobjectionable and the practice contributes directly to their education and wellbeing. Such an approach is illiberal or partisan and opposes the liberal belief that the community of science should seek the truth and leave a search for the good to others – for example, the family or the Church.

In giving women a voice, Oakley seems to be doing perfectionist research; but in rationalizing their participation in terms of traditional research interests, she seems to be doing traditional, liberal research and only deviating from the norms in order to continue to use her subjects in an attempt to acquire good data. In chapter 10, I describe some feminist research that is clearly and overtly partisan and that opposes the liberal distinction between the true and the good.

Though liberals attempt to free their data of values, they cannot do so, for, as I explained earlier, their standards of reliability and validity require them to pass the community's values through to their data. Moreover, their idea of neutrality is too narrow. On the liberal view, as long as psychologists or sociologists do not speak the words of morality, their contributions are value-neutral; but neutrality is not simply a matter of words, it is also a matter of deeds or, as I explain in chapter 9, a matter of what the protocols command as well as how they command it. When protocols direct a researcher to do something which happens to be morally wrong – for example, subordinate, deceive, or even, as in the Nazi case, torture a subject – liberals think that the protocols are neutral, provided they do not include moral terms or morally condone or condemn the conduct. But the protocols are not neutral, for they favor one conception of the good over another and, in particular, a conception of the good which places expected social welfare over the welfare or autonomy of the participant subject. So long as they require the subordination of the respondents or experimental subjects, the protocols reduce the subjects' capacity for self-determination and, somewhat ironically, oppose a conception of the good that, as I explained in chapter 1, is a basis for the liberal approach to the social sciences.

The conduct of experiments

The work of the social psychologist Stanley Milgram provides an interesting example of how commitment to the ideals of good data can prevent social scientists from recognizing the partisanship of their science. Some years ago, Milgram conducted a number of experiments to collect data about obedience to authority.[40] The question he hoped to answer was how far his subjects would comply with instructions to cause others serious harm. According to Milgram, the data from his experiments show that there is no limit to how far subjects will comply, and, since he assumes that his data are externally valid, almost no limit to how far people will go before refusing to comply with the instructions of authorities. "It is the extreme willingness of adults to go to almost any lengths on the command of an authority that constitutes the chief finding of the study and the fact most urgently demanding explanation."[41]

Milgram's research did not end with gathering the facts but went on to look for an explanation. His subjects' obedience, he found, could not be explained by a failure to understand that the actions were wrong, for they obeyed commands even when they knew that what they were being commanded to do was wrong.

> The force exerted by the moral sense of the individual is less effective than social myth would have us believe. Though such prescriptions as "Thou shalt not kill" occupy a pre-eminent place in the moral order, they do not occupy a correspondingly intractable position in human psychic structure . . . even the forces mustered in a psychological experiment will go a long way toward removing the individual from moral controls.[42]

Milgram goes on to explain that the forces that cause individuals to obey the commands, even when their conscience tells them otherwise, are a set of "binding factors" that lock the subject into his situation. The binding factors cause the subjects to attribute all initiative to the authority and to see themselves as instruments rather than agents. Such a mode of thinking – that only the authority is able to initiate an action – is, according to Milgram, "a fundamental mode of thinking for people once they are locked into a subordinate position in a structure of authority."[43]

Although Milgram believes that psychological factors are among the binding factors, he does not believe that they are all of them, for the problem of obedience, he allows, is not wholly psychological. Social norms, such as politeness and deference to experts, discourage resistance to authorities, and the organization of work in the society limits a person's responsibility to only small parts of any activity. These sociological factors make it easier for subjects to agree to do wrong or to hide from themselves the wrong they are doing.

Milgram's experiments have been criticized for their use of deception and for having been carried out without the informed consent of the experimental subjects.[44] His subjects were told lies about the experiment, and their consent to participate was not informed by a correct understanding of what they were being asked to do. Milgram is not indifferent to this deception. He allows that doing science should be constrained or limited by codes of ethics and that the use of deception is a legitimate ethical concern. However, he thinks that his deception was slight and that the harms were lessened by the briefing following the experiments and offset by the gains to science that came from his findings. He sees the manipulation of his subjects in the larger context of pursuing scientific knowledge, and in that larger context the harm looks slight to him. He does not see, as his critics do, that he is violating his subjects' rights and that he is not a disinterested judge of the harm his experiments caused.

A social psychologist would wonder why Milgram did not see his experiment in a harsher light and might look for the "binding factors" that locked Milgram into his situation and caused him to attribute all initiative to the demands of science and to see himself as a handmaiden. Milgram explains that the human agent fades from the picture in his experiment and that the experiment acquires an impersonal momentum of its own: "The psychological laboratory has a strong claim to legitimacy and evokes trust and confidence in those who perform there."[45] However, he fails to see that the psychological laboratory has as strong a claim to legitimacy for him as it does for his subjects and evokes his trust and confidence as much as it does theirs, or that the causes of his own selective vision are not entirely psychological and include norms of the psychological laboratory. According to these norms, data are good even if collected using deceit and deception, and any harms caused to the subjects are offset by the truths the data are expected to reveal.

There is more at work in Milgram's experiment than deceiving a subject. The experiments can help to increase the subjects' indifference to moral considerations and strengthen their disposition to obedience. His experiments show, Milgram says, that "moral factors can be shunted aside with relative ease by a calculated restructuring of the informational and social field."[46] He ignores the fact, however, that they show this by shunting aside the moral concerns of his own experimental subjects with a calculated restructuring of their informational and social field. Moreover, he is unaware that his experiments restructure his own informational and social field and shunt his own moral concerns or inhibitions aside.

Milgram does not realize that the authority of science – the demands for reliable and valid data – places him in a position like the one in which he is placing his own subjects. He writes:

> Although a person acting under authority performs actions that seem to violate standards of conscience, it would not be true to say that he loses his moral sense. Instead, it acquires a radically different focus. He does not respond with a moral sentiment to the actions he performs. Rather the moral concern now shifts to a consideration of how well he is living up to the expectations that the authority has of him.[47]

Milgram does not imagine that his words apply to himself and others who are engaged in doing social research, but they do. A researcher acting under some of the protocols for conducting experiments or interviews in the social sciences performs actions that violate standards of conscience. The researcher does not lose his moral sense, but he shifts his moral focus. His concern shifts to how well he is living up to the standards of good science and to the expectations of the scientific community. His liberal views – his view that science and ethics are entirely heterogeneous – assure him that even if his ethics are questionable, his science is redoubtable.

Milgram forgets that he is one of the people who comes to perform in the laboratory and that the laboratory has as strong, if not stronger, a claim on him as on his subjects. An action such as deceiving someone, which in isolation appears wrong, acquires a totally different meaning when placed in the scientific setting. As Milgram says, "Allowing an act to be dominated by its context, while neglecting its human consequences, can be dangerous in the extreme."[48] The laboratory creates a context in which Milgram's actions become so dominated by the ideals of good science that he minimizes their human consequences.

Milgram sees that the form and shape of society and the way it is developing influence a person's responses to authority.

> There was a time, perhaps, when men were able to give a fully human response to any situation because they were fully absorbed in it as human beings. But as soon as there was a division of labor among men, things changed. Beyond a certain point, the breaking up of society into people carrying out narrow and very special jobs takes away from the human quality of work and life. A person does not get to see the whole situation but only a small part of it, and is thus unable to act without some kind of over-all direction. He yields to authority but in doing so is alienated from his own actions.[49]

The separation of the standards of good science from ethics and politics, the ideal of value-neutrality, is part of the development that Milgram is talking about. Our society is broken up into people carrying out pure research and people applying the findings in the service of some public or private interest in the clinic, school, factory, court, or legislature. Protocols of science are separated from codes of ethics. The separation helps the researchers to see what they want to see. They yield to the authority of their science and the ideal of neutrality and, in doing so, ignore the values that their practice is furthering or passing through.

According to Milgram, the factors that lead to immoral acts being carried out in the name of obedience include the devaluation of the victim.[50] He is thinking of the violence against Jews by Nazi soldiers who were only carrying out their orders. However, he does not consider what in the structure of social life contributes to the devaluation of a subject. I am trying to show how the structure of social science contributes. Milgram, like the interviewer in directive interviews, devalues his subjects. His concerns or interests determine who knows, says, and does what, while the concerns or interests of his subjects are observed or measured but not allowed to control or influence the experiment. The design of the experiment encourages Milgram and his subjects to believe that they should be deferential and that the interests of science – as represented by the experimenter, the laboratory, the professional journal, and the research university – are more important than their own.

Using deception to move young college students to obey authority figures in psychological experiments may add to our knowledge, and Milgram maintains that it causes no great harm. But his judgment of harm is uninformed by any consideration of the subjects' rights and is not backed by any data on the lasting effects of deception or submission to authority in scientific experiments.[51] Playing the role of experimental subject may not influence how a person behaves outside the laboratory, but the role, even if limited to the laboratory, does contribute to a practice that Milgram and other social psychologists look upon with regret: that of blindly accepting and not questioning or resisting authority. Moreover, were participant subjects to question or resist authority in experiments or interviews in the social sciences, the data collected would not be good, for the experimenter or interviewer would no longer be able to follow his protocols and ensure that the data were reliable and valid.

Obedience and nonpartisanship

Milgram's experiments were designed to yield reliable and valid data about obedience to authority that would reveal the causes of obedience and explain why many adults are willing to go to almost any lengths on the commands of those they perceive to be authorities.[52] Obedience to authority is just one of many facts of social life that Milgram, as a social psychologist, might choose to study. His decision to study obedience is based on his assessment of the moral or political significance of obedience vis-à-vis the other facts that he might have chosen to study instead. Though personal values clearly influence the decision, most social scientists would say, following Weber, that this is a matter of value-relevance and that as long as Milgram does not include judgments of value in his findings, the research is free of his values and is value-neutral.[53]

Milgram believes that, though obedience is a basic element in the structure of social life, blind obedience is morally and politically objectionable.

Placing his interest in obedience in the context of the Holocaust, he writes:

> It has been reliably established that from 1933 to 1945 millions of innocent people were systematically slaughtered on command. Gas chambers were built, death camps were guarded, daily quotas of corpses were produced with the same efficiency as the manufacture of appliances. These inhumane policies may have originated in the mind of a single person, but they could only have been carried out on a massive scale if a very large number of people obeyed orders.[54]

> The Nazi extermination of European Jews is the most extreme instance of the abhorrent immoral acts carried out by thousands of people in the name of obedience. Yet in lesser degree this type of thing is constantly occurring: ordinary citizens are ordered to destroy other people, and they do so because they consider it their duty to obey orders.[55]

Milgram intends his research to be relevant to his moral concerns, but he does not want his concerns to influence the conduct of his experiments; for if they do, then his data will not be good. "The legal and philosophic aspects of obedience are of enormous import, but an empirically grounded scientist eventually comes to the point where he wishes to move from abstract [moral] discourse to the careful [objective] observation of concrete instances."[56] The protocols he adopts for conducting the experiments are intended to insure that his moral concerns will have no influence and that his data will present the facts of obedience as they are, rather than as we would prefer them to be.

However, in spite of his concern with the ordinary German citizens or soldiers who shunted moral considerations aside and acted in the name of obedience, his own obedience to good science led him to shunt aside moral considerations and deceive his own subjects and encourage them to blindly obey the orders of the experimenter. Ironically, he has to mock his own moral concerns and oppose the values which give his experiments their relevance in order to obey the ideals of his science.

Illiberal or perfectionist science does not require the researcher to alienate himself from his own social concerns or moral values. A researcher who is concerned, as Milgram was, to discourage blind obedience to authority but is committed to the perfectionist rather than the liberal approach could include his concerns in his research. He could educate his subjects about the problems of obedience and teach them to question or resist authority, including the authority of the experimenter and the psychological laboratory.

Of course, if Milgram were a devil, perfectionism would license his misdeeds. The protocols of his science could include inflicting misery on his subjects as a norm. Nothing in either liberal or perfectionist approaches to the social sciences assures that research will do more good than harm; but, on the perfectionist approach, doing good (according to some conception of the good) is an ideal of science and a measure of a scientist's data and the protocols she uses to gather them. On the perfectionist approach, doing good science and doing good overlap, and not by chance or as if by an invisible hand, but by design.

(unpersuasively)

Conclusion

Data are the stuff of science. Science must have them, but must have them collected in the proper way. The proper way, on the liberal view, yields reliable and valid data and is free of moral, cultural, and political value. I have argued in this chapter that the protocols for acquiring reliable and valid data are not value-neutral and that, no matter what the scientists' intentions, their data are often partisan.

In seeking protocols that are nonpartisan, the liberal scientist has chosen some that permit – and may even require – moral wrongdoing in the service of science. Their liberal ideals permit or require them to engage in an unethical practice but prohibit them from judging that the practice is unethical. To do good science, they must free their work of ethics and politics in word but may flout ethics or endorse politics in deed. The perfectionist approaches I describe in chapter 10 aim at being ethical and political in word and at backing up the words with deeds. According to these approaches, "good data" means, in part at least, data collected to advance some conception of the good or contribute to some ideal of human perfection; and, even when used in social science, "good" is to be seen as an overtly partisan term.

NOTES

1 L. H. Kidder, *Sellitz Wrightman and Cook's Research Methods in Social Relations*, 4th edn (Holt, Rinehart and Winston, 1981), p. 161.
2 S. A. Richardson, B. S. Dohrenwend and D. Klein, *Interviewing: Its Forms and Functions* (Basic Books, 1965), p. 44.
3 Kidder, *Sellitz Wrightman*, p. 266.
4 Ibid., p. 186.

5   See ibid., p. 6, for a discussion of the concepts of reliability and validity in the social sciences.

6   Richardson et al., *Interviewing*, pp. 130–1.

7   L. E. Tyler, *Tests and Measurements*, 2nd edn (Prentice-Hall, 1971), pp. 25–8.

8   My discussion of this test is based on the *1990–91 GRE Guide to the Use of the Record Examinations Program* (Educational Testing Service, 1990).

9   Ibid., p. 7.

10 The predictive validity of the test is the correlation between the GRE score and the indicator of success in graduate school. According to the ETS, the most commonly used indicator is graduate first-year grade point average. A very low correlation coefficient would indicate that the scores provide little information about grades in graduate school, and a very high coefficient that they provide much information. The correlation coefficient for a weighted composite of the scores on the verbal, quantitative, and analytic parts of the exam was 0.33, according to a study conducted by the ETS between 1985 and 1989. Such a coefficient is high for aptitude tests.

11 Weber, *Methodology*, p. 52.

12 Quoted in R. L. Beales, *Politics of Social Research: An Inquiry into the Ethics and Responsibility of Social Scientists* (Aldine, 1969), p. 1.

13 Robert Pozos presents such a view in "Can Scientists Use Information Derived from Concentration Camps?," paper read at the Conference on the Meaning of the Holocaust for Bioethics, Minneapolis, May 17–19, 1989 (transcription of official recording, Center for Biomedical Ethics, University of Minnesota, 1989, pp. 1–17). Recently the validity of the data has been challenged by Robert Berger in a paper, "Nazi Science – The Dachau Hypothermia Experiments," *New England Journal of Medicine*, 322 (1990), 1435–40. Berger argues that the Dachau experiments contain serious shortcomings in scientific content and credibility. He writes: "On analysis, the Dachau hypothermia study has all the ingredients of a scientific fraud, and rejection of the data on purely scientific grounds is inevitable. They cannot advance science or save human lives." But Berger, like Pozos, assumes that there are two separate grounds on which experiments in science may be rejected – viz., scientific and ethical – and the fact that an experiment is unethical is not a ground for concluding that it is unscientific.

14 See, e.g., R. Proctor, *Racial Hygiene: A History of Nazi Medicine* (Harvard University Press, 1988), pp. 5 and 285.

15 M. Weber, "Science as a Vocation," in *From Max Weber*, ed. H. H. Gerth and C. Wright Mills (Oxford University Press, 1946), p. 146.

16 H. Kelman, "Human Use of Human Subjects: The Problem of Deception in Social Psychological Experiments," *Psychological Bulletin*, 67 (1967), pp. 1–11.

17 A. J. Kimmel, *Ethics and Values in Applied Social Research* (Sage, 1988), p. 72.

18 For a discussion of the need for concealment and deception in psychological research, see J. M. Suls and R. L. Rosnow, "The Delicate Balance between Ethics and Artifacts in Behavioral Research," in *New Directions for Methodology of Social and Behavioral Sciences*, vol. 10 (Jossey-Bass, 1981),

pp. 56–67. Surveys of articles published in major journals in the field of social psychology indicate that deception is employed in over half the studies; but the incidence of deception is hard to measure, for most journals do not require that deception or concealment be reported (R. J. Levine, *Ethics and Regulation of Clinical Research*, 2nd edn (Yale University Press, 1988), p. 213, and J. G. Adair, T. W. Dushenko and R. C. L. Lindsay, "Ethical Regulations and their Impact on Research Practice," *American Psychologist*, 40 (1985), pp. 59–72).

19 Richardson et al., *Interviewing*, p. 118.

20 According to the APA code, psychologists have a "special responsibility to (1) determine whether the use of such techniques is justified by the study's prospective scientific, educational, or applied value; (2) determine whether alternative procedures are available that do not use concealment or deception; and (3) ensure that the participants are provided with sufficient explanations as soon as possible" (*Ethical Principles in the Conduct of Research with Human Participants*, American Psychological Association, Washington, D. C., 1982, p. 6); but techniques of concealment and deception are permitted when these conditions are met.

21 According to the moral codes, the only issue is whether the harm to the subject is minor; but decisions whether the harm is minor are not disinterested, for they are not made by the subjects but by the researchers. With the APA code, the psychologist is permitted to decide whether the use of deception is justified by the study's prospective scientific or educational benefits as long as the participants are debriefed or provided with explanations of the deception after the experiment is over.

22 Levine, *Ethics*, pp. 7–20.

23 Ibid., pp. 425–6.

24 See, e.g., E. Diener and R. Crandall, *Ethics in Social and Behavioral Research* (University of Chicago Press, 1978), pp. 50–1.

25 Richardson et al., *Interviewing*, p. 133.

26 Ibid., pp. 18–39.

27 A. Oakley, "Interviewing Women: A Contradiction in Terms," in *Doing Feminist Research*, ed. H. Roberts (Routledge and Kegan Paul, 1981), pp. 30–61.

28 Richardson et al., *Interviewing*, p. 318.

29 The sociologist reasons that if every interviewer is equally blank-faced and impassive, the responses will not vary from one interviewer to another, and, as a result, the data collected by any interviewer will be reliable. But here reliability opposes external validity, for the directive interview reveals how subjects respond to *any* blank-faced, impassive interviewer – not how subjects really are, unless we believe that the way people really are is the way they are when they are treated impassively or coldly. I owe this point to Naomi Scheman.

30 Oakley, "Interviewing Women," p. 35.

31 G. Sjoberg and R. Nett, *A Methodology of Social Research* (Harper and Row, 1968), p. 210.

32 Oakley, "Interviewing Women," p. 31.

33 Ibid., p. 38.

34 Ibid., p. 39.

35 Ibid., p. 40.
36 Ibid., p. 48.
37 Ibid., pp. 44–5.
38 B. Laslett and R. Rapoport, "Collaborative Interviewing and Interactive Research," *Journal of Marriage and the Family*, 37 (1975), pp. 968–77.
39 Oakley, "Interviewing Women," p. 41.
40 S. Milgram, *Obedience to Authority* (Harper and Row, 1974), pp. 1–12.
41 Ibid., p. 5.
42 Ibid., p. 7.
43 Ibid., p. 9.
44 See, e.g., S. Bok, *Lying: Moral Choices in Public and Private Life* (Pantheon, 1978), pp. 192–201.
45 Milgram, *Obedience*, p. 9.
46 Ibid., p. 7.
47 Ibid., p. 8.
48 Ibid.
49 Ibid., p. 11.
50 Ibid., p. 9.
51 There is evidence that the harmful effects of concealment and deception persevere and resist efforts to eliminate them through debriefing and desensitization. See, e.g., L. Ross, M. R. Lepper and M. Hubbard, "Perseverance and Self-Perception and Social Perception: Biased Attributional Processes in the Debriefing Paradigm," *Journal of Personality and Social Psychology*, 32 (1975), pp. 880–92.
52 Milgram, *Obedience*, p. 5.
53 Weber, *Methodology*, pp. 21–2 and 60–1.
54 Milgram, *Obedience*, p. 1.
55 Ibid., p. 2.
56 Ibid.

7

Sorting data into kinds

The facts gathered through interviews or experiments are sorted and organized. The subjects of these interviews and experiments are kinds of subjects. They are selected, observed, tested, or interviewed as subjects with a sexual preference, marital status, educational history, religious affiliation, occupation, income, wealth, or employment record. Sociologists who study suicide, stress, personality disorders, addiction, or depression among single and married adults over 65 sort their subjects by age, marital status, and state of mind. Political scientists who study the political party loyalty of Polish Americans and Irish Americans in a Presidential election sort theirs by political affiliation, ethnicity, and level of political interest.

Every social scientist sorts her subjects by one set of kinds or into one set of categories rather than another – for example, by race rather than sex, sex rather than class, or class rather than education – and chooses one definition of sex, race, class, or educational level over many possible others. The practice of sorting, I argue in this chapter, is not value-neutral. Nevertheless, Weber's distinction between value-relevance and value-freedom does nothing to reveal or highlight the partisanship or role that values play in sorting the data and organizing the facts; for the selection of kinds is a matter neither of selecting a question to study nor of remaining silent on questions of value, but rather of deciding who the subjects of the study are and how they are to be represented.

My purpose in this chapter is to highlight the partisanship – to show how values influence the choice of kinds in the social sciences and how kinds play a role in normalizing human subjects and regulating social practice. First, however, I survey some recent discussions of natural kinds in science and consider whether any of the kinds in the social sciences are natural kinds. Second, I consider the claim that social scientists do not discover, but rather invent or construct, the categories or kinds into which they sort their data. Next, I explain how, in sorting their data into kinds, social scientists pass the values of the community on to the data and how, in employing the kinds to observe, examine, and train their subjects, social scientists pass the values back to the community.

Naturalism and nonnaturalism

What is the relationship between the social sciences and the kinds into which they classify or sort their subjects? Are the kinds in the social sciences invented or discovered by the social scientist? On one view of the social sciences, the naturalistic view, most are discovered; for they are natural kinds and exist independently of the social scientists' efforts to identify or sort individuals, groups, practices, or institutions by kind. Kinds like age, race, or sex, on this view, are independent of the scientists' practice of sorting subjects by age, race, or sex.

According to the naturalist, social scientists discover what kinds their subjects are – homosexuals, alcoholics, adolescents, blacks, whites, or middle class – just as natural scientists discover electrons, atoms, molecules, elements, planets, volcanoes, and biological species, and both adolescents and planets are naturally occurring and proper subjects for science to study. There were adolescents, on the naturalist view, just as there were planets before there was a science to identify, record, compare, classify, measure, or understand them.

On another view of the social sciences, the nonnaturalist view, most of the kinds of the social sciences are invented, constructed, or made up rather than discovered, detected, or unearthed. The kinds of people, roles, aspirations, life-styles, sexualities, ideologies, sexes, races, affiliations, statuses, and relationships described in the social sciences would not be as they are had the practice of collecting, recording, comparing, organizing, and analyzing anthropological, sociological, economic, historical, psychological, or political data been different or not existed. The kinds the social scientists identify, on this view, do not represent an independently existing social reality or any real unity between things, but a reality made up by the scientists' own practices or a diffuse motley held together by the scientists' own projects and interests.

Abnormal psychology is a source of many of the nonnaturalist's examples. In the nineteenth century, it seems, psychiatrists made up many different kinds of sexual perversion. As Michel Foucault writes:

> The homosexual was now a species. . . . So too were all those minor perverts whom nineteenth-century psychiatrists entomologized by giving them strange baptismal names: there was Krafft-Ebing's zoophiles

and zooerasts, Rohleder's auto-monosexualists; and later, mixoscopophiles, gynecomasts, presbyophiles, sexoesthetic inverts, and dyspareunist women. These fine names of heresies referred to a nature that was overlooked by the law, but not so neglectful of itself that it did not go on producing more species, even where there was no order to fit them into. The machinery of power that focused on this whole alien strain did not aim to suppress it, but rather to give it an analytical, visible, and permanent reality: it was implanted in bodies, slipped in beneath modes of conduct, made into a principle of classification and intelligibility, established as a *raison d'être* and a natural order of disorder. Not the exclusion of these thousand aberrant sexualities, but the specification, the regional solidification of each one of them. The strategy behind this dissemination was to strew reality with them and incorporate them into the individual.[1]

On Foucault's view, Krafft-Ebing did not discover zoophiles and zooerasts but invented them. If auto-monosexualists and sexoesthetic inverts were kinds of patients in Rohleder's examining rooms, their aberrant sexualities were due as much to Rohleder's practice of sorting them as to anything in their minds or out in nature; and if Foucault is correct, then zoophiles, zooerasts, auto-monosexualists, and sexoesthetic inverts are not natural kinds studied by psychologists but nonnatural kinds invented by them in the course of diagnosing and treating the ills of their clients.

Natural kinds

In the eighteenth and nineteenth centuries, biologists wondered whether their taxonomies of plants and animals were natural. Were kingdoms, phyla, classes, orders, families, genera, species, and varieties in nature or merely in the way that biologists had chosen to think or talk about nature? If vertebrates are a natural kind of animal, then biologists discover them; but if they are merely an assortment of animals that biologists have chosen to lump together for practical reasons, like animals amusing to children, run over by cars, or eaten by Englishmen, then vertebrates are the biologists' invention.

A similar question arises in chemistry. The periodic table of chemical elements includes 103 kinds of elements. Did chemists discover the table or invent it? If the elements are natural kinds, then the chemists discovered the table; but substances can be sorted in many ways – by atomic number or by more tangible properties like color, luster, hardness, ductility, corrosiveness, odor, and toxicity. The question is, which reflect the order of nature and which the nature of the interests of the chemists who are sorting them. Kinds that are in nature or reflect the natural order of things are called "natural kinds," while those that reflect some human interest or the way a group of people have chosen to think or talk about nature are nonnatural or constructed.[2] The distinction between natural and nonnatural kinds is important in natural sciences like biology and chemistry, for a central aim of these sciences is to discover the laws of nature, and the laws of biology and chemistry cannot be true of any odd mix or assortment of things – for example, silver-colored metals, soda pop, weeds, house pets, or road kills – but only of things with some common, underlying causal history or structure – for example, platinum, potassium, and polonium, or orchids, oaks, and oats.

The distinction between kinds – natural versus made up – does not travel well from the natural to the social sciences; for most of the kinds into which the social sciences sort their subjects are based on human interest or invention and seem not to reflect nature at all, but rather the way in which communities of men and women have chosen to organize and regulate their lives. Subjects of the social sciences may be sorted by age, sex, race, class, gender, marital status, occupation, religion, political affiliation, citizenship, school grade, or criminal record, but the existence of most if not all of these kinds depends as much on the surrounding social conventions or legal regulations as on anything in the subjects themselves. In a state of nature – that is, in the absence of all social and political regulation and authority – people would have no marital status, gender, occupation, citizenship, religion, race, or class and arguably even no sex.[3]

The kinds of crimes enumerated in our criminal codes are the result of our efforts or our ancestors' efforts to devise and maintain a particular system of criminal justice. Forgers, swindlers, arsonists, pornographers, and extortionists were created, not discovered, in the course of drafting and enforcing criminal laws and regulations. Marital status is a kind in the social sciences, but since it relies on the social and legal institutions of marriage and divorce, we can hardly call it "natural." Had the laws or conventions that give people a marital status not been invented or adopted, no one would be single, married, widowed, or divorced, and there would be no husbands or wives for sociologists or psychologists to sort. If natural kinds must be independent of human interest and invention, few of the kinds into which social scientists sort their subjects are natural kinds or kinds in nature.

To speak of natural kinds in the social sciences, the notion of "natural" must be adjusted to reflect the fact that how a social scientist sorts her subjects almost always depends on some past or present choice of norms or regulations. A distinction between natural and nonnatural kinds must be a distinction between kinds discovered and kinds invented by the social sciences. Both sociology and criminal law sort people as minors or adults, as swindlers, forgers, arsonists, or sex offenders, but if the existence of these kinds was established by the law before people were sorted thus by the sociologist, then, in relation to sociology, the kinds could be called "natural." What the one institution invents, the other can discover or observe; so, once the law invents the forger and the arsonist, sociology can discover them.

A kind that is made up or invented by the state or the Church, on this view, can be naturally occurring in relation to a science. Relative to sociology, for example, the distinction between minors and adults is naturally occurring if sociology has no hand in the laws or regulations that invent and sustain that distinction. In relation to the voting rights and regulations of a community, the distinction between eligible and ineligible voters is not naturally occurring; but if the rights and regulations are free of the hand of political science, the distinction is naturally occurring relative to the science. The distinction is no longer between invented and discovered kinds but between kinds invented and those discovered in the course of doing social science.

Evolutionary biologists, in treating a cluster of characteristics as a trait and asking whether it is adaptive, are treating the cluster as a natural kind.[4] Richard Lewontin questions whether these clusters are natural kinds by calling attention to the role of human interest in drawing the characteristics together as a kind.

> Hidden in adaptive analyses are a number of assumptions that go back to theistic views of nature and to a naive Cartesianism. First, it must be assumed that the partitioning of organisms into traits and the partitioning of the environment into problems has a real basis and is not simply the reification of intuitive human categories. In what natural sense is a fin, leg or wing an individual trait whose evolution can be understood in terms of the particular problem it solves? If the leg is a trait, is each part of the leg also a trait? At what level of subdivision do the boundaries no longer correspond to "natural" divisions? . . . As we move from anatomical features to descriptions of behavior, the danger of reification becomes greater. Animal behavior is described by such categories as aggression, altruism, parental investment, warfare, slave-making, and cooperation, and each of these "organs of behavior" is provided with an adaptive explanation by finding the problem to which it is a solution.

Alternatively, "the problems" to be solved in adaptation also may be arbitrary reifications.[5]

If the parts of a fish that make up a fin or the stretches of behavior that constitute warfare do not have any real basis but are reifications of intuitive human categories, then fins and warfare are not natural kinds. Moreover, adaptive explanations of fins or warfare would be explanations not of any natural occurring phenomena but only of phenomena as interpreted or individuated to serve some human purpose or interest.[6]

Nevertheless, fins and warfare could be natural kinds in relation to biology; for we could ask whether the phenomena were individuated thus before biologists began to study them. Here the distinction is not between invented and discovered kinds but between kinds invented and kinds discovered by the biologist. However, only biological traits are subject to biological evolution, and a cluster of characteristics is not a biological trait unless the characteristics form a natural kind *tout court* – that is, a kind discovered by the biologist and invented by no one before her. Fins, for example, are not biological traits or selected for by evolution if the practice of sorting parts as fins was invented by taxidermists or fishermen; and aggression is not a biological trait if the practice of sorting behavior as aggressive was invented by policemen or psychologists. Lewontin's point is that many traits that biologists call "adaptive" are not biological traits at all, because the cluster of characteristics is a kind held together not by nature but only by human and often ideological interests.

A cluster of characteristics not held together by nature – not a natural kind *tout court* – is not a proper subject for a biological theory, but can be a proper subject for a theory in the social sciences. Forgers, swindlers, and arsonists are nonnatural kinds. The individuals who are sorted together as criminals or criminals of a certain kind are held together not by nature but by the criminal laws and the various interests served by the laws. The kinds were invented; but as long as they were not invented by the particular science, the scientist can offer a theory about them. Her theory will have limited application; it will be relevant only in the presence of the laws and only within a society in which criminals are so finely sorted. Nevertheless, within these limits, the social scientist can use her theory to predict or explain facts about forgers, swindlers, and arsonists; outside the limits, however, her theory predicts and explains nothing at all.

On Michel Foucault's view, the hands of the social scientists are everywhere, for most of the kinds they employ they have some hand in devising. The kinds of aberrant sexualities described by psychiatrists in the nineteenth century were made up by the psychiatrists and then adopted by their subjects. Many kinds of deviant behavior are recognized by both the law and the social sciences – for example, sexual assault, drug abuse, and clinical depression – but, as Foucault sees it, the sciences did not discover what the law invented but invented what the law subsequently discovered. Foucault's views are controversial, not only because he says that so many kinds of people are made up but also because he says that so many are made up by the social sciences. The role of the sciences in making up kinds of people or traits can be made clearer by employing the philosopher's distinction between nature and convention.

Institutional and brute facts

In the *Republic*, Plato draws a distinction between brute facts – nature – and institutional facts – convention. Socrates wants to know whether moral facts – that is, facts about what constitutes a just man or a just action – are brute or institutional.[7] The existence of institutional facts, as John Searle explains:

> presupposes the existence of certain human institutions. It is only given the institution of marriage that certain forms of behavior constitute Mr. Smith's marrying Miss Jones. Similarly, it is only given the institution of baseball that certain movements by certain men constitute the Dodgers' beating the Giants 3 to 2 in eleven innings. And, at an even simpler level, it is only given the institution of money that I now have a five dollar bill in my hand. Take away the institution and all I have is a piece of paper with various gray and green markings.[8]

The issue for Socrates is whether justice is like a five-dollar bill, whether the facts about who is just and unjust remain the same when human institutions and conventions change. Is giving each man his due just when the norms and regulations are those of Sparta, he asks, or only when they are those of Athens?[9]

Plato's distinction between brute and institutional facts is useful in sorting the kinds employed in the social sciences. The fact that anyone under the age of 21 is a minor is an institutional fact. It is only in virtue of our present laws that people in this age-group are minors rather than adults. As a result, the fact that people can be sorted into the two kinds, minors and adults, is an institutional fact. On the other hand, the fact that they can be sorted into the two kinds – those under and those not under 21 years of age – is not an institutional but a brute fact. Natural kinds are brute, while nonnatural or constructed kinds are institutional.

Most of the kinds in the social sciences are institutional, since the fact that they sort the subjects of the sciences is a fact only in relation to some social institution(s). Social scientists cannot expect to find that people are either minors or adults, employed or unemployed, voters or nonvoters, married or unmarried, in every society or culture they study. The distinction between being an employed and an unemployed person, for example, as important as it is to the study of capitalist societies, has no application to a hunting-gathering society.

Kinds, I am suggesting, can be brute (natural) in the context of one institution and institutional (made up) in the context of another. Nuns, for example, are natural kinds in relation to US law but made up in relation to the Church; for the fact that no males are nuns or that no nuns are married is a brute fact in the context of US law but an institutional fact in the context of the Church. To sort a kind in a social science as natural, it is not necessary that the supporting facts be brute, but only brute in relation to that science.

To take an extended example, childhood as a period or stage in life is treated as a brute fact by a number of social sciences. Psychologists and sociologists sort the ages between 4 and 12 as ages of childhood, and formulate and test hypotheses about people in this stage of their lives – for example that the first stages of morality are acquired during childhood. In terms of traits important to the science, each person between 4 and 12 is thought to be more like every other than like any person either older or younger.

The social historian Philippe Aries maintains that during the Middle Ages there was no childhood and that the years between 4 and 12 were not a stage in life; hence childhood is not a brute but an institutional fact.[10] In the tenth, eleventh, and twelfth centuries, as the young were weaned, so they began to take on the burdens, dress, and roles of adults, he says, and there was no period of transition between child-in-arms and adulthood:

> The men of the tenth and twelfth centuries did not dwell on the image of childhood, and the image had neither interest nor even reality for them. It suggests too that in the realm of real life, and not simply in that of aesthetic transposition, childhood was a period or transition which passed quickly and which was just as quickly forgotten.[11]

The group of people between 4 and 12 were not seen as forming a kind; no one's identity was tied to being at this stage in his or her life.

At the end of the Middle Ages, as the demands of adult life began to change, it came to be believed that 4- to 12-year-olds were not ready for adult life and should be subjected to special treatment and afforded special care before being allowed to join adults. The core of this special treatment, according to Aries, was schooling; and at the beginning of the fifteenth century, there was a great growth of interest in education among churchmen, lawyers, and scholars. The school removed 4- to 12-year-olds from adult life and helped to construct a stage in life between child-in-arms and adult where there had been none before. Childhood as a kind was further shaped by the invention of modern sciences such as psychology and pediatrics which adopted childhood as a category. "New sciences such as psycho-analysis, pediatrics and psychology devote themselves to the problems of childhood, and their findings are transmitted to parents by way of a mass of popular literature. Our world is obsessed by the physical, moral and sexual problems of childhood."[12] The existence of childhood as a kind is due, on Aries's view, to changes or developments in a number of social institutions, including education and science.

Childhood, on Aries's analysis, is not a natural kind, for the fact that 6-year-olds are in their childhood is not a brute but an institutional fact.[13] Churchmen, lawyers, scholars, educators, and scientists did not discover childhood but invented it. But if churchmen deserve most of the credit and science very little, then there is reason to say that childhood was nonnatural and made up in relation to the Church but natural and discovered relative to the sciences.

As a second example, consider prostitution. Until the latter part of the nineteenth century, prostitution in Europe was something poor women moved in and out of as they did other forms of labor. As one social historian writes about fifteenth-century France:

By the age of thirty, most prostitutes had a real chance of becoming reintegrated into society. . . . Since public opinion did not view them with disgust, and since they were on good terms with priests and men of the law, it was not too difficult for them to find a position as servant or wife. To many city people, public prostitution represented a partial atonement for past misconduct. Many bachelors had compassion and sympathy for prostitutes, and finally, the local charitable foundations of the municipal authorities felt a charitable impulse to give special help to these repentant Magdalens and to open their way to marriage by dowering them. Marriage was definitely the most frequent end to the career of communal prostitutes who had roots in the town where they have publicly offered their bodies.[14]

A prostitute was seen not as a kind of woman – the way a noble or aristocratic woman might have been – but as a poor woman trying to support herself through work. As Carol Pateman writes, "Prostitutes were not seen as a special class of women, nor were they isolated from other workers or working-class communities; there was no specialized 'profession' of prostitution."[15] But attitudes towards prostitution changed as a result of changes in the way in which prostitution was regulated.

> In Britain, for example, prostitution in the contemporary sense emerged from developments precipitated by the Contagious Disease Acts (1864, 1866, 1869). Under the Acts, women in military towns could be identified as "common prostitutes" by plain-clothes policemen, compulsorily subjected to gynaecological examination for venereal disease and, if infected, confined to a lock hospital.[16]

The new laws and the practices of observation, examination, separation, and incarceration that served to enforce them created a new way for a woman to be a woman: she could be a prostitute, but as such she would be unfit for other womanly work or marriage and unsuited for compassion or sympathy. As a prostitute, she would deserve special attention, supervision, treatment, or punishment and be made to stand apart from other women who were in most respects – young, poor, and powerless – the same.

The study and regulation of prostitution after the passage of the Contagious Disease Acts became a cottage industry, and prostitutes came to be seen increasingly in social scientific terms – for example, as sociopaths and psychological deviants – and less in medical terms – for example, as carriers of venereal disease.

> There is a huge literature on the subject of prostitution, including many official reports, and a good deal of attention has been devoted to the psychology and psychopathology of the prostitute. In 1969 a pamphlet widely read by probation officers in Britain talked of the "proof that prostitution is a primitive and regressive manifestation"; and a Home Office report in 1974 stated that the "way of life of a prostitute is so remarkably a rejection of the normal ways of society as to bear comparison with that of a drug addict."[17]

With the flood of literature, reports, and studies of prostitution, prostitutes became important subjects in the social sciences as well as prominent objects of legal control and regulation. They were now a kind of woman in the laboratories and examining rooms of the sciences, as well as in the law courts and prisons of the state.

Before the passage of the Contagious Disease Acts, women were not sorted as prostitutes, but after passage they were. Parliament and the Home Office didn't discover but invented prostitutes. Of course, there was prostitution before laws were passed to regulate and control it, but the laws did more than attempt to control acts of prostitution; they attributed the acts to a kind of woman and devised means to make her a major object of public policy and law enforcement. Whereas, before the regulation, there had been only acts of prostitution, after the regulation, there were prostitutes – a kind of person for the individuals who engaged in prostitution to be.

Prostitutes, if Pateman is right, are not a natural kind; for the fact that women who receive money for sex are prostitutes is not a brute but an institutional fact. The invention of prostitutes was motivated by an interest in controlling the sexual lives of women and preventing the spread of sexually transmitted diseases. If Parliament and the Home Office deserve most, and psychology little, of the credit for the invention, there is reason to say that prostitutes are nonnatural or made up in relation to law but natural and discovered in relation to psychology.

The issue raised by Foucault's work is whether kinds invented by the modern state are ever invented without some assistance from the social sciences, or, in other words, whether the institutional fact that two people share the same marital status, religious affiliation, academic degree, criminal record, or tax bracket would have been a fact had the social sciences not existed or had they not sorted people by marital status, religious affiliation, and so on. On Foucault's view, the institutions of the state – the schools, clinics, military, and prisons – are dependent on the social sciences, and would not be able to sort people the way they do without the work done by these sciences. As a result, on his view, few if any of the kinds into which social scientists sort their data are natural in relation to the social sciences.[18] *— obviously false*

[margin: very weak grounds on which to rest this argument – social disturbances obviously existed before there was social science –]

Social reality

Though few of the kinds or categories of the social sciences reflect the natural order of things – one that exists independently of anyone's attempts to classify or sort them – they are not myths or fictions; for the social world adjusts to fit our descriptions of it in a way that the natural world does not. As Foucault writes about the category of the individual:

The individual is no doubt the fictitious atom of an "ideological" representation of society; but he is also a reality fabricated by this specific technology of power that I have called "discipline." We must cease once and for all to describe the effects of power in negative terms: it "excludes," it "represses," or "censors," it "abstracts," it "masks," it "conceals." In fact, power produces; it produces reality; it produces domains of objects and rituals of truth. The individual and the knowledge that may be gained of him belong to this production.[19]

The same point could be made about the category of childhood. The invention of childhood influenced attitudes towards 4- to 12-year-olds, and the attitudes, in turn, influenced the way they behaved. The invention was also enforced by regulations. The sexuality, dress, play, and training of people in this age-group were directed and limited by regulations governing the treatment and behavior of children. Over time, people in this age-group accommodated themselves to these regulations and became the kind of people that educators and churchmen had decided they ought to be. As Ian Hacking explains, categories of people can come into existence, and kinds of people can come into being to fit them.[20]

The social world changes to fit our ways of classifying it, because the world is constituted of agents, and agents interpret some classifications as norms to which to conform their behavior. As people at the end of the Middle Ages conformed to the regulations of childhood, those called "children" came to share a distinctive cluster of characteristics. Moreover, the characteristics seemed to hang together and form a trait, because each was sustained by the same system of regulation governing the behavior and treatment of 4- to 12-year-olds.

The categories of homosexual and heterosexual offer another example of how people can change to match the way in which authoritative people talk about them. According to Foucault:

> As defined by the ancient civil or canonical codes, sodomy was a category of forbidden acts; their perpetrator was nothing more than the juridical subject of them. The nineteenth-century homosexual became a personage, a past, a case history, and a childhood, in addition to being a type of life, a life form, and a morphology, with an indiscreet anatomy and possibly a mysterious physiology. Nothing that went into his total composition was unaffected by his sexuality. It was everywhere present in him: at the root of all his actions because it was their insidious and indefinitely active principle; written immodestly on his face and body because it was a secret that always gave itself away. It was consubstantial with him, less as a habitual sin than as a singular nature.[21]

Though men have had sex with one another from the earliest times, those actions did not identify a kind of person until the nineteenth century. There were no homosexuals, heterosexuals, or bisexuals in ancient Greece, despite the facts of man–boy love and sodomy; for there was no practice there of sorting people by how and with whom they were sexually active.[22]

In the nineteenth century, as Foucault tells it, sex was spoken, written, speculated, fantasied, confessed, warned, worried, complained, and cautioned about in new ways and in infinite and intimate detail.

> Rather than the uniform concern to hide sex, rather than a general prudishness of language, what distinguished these last three centuries is the variety, the wide dispersion of devices that were invented for speaking about it, for having it be spoken about, for inducing it to speak for itself, for listening, recording, transcribing, and redistributing what is said about it: around sex, a whole network of varying, specific, and coercive transpositions into discourse. Rather than a massive censorship, beginning with the verbal proprieties imposed by the Age of Reason, what was involved was a regulated and polymorphous incitement to discourse.[23]

As part of the new preoccupation with sex and the profusion of language about sex came a technology for observing, comparing, measuring, detecting, unmasking, revealing, recording, collecting, examining, and investigating facts about sex. The devices intended to prohibit people from becoming certain kinds of sexual subjects – for example, lusty women or homosexual men – made it possible for them to become nymphomaniacs or homosexuals; just as the devices for protecting children, according to Aries, had the effect of making it possible for them to become children in need of protection. The language, the preoccupation, and the technology gave rise to new ways for people to be sorted and new kinds for people to be. The homosexual was one of these new kinds, and the regulative force of the language used to describe him made men who have sex with one another into homosexuals.

Value-neutrality and the invention of kinds

Value-freedom is an ideal for naturalists and nonnaturalists alike. Social scientists like John Stuart Mill, who believe that the social scientist's kinds are discovered, and nonnaturalists like Weber, who believe that they are invented, both believe that social scientists should describe but not prescribe the facts of social life.[24] The issue between Mill and Weber is not whether the social sciences should include judgments of political value but whether only ordinary class-terms should be employed in the social sciences. Weber, as I explain in chapter 2, maintains that the social sciences should employ ideal-types as well as ordinary class-terms but that, when employing the types, social scientists should not say that their subjects ought to conform to them.

Foucault agrees with Weber that kinds in the social sciences are ideal-types and so are invented rather than discovered, but he believes that kinds are laden with political values.[25] On his view, when social scientists employ their ideal-types, they prescribe how society ought to be, as well as how it is. The choice of kinds and the practice of sorting people in economics, psychology, and sociology, according to Foucault, are part of the rise and deployment of a form of political power and control – the decentralized and anonymous power characteristic of the modern industrial state.[26] Since their rise in the eighteenth and nineteenth centuries, the social sciences, he argues, have been a part of a "regime of power" – along with the Church, the military, the school, the prison, and the clinic – that have introduced new ways of maintaining social control and public order.

The social sciences are disciplines, branches of knowledge and teaching, but the knowledge they offer is knowledge with which to discipline – that is, isolate, examine, treat, regulate, and manage their subjects.

> The juridico-anthropological functioning revealed in the whole history of modern penalty did not originate in the superimposition of the human sciences on criminal justice and in the requirements proper to this new rationality or to the humanism that it appeared to bring with it; it originated in the disciplinary technique that operated these new mechanisms of normalizing judgment.[27]

On Foucault's view, there is no distinction between pure and applied research or between theory and practice in the social sciences, for in sorting subjects as criminals, inmates, and sexual deviants, social scientists are engaging in a form of politics. No boundary can be drawn between where the work of the social sciences ends and the work of the other centers of power, such as schools, clinics, and prisons, begins.

Whereas on the liberal's view, the choice of kinds in the social sciences serves every political interest or program equally well; on Foucault's, the choice depends on how well the kind serves the society's interests in social control. Because the social sciences are an instrument of a particular kind or variety of political power, they are not, on Foucault's view, politically neutral.

The issue, for Foucault, is not whether social scientists personally favor the political practices or arrangements served by their inventions but whether their inventions favor these arrangements. On Foucault's account, the inventions not only favor the rise and growth of the bureaucratic state; they favor the ideals of such a state by making up people as clients, patients, welfare-recipients, legal and illegal aliens, employed and unemployed, graduates and dropouts.

Liberals would separate the social scientists' reasons for inventing or choosing their ideal-types from the values served by their use in the context of a political practice. The types are free of political values, on their view, unless the values on which social scientists base their choice of types are political. Foucault denies such a separation. On his view, the scientists' own reasons or intentions matter less than the ends their choices serve. Since, on his view, they serve the ends of domination and control – for example, of children by adults, the mentally incompetent by the competent, the sexually maladjusted by the sexually adjusted, the law enforcer over the lawbreaker, doctors over patients, teachers over students – the ideal-types or kinds invented or chosen in the social sciences are not neutral on the value of one kind of person dominating or being dominated by another.

Normalizing judgments and invented kinds

Weber's quarrel is with social scientists who advocate or attempt to impart political values from their pulpits. On Foucault's view, there can be no neutrality from the pulpit, for the kinds employed in the social sciences do not merely sort the subjects of the science but normalize and regulate them as well. Kinds like the insane, the juvenile delinquent, the learning-disabled, the alcoholic, the sexual abuser, or the rational economic man are not merely organizing but normalizing concepts, for they do not merely draw together what is; they prescribe what ought to be and bridge the division liberals draw between the realms of fact and value.[28]

Take as an example the category of public opinion, which is often cited to legitimate the policies of the modern democratic state. Opinion research presents itself as an objective way of measuring public opinion. Social scientists teach that opinion research enables institutions to operate more democratically, for it can be used to supplement the market and the voting booth as a ground for democratic, public choice.

However, public opinion is not a natural kind, even in relation to the science or discipline of opinion research.[29] The individual opinions that opinion research samples and records are constructed, rather than discovered, by the procedures that record them; for subjects are encouraged to express opinions even when they have none, and the opinions they express are often stereotypes offered in place of, rather than as a reflection of, any understanding or convictions of their own. Finally, there is nothing really public about the opinions collected in opinion research, for, as the social scientist uses the term, "public" means no more than a collection of individual or private opinions. Opinions are sorted as public even though they are not based on any process of public discussion or debate. In short, the fact that public opinion supports American policies in the Middle East is an institutional rather than a brute fact about the attitudes and values of American citizens, and the institutions that invent the fact include the discipline of opinion research.

Though public opinion is invented rather than discovered by opinion research, it serves as a norm against which public policy and choice are judged to be legitimate or illegitimate. Policies on taxes, health care, child care, housing, employment discrimination, privacy, flag burning, pornography, and mergers and acquisitions are formulated, revised, and defended in light of public opinion, and the scientists' invention is offered in support of the practices of business and government. Though the researcher does not recommend public policy or argue that public policy should reflect public opinion, her practice of devising opinion surveys and sorting public responses is not neutral on questions of political legitimacy, for it creates the illusion of a democratic process in the absence of the reality.

Once subjects are sorted into one of a fixed number of kinds, the kinds guide those with the authority to administer public policy or regulate public life. Teachers, lawyers, doctors, managers, and government officials observe, examine, treat, counsel, discipline, advise, employ, or educate the subjects as if they fit smoothly and neatly into the scientific categories. As Murray Edelman observes:

> Any categorization scheme that consigns people to niches according to their actual or potential accomplishments or behavior is bound to be political, no matter what its scientific function is. IQ's; psychiatric labels; typologies of talent, skills, or knowledge; employment statuses; criminal statuses; personality types – all exemplify the point. . . . Once established, a categorization defines what is relevant about the people who are labelled. It encourages others to seek out data and interpret developments so as to confirm the label and to ignore, discount, or reinterpret counter-evidence.[30]

Housing, clothing, entertainment, employment, education, social work, law enforcement, publishing, broadcasting, art, medical care, religion, and politics are tailored, pitched, shaped, adjusted, or developed to respond to the subjects of the liberal sciences as if they were completely and accurately described as child-abusers, psychotics, co-dependents, prostitutes, rational economic men, homosexuals, alcoholics, underachievers, overachievers, or handicapped – that is, by the idealized language of the sciences.

The sorting carried out by the sciences is reproduced and reinforced by the labelling and targeting of the helping professions, business, government, and the media, and the more the categories direct public and private response to the subjects and affect their standing in the community, the more they serve as a norm.

> The language of "reinforcement" and "help" evokes in our minds a world in which the weak and the wayward need to be controlled for their own good. The language of "authority" and "repression" evokes a different reality, in which the rights of the powerless need to be protected against abuse by the powerful. Each linguistic form marshals public support for professional and governmental practices that have profound political consequences for the status, the rights, and the freedom of professionals, of clients, and of the wider public as well.[31]

The cutting, trimming, and molding of the subject begun in the course of pure research is continued when the findings are used to administer public policy, engage in clinical practice, or carry out the work of a profession.

Moreover, the kinds are guides not only as to how others should treat or view the subjects but also as to how the subjects should comport or view themselves; they serve as norms against which the subjects correct and appraise not only the behavior of others but their own as well. When economists sort firms by how well they maximize profits, sales, or market share, the firms take increased profits, sales, or market share as the norm; for within schools of business, banks, brokerage houses, and offices of government they are a measure of the health or quality of the firm. Economists need not say that a firm ought to increase profits, for, in the context of the prevailing teaching and writing about the market behavior of firms, sorting firms by profit is to appraise them.

The inventions of the social scientist influence her subjects, and those that are used in the helping professions to discipline, reform, cure, or educate students, clients, patients, or inmates serve to evaluate them as well. In sorting subjects as heterosexual or homosexual, social scientists not only make up people; they also direct the helping professions to change them and make them better, for in the clinic, barracks, church, and school, homosexuality is treated as a pathology or deviation from an accepted and valued norm. When people are sorted as homosexuals, the clinic has a reason to treat them, the military a reason to exclude them, and the Church a reason to deny them grace.

Psychiatry, until recently, defined homosexuality as a mental illness, and, given the aims of psychiatry – namely, to treat the mentally ill and adjust the psychologically maladjusted – a judgment made in a psychiatric clinic that a patient was homosexual was a recommendation for treatment. For the psychiatrist, homosexuals were not only a kind of person, they were a kind of ill or maladjusted person – one in need of a cure. To describe a person as a homosexual was not itself a reason for a doctor's intervention; but to so describe her in the examining room of a psychiatric clinic was a reason, and the description directed doctors to remake their patients into new, more acceptable kinds of sexual beings.

According to the liberal view of the social sciences, the meaning of a kind can always be distinguished from its use. As a result, the fact that the kinds of the social sciences are used in partisan ways to examine, treat, or discipline some subjects does not show, liberals would say, that the kinds are themselves partisan. In merely sorting men as homosexuals, the psychiatrist is not endorsing any of the practices that await those men as a result of their being so sorted.

In chapter 9, I raise general objections to the liberal's distinction between the meaning and use of kinds or categories in the social sciences; but here, where the kinds in question are nonnatural or invented by social scientists, the distinction is especially lame, for the kinds were invented for a use and, as a result, when the social scientists sort their subjects, they endorse the uses their inventions are intended to serve. If psychiatrists invent a category of sexual deviants in order to diagnose and treat some of their clients, they can't maintain, while sorting the latter as deviants, that they don't endorse the diagnosis or support the treatment.

Normalizing judgments and discovered kinds

According to his critics, Foucault overestimates the influence of the social sciences in creating and sustaining the modern state. But even if Foucault's critics are correct, the question of whether kinds like the homosexual or the alcoholic are invented remains open; for even if they were discovered by the social scientist, they were invented by other authorities as part of the practice of medicine, religion, schooling, or the law. Even if there are bigamists, adulterers, sodomites, prostitutes, pornographers, forgers, swindlers, arsonists, or perjurers in possible worlds that do not include the social sciences, there are none in worlds that do not include a criminal justice system. A person can be one of these kinds of offenders only because authorities within the criminal justice system sort violators of the law in this way.

Kinds invented in the practice of religion, law, or schooling are not value-neutral. They serve the political values and policies of the Church, legislature, courts, offices of law enforcement, prison system, and schools. For example, according to Foucault, in the eighteenth century governments began to sort groups of people as a population, and the practice of sorting influenced and was influenced by policies designed to maintain a new form of social and political order.

> One of the great innovations in the techniques of power in the eighteenth century was the emergence of "population" as an economic and political problem: population as wealth, population as manpower or labor capacity, population balanced between its own growth and the resources it commanded. Governments perceived that they were not dealing simply with subjects, or even with a "people," but with a "population," with its specific phenomena and its peculiar variables: birth and death rates, life expectancy, fertility, state of health, frequency of illness, patterns of diet and habitation. All of these variables were situated at the point where the characteristic movements of life and the specific effects of institutions intersected.[32]

In calling subjects or a people "a population," governments were not only describing them but recommending that they be continuously observed, surveyed, measured, recorded, registered, and documented; and their interest in recommending such treatment was in making the surveillance and discipline of parents, children, debtors, paupers, tradesmen, churchmen, laborers, citizens, and aliens easier, more reliable, and exacting.

In taking kinds over from the law, the schools, and the Church, the social sciences accept their normalizing judgments and help to maintain the discipline. Consider, for example, the one kind of domestic partnership recognized by the law – namely, marriage. Governments sort adults who share a household into one of two categories: married or unmarried. Public policy is not neutral on marriage, for married couples are accorded powers and statuses and are eligible for benefits unavailable to unmarried ones. Given the regulation of marriage and the prohibition against same-sex marriages, lifelong homosexual couples must be sorted with other pairings not sanctified by the marriage laws. As a result, the practice of sorting couples into married and unmarried kinds is not politically neutral, but favors both married people and heterosexuals.

When social scientists follow the lead of governments and accept the legal distinction between married and unmarried couples, they accept the politics that goes along with it. Though they may remain silent on the value of the differences in privilege and status or may even personally disapprove of those differences, their discovery of married and nonmarried as kinds of couples and their use of the kinds in their own teaching and research help to maintain the inequalities of economic and political power arising from the marriage laws. Though they may not intend to make marriage the norm, their decision to accept the legal or official way of sorting couples, rather than to sort them on the basis of the length of the relationship or degree of emotional commitment, helps to make it so.

Sociologists who study whether crime, suicide, depression, unemployment, church attendance, or political participation is higher for married than for unmarried couples do not invent marriage or speak in favor of marriage as an institution; but they are supporting the prohibition against homosexual marriage and discrimination against homosexual couples by deciding that the only kinds of couples of importance to their science are the married and unmarried, or heterosexual ones. Even sociologists who study marriage in order to show the political and economic inequalities arising from the marriage laws contribute to the practice of sorting couples in accordance with those laws.

Their practice supports the legal judgment that married partners are more like each other in socially relevant respects than they are like any domestic, unmarried couples. Though these sociologists do not intend to endorse marriage when they sort their subjects as married or unmarried, and, in their own minds, may oppose the marriage laws, the effects of their practice matter more than their intentions, for the issue is not whether the sociologists *intend* their sorting to be nonpartisan but whether it *is* nonpartisan.

Because value-neutrality forbids social scientists to advance their own values, they usually adopt or reproduce in the design of their research the kinds that are in place and in use in the subjects' own community. But, in doing so, they also adopt and affirm the politics on which the kinds are based. The alternative is for social scientists to invent their own kinds and use them in place of the community's. That is, if the social scientist does not approve of the community's discrimination against homosexuals or its preference for married over unmarried domestic partners, she can decide not to sort her subjects as heterosexual or homosexual or as married or unmarried and sort them instead into kinds she approves of. Instead of studying whether men who live with wives are less likely to suffer some pathological condition – for example, clinical depression or hypertension – than those who don't, she can study whether men with domestic partners are less likely to suffer the condition.

However, social scientists cannot through their own efforts alone invent kinds like "domestic partners" for couples to be; in order for the partners to be a kind of couple, more is needed than a scientist's label. The partners must be seen by others in the community and see themselves as deserving of special consideration and respect. They must be placed in the community's records – medical, employment, tax, school, credit, criminal, police, military, and financial records – as domestic partners and be eligible for benefits that the community reserves for relationships that it recognizes officially and takes seriously.

The scientist cannot invent "domestic partners" and decide to study whether the incidence of clinical depression in some community is higher for men with domestic partners than for men without them. To study the question, the fact of domestic partnerships has to be a fact for members of the partners' community; for unless the partnerships have some social standing, there will be no data to collect – no records of which men do and do not have domestic partners and no way to determine which men to examine or investigate – and no reason to suspect that the partnerships have any effect on the physical or mental condition of men in that community.

The social scientist who does not approve of the way in which men are sorted by the government or in the economy cannot merely interpose her values between the men and the practice of sorting them; she must undertake to change the practice itself. She cannot remain disinterested and stand apart from the lives of her subjects, but must join forces with them and work for social change. To add domestic partnerships to the categories of her science, she must see that the government or economy adds them to the ways it records, examines, normalizes, and regulates people.

The idea that a scientist should join forces with her subjects – give them power and authority over the conduct of her research or work with them to bring about changes in their lives – opposes the ideals of liberal science. In particular, it opposes the ideals of value-neutrality and objectivity and the distinction between studying the world – that is, observing it as it is – and trying to change it – that is, trying to make it as it ought to be – that lies at the heart of a liberal philosophy of science. A social scientist who does not wish to limit herself to the kinds she has discovered, because she does not wish to affirm the values that lie behind them, must trade her liberal ideal for a perfectionist one. She cannot merely change her scientific practice; she must also change the aims and ideals of her science.

In chapter 10, I take up the matter of perfectionist science and explain how some perfectionist approaches to science require the scientist to be more than an observer and her subjects to be more than objects of observation. However, what matters here is that there is a way for the social scientist to sort her subjects that does not affirm values she does not approve of; but it is a way that she can find only by giving up the myth of nonpartisanship and the ideal of neutrality.

[handwritten margin notes: the entire argument rests or falls on logic and or the particular examples used — it moves way too quickly]

Conclusion

Social scientists must decide how to sort their data. Usually they decide to be uncritical and to merely appropriate the categories employed in their subjects' own community; but sometimes they invent their own categories and sort their subjects differently from the way they are sorted at home. In either case, their decisions are not value-neutral, for they normalize the subject and support those political or social policies that are made possible by the norms. Social scientists are not only describing their subjects when they sort them by kind; they are directing their treatment by others and limiting the choices that it is reasonable for those subjects to make.

NOTES

1   Foucault, *Discipline and Punish*, pp. 44–5.
2   See L. Reznek, *The Nature of Disease* (Routledge and Kegan Paul, 1987), p. 33, for a discussion of the distinction between natural and nonnatural kinds and its application to medicine, and M. Ruse, "Definitions of Species in Biology," *British Journal of the Philosophy of Science*, 20 (1969), pp. 97–119, for a discussion of whether the kinds of biology and, in particular, whether species are natural or nonnatural kinds.
3   For a discussion of whether sex is a natural or nonnatural kind, see S. J. Kessler and W. McKenna, *Gender: An Ethnomethodological Approach* (University of Chicago Press, 1978), pp. 42–80.
4   See chapter 4 for a discussion of adaptive explanations in biology and the social sciences.
5   Lewontin, "Adaptation," pp. 241–2.
6   For more on Lewontin's criticisms of adaptationism, see chapter 4.

7 See Plato, *Republic*, Book I, 338c–354c.

8 J. Searle, *Speech Acts* (Cambridge University Press, 1969), p. 51.

9 The distinction between brute and institutional facts is also discussed by G. E. M. Anscombe in "On Brute Fact," *Analysis*, 18 (1958), pp. 69–71.

10 P. Aries, *Centuries of Childhood: A Social History of Family Life*, tr. R. Baldick (Alfred Knopf, 1962).

11 Ibid., p. 34.

12 Ibid., p. 411.

13 Aries's history is controversial. Most of his evidence concerns the representation of children in paintings of the Middle Ages. He writes, e.g.: "Medieval art until about the twelfth century did not attempt to portray [childhood]. It is hard to believe that this neglect was due to incompetence or incapacity; it seems more probable that there was no place for childhood in the medieval world" (p. 33). Since there are other explanations for his observations about paintings that do not suggest that there was no place for childhood in the medieval world, there is reason to doubt his claim about the absence of childhood. My interest is not in the truth of the claim but in its usefulness in illustrating my discussion of kinds. For a critical discussion of Aries's history, see D. Herlihy, "Medieval Children," in *The Walter Prescott Webb Memorial Lectures: Essays on Medieval Civilization* (University of Texas Press, 1978), pp. 109–42.

14 J. Rossiaud, "Prostitution, Youth, and Society in the Towns of Southeastern France in the Fifteenth Century," in *Deviants and the Abandoned in French Society: Selections from the Annales économies, sociétiés, civilisations*, ed. R. Forster and O. Ranum, tr. E. Forster and P. Ranum (John Hopkins University Press, 1978), p. 21.

15 C. Patemen, *The Sexual Contract* (Stanford University Press, 1988), p. 196.

16 Ibid.

17 Ibid.

18 Whether he is correct or not is a historical question best answered by studying the exact role of the social sciences in the genealogy of each of the kinds employed in those sciences. Many historians believe that Foucault, like Aries, has overstated the case for complicity.

19 Foucault, *Discipline and Punish*, p. 194.

20 Ian Hacking calls this phenomenon "dynamic nominalism." See I. Hacking, "Five Parables," in *Philosophy in History*, ed. R. Rorty, J. B. Scheewind and Q. Skinner (Cambridge University Press, 1984), pp. 103–24, and "Making Up People," in *Reconstructing Individualism*, ed. T. Heller, M. Sosna and D. Wellbery (Stanford University Press, 1986), pp. 222–37.

21 M. Foucault, *The History of Sexuality*, vol. 1, tr. R. Hurley (Vintage Books, 1980), p. 43.

22 Foucault talks about homosexuals but seems to equate homosexuality with male homosexuality and, on the topic of sexuality, as on most others, pays little attention to females.

23 Foucault, *History of Sexuality*, vol. 1, p. 34.

24 For Mill's naturalistic view of the social sciences, see J. S. Mill, *On the Logic of the Moral Sciences* (Bobbs–Merrill Company, 1965).

25 Foucault would not accept the liberal's distinction between scientific and political values. See *Discipline and Punish*, pp. 170–95.

26 In *Discipline and Punish*, Foucault offers a functional analysis of the kinds employed in "the objectifying social sciences" and in *The History of Sexuality* an analysis of those employed in the "subjectifying or interpretive social sciences." The interpretive social sciences deal with meanings that are hidden from the subjects of the science but accessible to interpretation by an expert. They make the subjects into therapeutic individuals and support a system of regulations and institutions for controlling them. Psychoanalysis is the prime example of a subjectifying social science, and the classifications and kinds of psychoanalysis function to produce a human being who can be treated in ways that he might not consciously approve of. While the function of the interpretive sciences is to produce "docile minds," the function of the objectifying social sciences is to produce "docile bodies." They make it possible to regulate and train bodies in new ways and to individuate subjects who, from the perspective of the state, had been indistinguishable. See H. L. Dreyfus and P. Rabinow, *Michel Foucault: Beyond Structuralism and Hermeneutics*, 2nd edn (University of Chicago Press, 1983), pp. 178–9, for a discussion of the distinction between objectifying and subjectifying sciences.

27 Foucault, *Discipline and Punish*, p. 183.

28 I borrow the term "normalizing concept" from I. Hacking, "The Making and Molding of Child Abuse," *Critical Inquiry*, 17 (1991), pp. 838–67.

29 See, e.g., Pollock, "Empirical Research."

30 M. Edelman, "The Political Language of the Helping Professions," in *Language and Politics*, ed. M. Shapiro (New York University Press, 1984), p. 49.

31 Ibid., p. 45.

32 Foucault, *History of Sexuality*, vol. 1, p. 25.

8

Explaining the data

When social scientists maintain that their explanations are value-neutral, they usually mean that they are value-free – free of value-judgments. Explanation 1 is value-free, but 2 is not.

1 The legislator voted against the tax cut because she believed the cut to be unjust.
2 The legislator voted against the tax cut because the cut is unjust.

While 2 includes a judgment of the justice of the tax cut, 1 does not; it reports a fact about the legislator's beliefs. Most social scientists would say that 2 is value-neutral. But explanations can be value-free and partisan. They can be partisan in favoring a particular conception of the good or in opposing the possibility of any one of a number of different conceptions of the good.

For example, in his book *A Theory of Justice*, John Rawls describes the circumstances under which justice is a moral virtue – what he calls "the first virtue of social institutions."[1] The circumstances of justice obtain, he says, when mutually disinterested persons put forward conflicting claims for the distribution of social advantages under conditions of moderate scarcity. In the absence of these circumstances, there is no occasion for the virtue.[2] Imagine, then, that a social scientist offers explanations of the behavior of the members of a social group according to which the members are not mutually disinterested or never put forward conflicting claims for the distribution of social advantages. That is, the explanations, if true, show that the circumstances of justice do not obtain. Though the explanation says nothing about justice, it is not neutral on whether some distribution of advantages to members is just; for the explanation is incompatible with every judgment of the justice or injustice of a distribution of advantages to the members of the group. The explanation is neutral between whether the tax cut is just or unjust, but partisan on the question of whether the cut is a matter of justice at all.

To take another example, Karl Marx did not believe that justice was a moral virtue. According to his theory of history, concepts of right and justice are part of the ideological superstructure of society.[3] He showed how they contribute to the mode of production of capitalism and how they rely on false assumptions about the freedom of labor in a capitalist economy.[4] His explanations of how coercion is built into the capitalist relations of production do not contain any judgments of the justice or injustice of capitalism; but they are, nevertheless, not neutral on questions of justice – for example, whether justice is a social virtue – for they oppose the assumptions – for example, those concerning the freedom of wage laborers – on which the judgments of justice and injustice depend.

My aim in this chapter is to show that many of the explanations offered by social scientists are partisan, not because they favor a particular conception of the good but because they are incompatible with a view of the subject on which many moral judgments and conceptions of the good depend. In particular, I argue that the explanations that many social scientists offer of the behavior of their subjects imply that our familiar moral concepts of responsibility, praise, blame, duty, obligation, respect, and resentment do not apply to them at all. If the social scientists' explanations of a subject's behavior are true, then many of our moral assessments of the subject or her behavior cannot be true, for the explanations imply that she lacks the kind of agency that many of our familiar moral concepts assume. First, however, I survey some of the prominent forms of explanation in the social sciences – namely, functional, covering-law, decision-theoretic, and hermeneutic – and explain how they oppose the rational explanations that the subject offers of her own behavior. Finally, I show how, in opposing her own explanations, these scientific explanations put the agency of the subject in doubt and, as a result, oppose most moral assessments of her conduct.

Scientific explanation

There is an idea common to a number of different social sciences that the participants in a social practice are benighted and that the accounts they offer of their own attitudes and actions are poor and should be discounted and replaced with other, richer, more enlightened or profitable lines of explanation. According to this idea, little or no credit should be extended to a participant's account of an action, and the entire inventory of these accounts should be marked down or written off as false or mistaken. Richard Nisbett and Timothy Wilson, for example, write in a paper in *Psychological Review*: "The evidence indicates it may be quite misleading for social scientists to ask their subjects about the influences on their evaluations, choices or behavior. The relevant research indicates that such reports, as well as predictions, may have little value except for whatever utility they have in the study of verbal explanations per se."[5]

This idea contrasts with our more ordinary, unscientific idea that while some participant accounts should arouse our suspicion, others should be afforded a full measure of our trust. According to our ordinary idea, we lose confidence in one account by gaining confidence in another, and when we set some accounts aside as false, we assume that others are the real coin. Participant accounts, according to our ordinary idea, should be marked down or depreciated not as a corporate body but singly, one account at a time.

The idea that participants do not understand themselves or that they are understood only by others invested with a science or a scientific theory opposes our ordinary practice of trusting and saving some participant explanations. It also opposes, I believe, our ordinary practice of treating participants as moral agents, as individuals who have moral rights and moral obligations or a conception of the good and towards whom it is appropriate to adopt a range of moral attitudes and emotions.

If the social sciences discount participant accounts, what is it that they are discounting? How do participants explain their own behavior? One common way is by offering a rational explanation.[6] People usually explain what they do by citing their reasons for doing it. A rational explanation of a person's behavior explains the behavior if it cites an intention that is the cause of the behavior and that, under some description of the behavior, rationalizes it or makes it seem reasonable. The reasons or intentions that people cite usually include beliefs and desires that are meant to show that what they did was a reasonable thing to have done in the circumstances.[7]

Of course, the fact that people explain some of their behavior by saying what their reasons were does not mean that their reasons explain their behavior. Sometimes we have a good reason to discount or look beyond a participant's own explanation and replace it with a different one of our own. Discounting is part of our ordinary, and not merely our scientific, practice. However, the everyday reasons we have for discounting are reasons to discount some participant accounts but not all; for when, as part of our ordinary practice, we discredit one account, it is usually because we credit another. In fact, our ordinary practice of setting aside or discounting participant accounts is based on the assumption that false or valueless accounts are the exception rather than the rule; for we assume that the participants in social, political, and economic life are rational (even if their behavior is sometimes irrational), and to assume

[handwritten margin notes: an empirical claim that I think is probably false, depends on what we mean by "what they do." Rs responses to "why are you successful?" will not be in terms of intentions —]

that participants are rational is to assume that as a rule their own reasons for their behavior explain it.

We may discount a participant's account because we believe that it is insincere and that she is hiding rather than citing the causes of her behavior; but part of our reason for doubting her sincerity is some prior knowledge of her intentions. Moreover, we may discount a participant's account because we believe she is self-deceived and is hiding from herself the cause of her behavior; but, again, among our reasons for believing that she is self-deceived are our own beliefs about her intentions. However, what we know of people's intentions we know, in part at least, because we believe that many of their accounts of their own behavior are true. When, as part of our ordinary practice, we replace a participant's own rational explanation with an explanation of our own, we assume that normally her judgments about her own intentions are true. The more error we impute to her, the less we understand of her thought or her talk and the less reason we have to think that her intentional explanations of her behavior are mistaken. That is, our own understanding of what she says or thinks relies on the principle of charity, the principle that another's judgments and intentions are not radically different from our own. According to the principle of charity, there is a limit to the mistakes that we can attribute to others in their judgments of their own intentions. The greater the difference between our judgments and theirs, the more reason we have to believe that it is we, rather than they, who are mistaken.[8]

Many social scientists put aside or look beyond participant accounts, because they believe that these accounts do not explain enough. For example, some social scientists are interested in explaining not the behavior of individuals but their intentions or in explaining collective or large-scale social events or some statistical findings about a group. In these cases, when the social scientists put participant accounts aside, they do not discount the accounts in the sense of "discount" that I am talking about, for they do not say that the participants' accounts are mistaken but only that they are not very deep or to the point. In such cases, the social scientists' account and the participants' accounts are compatible, for there is no implication that what the participants say is false. When I speak of discounting a participant's explanation, I mean offering an explanation that is inconsistent with, not merely different from, the participant's own. To discount is to imply that the reasons that participants offer in trying to explain their own behavior are not a reason for a cause of their behavior. For social scientists to discount, in this sense, implies more than that they know something the participants don't; it implies that the participants have false beliefs about their own intentions.

When psychologists maintain, for example, that the causes of a sub-

fallacy of equivocation

not synonymous

ject's behavior are not her intentions but processes or events that are hidden from her view, they discount a subject's account of her behavior in the sense I am talking about. Thus, Latane and Darley, in their study *The Unresponsive Bystander: Why doesn't he Help?*, discount when they maintain that bystanders who come or fail to come to the aid of people in distress are mistaken about the causes of their behavior.[9] It is the presence or absence of other bystanders, according to Latane and Darley, rather than the intentions the bystanders cite, that explain their behavior. Storms and Nisbett, in their study "Insomnia and the Attribution Process," discount when they argue that it is the presence of hidden causes – for example, an overheated room or a tendency to work or smoke before going to bed – that explains the behavior of insomniacs rather than the worries or concerns that insomniacs give as reasons for their not sleeping.[10]

Social scientists who offer neurophysiological explanations of behavior for which subjects offer rational accounts, on the other hand, do not discount if the intentions that the subjects cite are type- or token-identical to the neurophysiological conditions or events cited by the scientists. Though the explanations are different, they are not inconsistent; for if an event in my brain is the cause of my arm going up and the brain event is identical with an intention of mine, then the intention causes my arm to go up as well.

Similarly, when Marx and Engels offer functionalist explanations of the behavior of factory-owners in England in the nineteenth century, they do not discount the owners' own rational explanations of their actions; for, although the owners might not accept the teleological explanations that Marx and Engels offer, the idea that their actions have a function or that the function is to increase the forces of production is consistent with the owners' understanding that their intentions – for example, to increase profits – are the cause of their behavior. According to Marx and Engels, the factory-owners' explanations are marked down not because what they say is mistaken but because they say too little: they do not explain the intentions.[11]

Four models of explanation

Though most social scientists agree that the subject's explanations are mistaken, their standards of correct explanation differ, and each standard offers a different reason for discounting the subject's account. Emile Durkheim writing on social causation, A. R. Radcliffe-Brown on ritual action, Sigmund Freud on the psychopathology of everyday life, and Gary Becker on the economic approach to human behavior each adopt a different standard – namely, covering-law (Durkheim), functional (Radcliffe-

Brown), hermeneutic (Freud), and decision-theoretic (Becker) – but the explanations of behavior that each offers are incompatible with the rational explanations that are offered by their subjects.

Durkheim stands in the Galilean tradition in the social sciences.[12] It is his view that every event, whether in the natural or the social world, is to be understood in terms of its efficient cause. To explain why some individuals join a church, commit suicide, or remain celibate throughout their lives, one needs to show that acting so is connected in a lawful way to some social fact. The task of social science for Durkheim is to discover the causal laws that describe the links between social facts and individual behavior.[13]

A. R. Radcliffe-Brown, on the other hand, stands in the Aristotelian tradition. It is his view that in order to explain why an individual engages in a religious practice or holds to a system of religious belief, it is necessary to discover the purpose or ultimate cause behind the practice or belief. The ultimate, rather than the proximate or efficient, cause is what explains the individual's behavior, and the ultimate cause is not the purpose of an individual but of a group.[14]

Gary Becker also stands in the Aristotelian tradition. However, the purposes that explain behavior, on his view, are always individual purposes – for example, the preference of the consumer or producer for more of some good over less. According to Becker, the task of social science is to show that in most areas of their lives people behave as if they were economic agents and were attempting to maximize individual utility or profit, even if increasing utility or profit is not their intention.[15]

Freud stands with one foot in each of these traditions. He believes that an individual's behavior is to be explained by its purpose, but that the purpose is an intended, though unconscious, purpose; and, according to Freud, an individual's unconscious purpose in doing something explains what she did only if it is the efficient cause of her doing it.[16]

What Durkheim, Freud, Becker, and Radcliffe-Brown have in common is that each offers explanations of social life that are incompatible with all or many of the explanations offered by the participants in that life. According to each, participants, unless enlightened by a social theory or tutored by those who have mastered it, do not understand the facts of their life clearly or deeply enough to be able to explain large parts of that life to themselves or to others.

Durkheim

Durkheim's practice was to explain actions not as actors do, by citing intentions, but by citing facts about social life that the actors are themselves unable to perceive but that are, on Durkheim's view, the causes of their actions. "I consider extremely fruitful this idea that social life should be explained not by the notions of those who participate in it, but by more profound causes which are unperceived by consciousness."[17] Durkheim maintained that intentions could not be the cause of an action, because he believed that there was no lawlike relation between intention and action.[18]

In his work *Suicide*, for example, Durkheim reasons that suicides cannot be explained by the desires of the victim, because there are other people who have the same desires and do not attempt to end their lives.

> We know that these individual [psychological] events [viz., some specific desires], though preceding suicides with fair regularity, are not their real causes. To repeat, no unhappiness in life necessarily causes a man to kill himself unless he is otherwise so inclined. The regularity of possible recurrences of these various circumstances thus cannot explain the regularity of suicide.[19]

Durkheim's idea is that desires cannot be the cause of actions unless there is a lawlike relation between desires and actions. Since, whatever the desire with which an agent performs an action, there are other agents who share the desire but do not perform the action, this shows, on Durkheim's view, that desires are not the causes of action.

Durkheim's argument in *Suicide* is meant to be general. Only if the intentions that agents cite when they attempt to explain their behavior are always followed by the behavior are they the cause of it. Since the behavior does not always follow the intentions, the latter cannot be the cause of the former. And if the intentions are not the cause, then they do not explain the behavior.

Durkheim's reasoning proceeds from a principle of causality similar to that which Donald Davidson calls "The Principle of the Nomological Character of Causality": that if one event is a cause of another, then there must be a law relating them.[20] If there are no laws relating an intention to an action, the intention cannot be the cause of the action; and if the intention is not the cause, then it cannot explain the action.[21]

Durkheim replaced the language of reasons, the language that participants use to explain their own actions, with a language of causes that are not reasons. Freud, by contrast, used the language of reasons in his explanations of behavior; however, the reasons he cites are not the participant's own; for although they belong to the participant and are part of her intention, she is not conscious of those intentions.[22]

Freud

According to Freud, a person has desires of a sexual nature that are incompatible with her thoughts of herself (with her ego). They arise from her animal instincts (her libido), and they conflict with the ethical or aesthetic standards by which she judges herself and her own worth (the superego); and, because of the conflict, the thought that she has these forbidden desires is too painful for her to bear. She cannot let on to herself, let alone to others, that such desires are her own. However, she cannot turn her back on them entirely, because these desires cannot forever remain unfulfilled.[23]

There are two mechanisms, according to Freud, by which a person can hide forbidden desires from herself and, at the same time, to some degree, satisfy them: repression and sublimation. Each defends the ego against the threat posed by the recognition of the desires, and each, at the same time, offers the desires an outlet. Through the mechanisms of repression and sublimation, the agent's forbidden desires are satisfied, though in a disguised and unrecognizable form.

The mechanism of repression, according to Freud, yields two kinds of actions: "faulty actions" and "inadvertent actions." Under the first label Freud includes acts of forgetting, slips of the pen or tongue, the losing or breaking of objects, bunglings, and misreadings. In doing these things, the agent is not conscious of having acted intentionally at all. For example, a young boy falls and, in falling, knocks over his parents' wedding picture. He sees this as an accident, as a movement of his body that was in no way intended. However, the boy, like any young boy, desires to replace his father in the conjugal bed (oedipal desire). This is a forbidden desire, and the boy has repressed it. Moreover, there is no description that the boy would apply to his behavior whereby the oedipal desire would give him a reason to fall and knock over the picture. The description under which the movements of his body are rationalized by that desire is a description that the boy would not apply to these movements: namely, "replacing father in mother's bed." The boy's oedipal desires are both a cause and a reason for his falling and knocking over the picture. However, the falling and knocking over are not understood by the boy to be an oedipal action, and, consequently, the boy is able to hide from himself that he has oedipal desires that cause and rationalize his movements.

Inadvertent actions, the second means of expressing repressed desires, are actions that the agents believe to be intentional movements but done without any aim or purpose. However, on Freud's view, they are not aimless, and the agents perform them with an intention, though not a conscious one, of satisfying a sexual desire. Freud cites humming tunes, fiddling with things, and fingering one's clothing as examples of inadvertent actions. When they finger or fiddle, agents don't believe that they are satisfying any sexual desires. However, the fingering or fiddling satisfies an unconscious sexual desire, although the description under which the behavior satisfies the desire is not a description that the agents believe to be true of their fingering, for it is not in any literal sense true of these movements of their body.

For example, a priest fiddles with his buttons while he listens to a man confess his sexual sins. He believes that he is fiddling with his buttons and that he is doing it intentionally, but he believes that he is doing it aimlessly and for no reason or purpose. However, the priest has a forbidden desire to do what the man confesses to having done, and, in fingering his buttons, the priest is satisfying this desire without seeming to do so. In fingering his buttons, the priest is removing his frock, the emblem of priestly privileges but also of priestly duties. These duties include abstinence. To be defrocked is to be stripped of this duty and to become, once again, a bare man who, at times at least, can satisfy his sexual desires. Understood this way, his movements are a means to a desired end. However, he doesn't understand them in this way and so does not believe that they are a means to any end that he desires. Through repression, the priest is able to satisfy his sexual desires and, at the same time, feel pure and free from sin. The priest does not literally remove his frock or engage in any sexual adventure, but, given the connection between the movement of his fingers on the buttons and the removal and the adventure, he is able to satisfy the desire for sexual adventure by remaining in his study or confessional and fingering alone.

Sublimation, according to Freud, is the other mechanism that allows agents simultaneously to hide and to act on their forbidden desires. With sublimation, the agents do not repress their forbidden desires but substitute for them desires that are culturally acceptable. Agents can act on these "acceptable" desires without revealing to themselves that they are acting on a forbidden desire. These acceptable desires are not just any stand-ins or substitutes for the forbidden ones; they are symbolic substitutes. Consequently, when the agents satisfy the stand-in, they satisfy the desire. That is, satisfying the stand-in is a means of satisfying the forbidden and hidden desire, on Freud's view, in virtue of the fact that the one is a symbol of the other.[24]

In his study of Leonardo da Vinci, for example, Freud explains how Leonardo sublimated his sexual desires into an urge for scientific research and, in particular, research on the nature of flight.[25] For this he chose to study birds, and his scientific papers include a detailed study of vultures.

Leonardo explained his studying vultures by citing his desire to learn about the nature of flight. However, according to Freud, this desire was a symbolic substitute for a forbidden, homosexual desire, and it is this forbidden desire that explains his interest in and study of these birds. On Freud's view, it is Leonardo's hidden or latent desire and not his manifest or cited desire, the desire he cites as his reason for acting thus, that is the cause of his behavior. Freud's explanation and Leonardo's are incompatible, and, as a result, Freud can be said to discount Leonardo's own explanations of his behavior.

In short, Freud discounts the accounts of participants because, on his view, many of their actions are faulty, inadvertent, or acts of sublimation. In the case of faulty actions, Freud discounts the participant's account because the participant believes that the behavior is unintentional. The movements of her body, so far as the participant understands them, are accidents; but according to Freud, she is mistaken. In the case of inadvertent actions, the participant believes that her movements are intentional, but she does not believe that she performs them for any reason or with any purpose; but here again the participant is mistaken. With both faulty and inadvertent actions, participants maintain that their actions were purposeless, while Freud discounts their view, maintaining that they were purposeful.

In the case of acts of sublimation, participants believe that their actions are purposeful; but Freud maintains that they do not understand the purposes that explain them. Only if Leonardo were to learn the psychoanalytic meaning of vultures would he be able to understand the purposes underlying his study. However, to understand this, Leonardo would need the theoretical language of psychoanalysis. According to Freud's theory of sublimation, there are wide expanses in our lives – namely, our creative or artistic efforts – which can only be rationally explained under descriptions that, without the aid of the theory, will seem to be false rather than true.

Radcliffe-Brown

According to Freud, the purposes that explain a participant's actions are often intended (though unrecognized) purposes. On the other hand, according to Radcliffe-Brown, the purposes are often unintended. In his studies of ritual behavior, Radcliffe-Brown sets aside the rational explanations that participants offer of their actions and focuses instead on the effects of the actions on the group. These effects, according to him, can be seen by the anthropologist but not by participants.

Let us suppose that we wish to investigate in Australian tribes the totemic rites of a kind widely distributed over a large part of the continent. The ostensible purpose of these rites, as stated by the agents themselves, is to renew or maintain some part of nature, such as a species of animal or plant, or rain, or hot or cold weather. With reference to this purpose we have to say that from our point of view the agents are mistaken, that the rites do not actually do what they are believed to do.[26]

My own view is that the negative and positive rites of savages exist and persist because they are part of the mechanism by which an orderly society maintains itself in existence, serving as they do to establish certain fundamental social values. The beliefs by which the rites themselves are justified and given some sort of consistency are the rationalizations of symbolic actions and of the sentiments associated with them.[27]

According to Radcliffe-Brown, in the case of ritual actions, it is always a mistake to explain the action by citing the participant's intentions.

The very common tendency to look for the explanation of ritual actions in their purpose is the result of a false assimilation of them to what may be called technical acts. In any technical activity an adequate statement of the purpose of any particular act or series of acts constitutes by itself a sufficient explanation. But ritual acts differ from technical acts in having in all instances some expressive or symbolic element in them.[28]

Participants in a rain dance, for example, explain their actions by citing their desire for rain. Early anthropologists like Sir James Fraser accepted these explanations at face value. They assumed that the dancing was a technical act and that the dancers desired rain and believed the dancing to be a cause of it. Finally, they assumed that the dancers' belief and desire were the cause of the dancing. Radcliffe-Brown objects. The dancing, he argues, is a ritual act, and it is unreasonable to think that the dancers have false beliefs about the causes of rain and that their false beliefs are the cause of their dancing.[29] The dancing is to be explained, on Radcliffe-Brown's view, by an ultimate rather than by any proximate cause.

On Radcliffe-Brown's view, a participant's stated beliefs and desires do not explain rituals, while on Freud's view they do not explain art. However, while for Freud art is explained by hidden desires, for Radcliffe-Brown ritual is not explained by any desires at all.[30] Radcliffe-Brown believes that it is wrong to look for a rational explanation of a participant's ritual actions, and because participants offer rational explanations, he discounts them.

Gary Becker

According to the economic approach to human behavior, people act so as to maximize expected utility on the basis of more or less stable preferences and coordinate their actions with the actions of others through markets.[31] According to Becker, the economic approach is applicable not only to behavior within the monetary market sector but to family life as well. On his view, it is the one approach in the social sciences that provides a unified framework for understanding all human behavior.

> All human behavior can be viewed as involving participants who maximize their utility from a stable set of preferences and accumulate an optimal amount of information and other inputs in a variety of markets.[32]

> I have come to the position that the economic approach is a comprehensive one that is applicable to all human behavior, be it behavior involving money prices or imputed shadow prices, repeated or infrequent decisions, large or minor decisions, emotional or mechanical ends, rich or poor persons, men or women, adults or children, brilliant or stupid persons, patients or therapists, business men or politicians, teachers or students.[33]

Whenever people choose between doing A and doing B – for example, marrying or staying single, working or stealing for a living, having a child or remaining childless, joining or not joining a church, becoming a Democratic or a Republican – they will choose A over B, according to the economic approach, if and only if the expected utility of A is equal to or greater than that of B. So, for example, people will marry if they can expect to raise their utility level above what it would be were they to remain single; and should the supply of mates increase, the cost of a mate will decrease, and, other things being equal, the number of marriages will rise.[34]

Becker does not assume that participants intend to maximize utility or can say what the expected value of one choice is over another. It is enough that they act as if they calculated and compared these values; it is not necessary that they understand themselves to be acting in this way. Most people do not view their decision to marry, steal bread, or bear children the way that Gary Becker does. However, according to Becker, this does not mean that their "personal" decisions are not a function of costs and benefits: "The economic approach does not assume that decision units are necessarily conscious of their efforts to maximize or can verbalize or otherwise describe in an informative way the reasons for the systematic patterns in their behavior."[35]

Though the explanations of family life that Becker offers are different from those that are offered by most participants, it is not clear whether Becker, in offering his economic explanations, is discounting the accounts of the participants. That is, it is not clear whether if what Becker says about their behavior is true, the participants' own rational explanations must be mistaken. It is not clear, because Becker sometimes speaks as if the economic approach describes the causes of a subject's action and, at other times, as if it merely describes the action.[36]

Subjects can be economic in either of two senses: one causal, the other not. They are economic in a noncausal sense if their choices are consistent with the maximization of a well-ordered function such as a utility or expected utility function, and in a causal sense if their choices are consistent with the maximization of the function because they intend them to be.[37] A business firm, for example, might decrease its production in a way that increases profit, even if what causes it to act in this way is not an intention to profit; for increasing profit might be an unintended consequence of the firm's behavior, and an economist might explain the firm's choice by citing the effects on profit and ignore altogether the questions of intention. In this case, though the economist ignores the firm's intentions, she is not discounting the firm's own, intentional account of its choice, for it is possible for both her account and the firm's to be true. Only if the economist explains that an intention to increase profits was the cause of the cut in production, while the firm explains that it was not, does her explanation discount the firm's, for only then are the two explanations incompatible.

However, this view of the economic approach is not entirely adequate, for there are two reasons to think that the question of whether subjects act so as to maximize some well-ordered function cannot be separated from the causal question of how they choose their action. First, effects on profits explain choice only if the relation between choice and profit is lawlike; for only then is the effect on profit a reason to expect the choice. But an account of the causes can be a reason to believe that the relation between choice and profit is not lawlike; for if, on the firm's own account, its choices are caused by intentions that are known not to result, as a rule, in any increase in profit, then there is reason to believe that the relation between choice and profit is not lawlike.[38]

Second, utility, unlike profit, is a psychological magnitude; it is a measure of preference, and preference is a state of mind that is identified by the participant's own account of her actions.[39] If we accept a participant's account that she is choosing a less over a more preferred alternative, we must conclude that she is not acting to maximize utility. She is doing what she intends to do but not what she prefers to do. However, the economic approach to human behavior assumes that participants never choose less over more and so only intend to do what they prefer to do.[40] Consequently, when the participant explains that her aim in choosing B over A is less over more and Becker explains her choice economically, he attributes preferences to her that are inconsistent with those that she attributes to herself. As a result, his economic explanation discounts her own account, even though it appears to be silent on the causes of her choices.

The subjects of morality

When we try to explain the behavior of people, we assume that, as a rule, they are able to explain it to themselves. Though we judge that some of their explanations are mistaken, our judgment is based on the belief that others are correct; for there is a limit to how much error we can attribute to a person's understanding of her own actions. Many social scientists, however, assume that the explanations their subjects offer are always or often mistaken. Yet, our practice of making moral judgments rests on our ordinary standards of explanation rather than on the social scientists'. As a result, as I argue in the following paragraphs, the subjects of morality cannot be as often mistaken about the causes of their own behavior as these social scientists assume, and, as a result, the subjects of morality cannot be the subjects of the social sciences.[41]

How frequently must a subject's conscious intentions explain her behavior for her to be a subject of morality? There is no sharp line here, no set number of mistakes that separates the subjects of the social sciences from those of morality. At one extreme is the thoroughly benighted subject: one whose conscious intentions are never a cause of her behavior. Durkheim's subjects are closer to the extreme than Radcliffe-Brown's. At the other extreme is the thoroughly lucid subject: one whose conscious intentions are always the cause of her behavior. The closer the moral subject is to the one extreme and the social science subject to the other, the clearer it is that they are incompatible. My position is that Durkheim's, Freud's, Becker's, and Radcliffe-Brown's subjects are close enough to one extreme and often benighted enough to make them strangers to morality.

I offer four arguments for this conclusion. The first, the argument from responsibility, is the most general and abstract. Here I argue that our concept of moral responsibility is such that it is only to subjects whose behavior is caused to a high degree by their conscious intentions that we can attribute moral responsibility. My argument here resembles the soft determinist's argument that moral responsibility is not only compatible with causal determinism but inconceivable without it. The second, the argument from conscious interests, and third, the argument from the good will, are less general. The point of these arguments is that the subject in the social sciences cannot have the interests assumed by Mill's utilitarianism or the will assumed by Kant's account of moral worth. Finally, in the fourth, the argument from moral emotion, I draw on an idea of Peter Strawson's that, as part of our moral practice, we adopt participant attitudes and feelings toward others, and argue that we cannot adopt these attitudes toward others whose conscious intentions do not, as a rule, explain their behavior.[42]

The argument from responsibility

To be a moral subject, much of a subject's behavior must be caused by her conscious intentions, for moral subjects are bearers of moral responsibility; but a subject bears moral responsibility for her behavior only if she is consciously rational, and she is consciously rational only if, as a rule, her conscious intentions are the cause of her behavior.

Some moral philosophers have argued that a person is morally responsible for what she does only if she would have done otherwise had she so intended.[43] I am claiming less. According to my argument, a subject is morally responsible for doing A only if some large (perhaps weighted) number of the things she does (which need not include A) would have been otherwise had her conscious intentions been otherwise.[44] On this view, we can hold someone morally responsible for an unintended or involuntary movement – for example, falling down or falling asleep – as long as enough of her other movements are intended or voluntary. The more a subject's movements are unresponsive or not subject to her conscious intentions, the less appropriate it is to hold her morally responsible for any one of her bodily movements. The reason for this, I contend, is that unless a large enough number of her movements are understood to be caused by her conscious intentions, we lose our reason to believe that she is a consciously rational subject; and unless we have reason to believe that she is a consciously rational subject, we have no reason to attribute intentions to her at all.[45] Subjects to whom we do not have good reason to attribute intentions are not the bearers of moral responsibility and, in that respect, are not subjects of morality.

Durkheim's subjects are not consciously rational, for were their intentions different, their behavior would remain the same. In arguing for social over psychological causes of behavior, Durkheim denies that there is a causal connection between conduct and intention and, as a result, offers us a subject whose behavior is not causally responsive to changes in her intentions. Such a subject is not a moral subject, and so Durkheim's subjects are not the subjects of morality.

Freud's subjects, unlike Durkheim's, are moved by psychological rather than social causes. Freud, unlike Durkheim, does not deny that intentions are explanatory; what he denies is that the intentions that participants cite are as a rule explanatory. According to Freud, there is no break or gap between intention and conduct, but only between conscious intention and conduct.

Because Freud's subjects, unlike Durkheim's, would very often do otherwise were they to intend otherwise, they would seem to be the subjects of morality. However, they are not moral subjects, for the intentions to which their behavior is responsive are too often intentions of which they themselves are not conscious. That is, the descriptions under which the behavior of Freud's subjects is intentional are very often descriptions under which they do not consciously intend their behavior. They very frequently hide from themselves the intentions that are the practical reasons for, and the causes of, their behavior. Moral responsibility, however, requires conscious rationality. It is only if some large (perhaps weighted) amount of a person's behavior varies with her conscious intentions that we hold her morally responsible for her behavior.

My argument is as follows. According to our idea of moral responsibility, morally responsible subjects are able to benefit from moral instruction. Given what they regard as very good reasons for revising their intentions, they can be expected to revise their behavior. The aim of moral instruction is to change what people do by changing their reasons for doing it. Freud's subjects are not the subjects of morality, because although their conscious reasons are open to moral instruction, these are very often not the cause of their behavior, and although their unconscious reasons are often the cause, these are not open to moral instruction, for the ego's mechanism of defense keeps the subjects from acknowledging that these unconscious reasons are theirs. "An unconscious wish cannot be influenced and it is independent of any contrary tendencies, whereas a conscious one is inhibited by whatever else is conscious and opposed to it."[46] When moral instruction causes changes in the conscious intentions of Freud's subjects, it often does not cause changes in their behavior, for the behavior is not caused by these intentions; and because the ego employs evasive strategies that screen the unconscious causes from the subjects' consciousness, it screens them from moral instruction.

> It is a long superseded idea, and one derived from superficial appearance, that the patient suffers from a sort of ignorance, and that if one removes this ignorance by giving him information (about the causal connection of his illness with his life, about his experiences in childhood, and so on) he is bound to recover. The pathological factor is not his ignorance in itself, but the root of this ignorance in his *inner resistances*; it was they that first called this ignorance into being, and they still maintain it now. The task of the treatment lies in combating these resistances. Informing the patient of what he does not know because he has repressed it is only one of the necessary preliminaries to the treatment. If knowledge about the unconscious were as important for the patient as people inexperienced in psychoanalysis imagine, listening to lectures or reading books would be enough to cure him. Such measures, however, have as much influence on the symptoms of nervous illness as a distribution of menu-cards in a time of famine has upon hunger. The analogy goes even further than its immediate application; for informing the patient of his unconscious regularly results in an intensification of the conflict in him and an exacerbation of his troubles.[47]

In short, the subjects of Freud's double consciousness are not the subjects of morality, because the doubling and the inner resistances hide the causes of their conduct and prevent them from becoming objects of reason or moral reform.

Leonardo, for example, at least in his artistic life, is not a moral subject; for, on Freud's view, he cannot understand that his artistic endeavors are acts of sublimation or that the homosexual intentions causing them are his own intentions. He cannot understand, because the intentions are hidden in his unconscious and because repression and sublimation include a mechanism – namely, resistance – that causes him to deny that a forbidden intention is his.[48]

Becker's subjects resemble Durkheim's. We have no reason to believe that were their intentions different, their behavior would be different; for, on Becker's view, a person will act so as to maximize utility even if he does not intend to do so and even if he intends not to. The subjects of economics can act with altruistic intentions, but the actual, as against the intended, effect of their action is to increase their own utility. Persuading Becker's subjects to act with altruistic rather than egoistic intentions will

The key is that post-factohoc stat recollections of intention are not good evidence of intention, not to mention actual causes.

– Anyway, per self-accounts of past behavior are not always in terms

not cause them to act other than economically or to act in a way that does not maximize utility.

Radcliffe-Brown's subjects resemble Freud's. Like Freud's, they lead a double life. When they engage in technical acts, they are consciously rational subjects. When they engage in ritual actions, they are not. So, as participants in the rituals of life, they are not moral subjects, for in being subject to ritual, their actions are not subject to their own intentions. Like Freud's subjects of repression and sublimation, the subjects of ritual actions are not able to benefit from moral instruction. Given what they regard as very good reasons for revising their intentions, they cannot be expected to revise their behavior, for their behavior is not caused by their intentions but, in some mysterious fashion, by the effects of the behavior on the structure of their group.

Moreover, given that the judgments by subjects of ritual about their own intentions are so often mistaken, there is reason to doubt that they are rational subjects or that we understand their intentions. Radcliffe-Brown objects to Sir James Fraser's interpretations of the participants' intentions, because they are uncharitable – Fraser attributes too many mistaken beliefs about nature to the dancers. But in discounting the dancers' accounts, Radcliffe-Brown is being uncharitable as well, for he is attributing too many mistaken beliefs to the dancers about the cause of their own behavior. A subject who, in some large and central area of her life, is not rational or whose thought and behavior in that area are not interpretable is not (or at least in that area is not) a subject of morality.

– we can discount b/o discounting intentions, since lots -- false beliefs about causes of my own behavior are not in terms of intentions.

The argument from conscious interests

There are some moral theories according to which what makes an action right is that it satisfies human desires. This was Mill's view: an action is right insofar as it adds to the satisfaction of human desires and wrong insofar as it detracts from them.[49] Mill assumed that the satisfaction of more human desires makes the world a better place than the satisfaction of fewer.

Mill says in *On the Logic of the Moral Sciences* that states of mind – that is, thoughts, emotions, and actions – are caused by other states of mind or by states of body.[50] He, like Durkheim, accepts the principle of the nomological character of causes. He believes that if one state of mind causes another, then the one must be regularly followed by the other, and that there must be a psychological law that links them. However, unlike Durkheim, he believes that there *are* such laws and that a science of psychology (he calls it a science of human nature) is possible; unlike Durkheim too, he accepts participant explanation, because he believes that the intentions that the participants cite are, as a rule, the causes of their behavior.

Like other states of mind, beliefs and desires, for Mill, are characterized by the role they play in causing behavior. According to Mill's philosophy of mind, states of mind that are never a cause of a person's thoughts, emotions, or actions are not states of belief or desire. So, on Mill's view, in denying that a person's intentions are a cause of her behavior, Durkheim is denying that she is in a state of mind that, according to utilitarianism, it is the business of morality to advance. No one is in a state of mind that, according to Mill, morally matters – namely, happiness – unless that state is one that causally matters.

Mill, like Davidson, believes that causality and intentionality go hand in hand.[51] Part of our reason for attributing intentions to a subject is that they are a cause of her behavior. Belief and desire, on his view, cannot be epiphenomenal or nomologically inert. So, if Durkheim is correct in maintaining that social rather than psychological facts explain a subject's behavior, the subject would not be a subject of utilitarianism, for she would not have the kind of mind that makes states of happiness possible.[52]

There is another reason for thinking that Durkheim's subjects are not the subjects of Mill's utilitarianism: only those subjects whose actions are explained by their intentions can choose to conform their behavior to the prescriptions or advice of utilitarianism. That is, if a person's intentions are not a cause of her actions, then the intention to increase human happiness could never move her to action. In such a case, utilitarianism could not be a theory to guide human conduct. At best, it would be a theory by which to evaluate it; but Mill thought that utilitarianism was both.

Mill's utilitarianism is incompatible with Becker's social theory as well as Durkheim's. Though Becker and Mill both assume that their subjects have a coherent set of desires or preferences, Becker imputes preferences to his subjects that discount their own account of their behavior; for in offering his economic explanations, Becker attributes preferences to them that are not consistent with those that, in offering their account, they attribute to themselves.

There are two issues here. One is whether Becker can so often overrule his subjects' judgments about their own preferences. If, as Davidson argues, the bearers of intention must be largely correct in their judgments of intention, then he cannot; for the more he discounts his subjects' own judgments, the less he can attribute preferences to them at all.

The second issue is whether Becker's subjects can choose to conform

recollections is better

their behavior to the prescriptions of utilitarianism. Can a person who always acts to satisfy his preferences be caused by the belief that A is more conducive to human happiness than B to choose A? The answer to this question depends on the economist's concept of preference. As "preference" is traditionally defined in economics, each participant's preferences are independent of every other's. According to this definition of "preference," the subjects of economics are purely self-interested. They are not moved by feelings of sympathy or envy. Purely self-interested subjects can act as if they were utilitarians, but their reasons for acting cannot be utilitarian. That is, their actions cannot be caused by the (ultimate) desire to increase the happiness of others, for that is precluded by the economist's assumption of independence. If the subjects of utilitarianism must be able to choose human happiness for the sake of human happiness, then they cannot be the subjects of such an economic theory.

Radcliffe-Brown's subjects lead two lives, and in one, their ritualistic life, they are not the bearers of human happiness; for in that life, their behavior is not subject to their beliefs and desires, and thus, in that life, there is reason to doubt that they have any desires at all. In addition, in their ritual lives, Radcliffe-Brown's subjects cannot act from any utilitarian desires, for their desires, if we can speak of them at all, are inert – are not a cause of any of their behavior.

The argument from the good will

Kant's moral theory, unlike Mill's, is not based on the effects of, but on the reasons for, an action. What gives an action moral worth, according to Kant, is that the agent performs it for the right reasons: out of a sense of duty. Moreover, duty may require a person to perform an action that is contrary to her own inclinations or desires; for, if it is morally right for a person to do something, it is right even if she would be happier (satisfy more of her desires) if she acted otherwise. Kant writes:

> Only something which is conjoined with my will solely as a ground and never as an effect – something which does not serve my inclination but outweighs it or at least leaves it entirely out of account in my choice – and therefore only bare law for its own sake, can be an object of reverence and therewith a command. Now an action done from duty has to set aside altogether the influence of inclination, and along with inclination every object of the will; so there is nothing left able to determine the will except objectively the *law* and subjectively *pure reverence* for this practical law, and therefore

the maxim of obeying this law even to the detriment of all my inclinations.[53]

It is part of Kant's moral psychology that a subject can be moved to act by the belief that she is morally obliged to and in the absence of a desire to; for, as Kant sees it, the absence of a desire is never a reason or an excuse for not doing what duty requires.[54]

On Kant's view, the moral quality of a person's action is dependent on the reasons why she performed it. Only if her reasons were moral reasons are her actions worthy of our moral respect. To comply with the moral law is a moral reason, according to Kant, while to increase one's own happiness or even the happiness of others is not. Consequently, if the intention to increase happiness, rather than the intention to comply with the law of promise keeping, explains why a person keeps her promise, her will to keep the promise is not a good will. Her intention to do what the moral law requires must explain why she keeps the promise before her will to keep it can be said to be good.

If a participant's reasons do not explain her behavior, her reverence for the law does not explain it. Consequently, in discounting wholesale the participant's account and in maintaining that her reasons do not explain her behavior, the social scientist denies that the participant's will is a good will. In discounting wholesale the participant's account, the social scientist removes our ground for believing that the participant is a consciously rational subject and that she is capable of acting from any of her reasons, and, *a fortiori,* that she is capable of acting from her reverence for the law.

To deny, as Durkheim does, that reasons or intentions explain is "to deny to the concept of morality all truth and all relation to a possible object."[55] The will of Durkheim's subject is never autonomous but always heteronomous (subject to external causes): it is never moved by the subject's intentions and thus never moved by her intention to comply with the moral law. As a result, the will of Durkheim's subject is never a good will, and his subjects are not the subjects of Kant's morality.

Freud's theory of double consciousness is also inconsistent with Kant's moral psychology; for if a subject's actions are often explained by desires that are buried in her unconscious and not by her conscious intentions, then she cannot act out of reverence for the law, for even if she has the conscious intention of doing what the law commands her to do, she is not acting with a good will, for it is the hidden desire rather than the intention that explains her action. Whenever Freud's subjects act from latent desires, their will is heteronomous. But because Freud's subjects so often act from latent desires, we lose our reasons for believing that their will is sometimes autonomous and that they sometimes act with the intention of complying with the law. We lose our reasons for believing that we understand their intentions or for believing that they sometimes act out of duty rather than to satisfy a sexual desire. As a result, there is reason to believe that Freud's subjects, no less than Durkheim's, are not the subjects of Kant's morality.

The point here, as in the preceding arguments, is that to accept a theory of human behavior according to which a subject's conscious intentions seldom explain her behavior requires a revision of our moral views. It requires that we revise that part of our moral view that is utilitarian and that we give up that part of our view that is Kantian as well. The psychology of Durkheim, Freud, Becker, and Radcliffe-Brown is not consistent with the moral theories of writers like Kant and Mill, for we cannot attribute to the subjects of their psychology the motivation needed for the behavior of these subjects to have moral worth or be conducive to human happiness. To discount, as a matter of general practice, participants' accounts of their own behavior is to deny morality, whether Kant's or Mill's, to its subjects.

The argument from moral emotion

Focused as it is on the notion of duty and on the idea of a moral law, Kant's moral philosophy emphasizes that part of our ordinary moral practice that is general and impersonal. It sets aside those emotions or sentiments which, in ordinary life, lead us to treat some subjects differently and more considerately than others. In his paper "Freedom and Resentment," Peter Strawson considers that part of our ordinary moral practice that takes some of these feelings and emotions into account. Strawson observes that although some of our ordinary moral practices require us to adopt a detached attitude toward others, the kind of attitude that Kant recommends, some other of our moral practices require us to adopt more personal and less detached, participant attitudes.[56] Instead of viewing subjects disinterestedly and measuring their performances against an impersonal standard of duty, we act out of friendship or personal concern. Our less detached or more personal attitudes are what make our interpersonal relationships possible. Strawson includes as examples such attitudes or feelings as forgiveness, gratitude, resentment, love, good will, esteem, contempt, and anger.

According to Strawson, there are two kinds of consideration which serve to modify or temper our normal participant attitudes or feelings toward subjects or their actions. One serves to discount the action, the other to discount the subject. The first leads us to excuse subjects for a harm that they might have caused us, without inviting us to think that they are the kind of subject toward whom it would be inappropriate to ever feel moral emotions like anger, gratitude, or resentment. The fact that their actions were inadvertent, unavoidable, or done without malice, for example, is a reason not to resent them for causing us this harm, but it is not a reason to think that they are subjects whose actions should never give us a reason to be angry or resentful.

The second consideration, by contrast, invites us to view a subject as someone towards whom it is never appropriate to adopt any participant attitudes at all. To believe, for example, that a man is insane or thoroughly irrational is to have a reason to suspend our participant attitudes toward him altogether – a reason not to get angry with him if he behaves badly or to get indignant with him if he seems insensitive to our feelings or concerns. We may be harmed by his boasts, lapses, or lies, but if he lies or boasts compulsively, we should not resent him or feel contempt. Unless we believe that a man is rational and that his conscious intentions, as a rule, are the cause of his behavior, we should not make him an object of our moral attitudes and feelings.[57]

Strawson's interest is in the thesis of determinism, and the question he asks himself is whether a belief in that thesis would give us a reason to suspend our participant attitudes toward subjects whom we classify as rational.[58] Would we have any reason to modify our ordinary practice of adopting participant attitudes toward some subjects and suspending them toward others if we believed that all actions and attitudes are causally determined? Strawson thinks that belief in such a general thesis would not give us any reason to withdraw these attitudes from every subject, rational and irrational, sane and insane alike. Belief in determinism, Strawson argues, is not a ground for switching from a participant to an objective attitude.

> For it is not a consequence of any general thesis of determinism which might be true that nobody knows what he's doing or that everybody's behavior is unintelligible in terms of conscious purposes or that everybody lives in a world of delusion or that nobody has a moral sense, i.e., is susceptible of self-reactive attitudes, etc.[59]

He goes on to say – correctly, I think – that, given the sense of "determined" required for the thesis of determinism, the fact that a subject's actions are determined gives us no reason to suspend our participant attitudes. The fact that a subject's actions are determined by her beliefs and desires and that her beliefs and desires, in turn, are determined by preceding states of mind or events does not give us a reason for with-holding feelings of affection, loyalty, or friendship towards her.

My concern, however, unlike Strawson's, is not whether determinism and resentment are compatible, but whether the social science explanation and resentment are, and my position is that they are not. Though it is not a consequence of any general thesis of determinism, it is a conse-quence of a wholesale discounting of participant accounts that nobody knows, to use Strawson's words, "what he is doing or that everybody's behavior is unintelligible in terms of conscious purposes or that everybody lives in a world of delusion or that nobody has a moral sense."

The consideration that the participants' own reasons as a rule do not explain their behavior (unlike the consideration that every thought and action is causally determined) is a reason, given our present moral prac-tice, to suspend our participant attitudes. We cannot appropriately feel resentment or gratitude towards subjects who behave in a way that harms or benefits us but whose behavior often has little to do with their con-scious intentions.

Because they so seldom understand the causes of their own behavior, Durkheim's, Freud's, and Becker's subjects are not the proper objects of anger, resentment, or respect; they are objects that we can observe, sur-vey, examine, study, classify, motivate, supervise, regulate, command, dis-cipline, treat, train, rehabilitate, or cure. A subject whose behavior is seldom explained by her own reasons for so acting is someone whom we might view as a burden, a ward, a client, a dependent, or a charge, but not as someone with a mind of her own, someone whose movements are actions of which she is the agent. We can try to improve her prospects by pulling her with carrots or pushing her with sticks, but not by putting stock in her own accounts of the causes of her own behavior.

If we interpret a subject out of our moral community by discounting her own explanations of her actions, we interpret her not only as someone towards whom we should not feel anger or resentment, but, in addition, as someone from whom we cannot expect anger or resentment either; for these emotions include intentions that can be imputed only to someone whose actions, as a rule, are caused by her intentions.

To discount a subject's own account of herself is to deny that she is a moral subject in two ways. It is to withhold from her our own moral emotions and also to withdraw from her *her* own emotions; for to dis-count her self-understandings is a reason for us not to feel resentment or anger towards her, but it is also a reason to think that she feels no resentment or anger towards us.

This last point is made by Marilyn Frye, who, in an essay entitled "A Note on Anger," points out that to be angry is to make a judgment.[60]

When I am angry with people for lying or boasting, I judge that they ought not to have lied or boasted. Frye's interest is in how we react to the anger of others, and, in particular, the ways we have of not taking their anger seriously. One way is to assume that the anger is not explained by their reasons for being angry, their judgment that someone did something wrong, but rather by some cause that is hidden from their view.[61]

Frye discusses the role that gender plays in our practice of discounting participants' accounts of their emotions. In our culture, she observes, a woman is more likely than a man to have her own explanation of her anger (and her other moral emotions) discounted. A man who explains that the reason why he is angry is that he believes that he has been treated unfairly is more likely to have that accepted as an explanation of his anger than a woman is. In ordinary life, we are inclined to think that women, more than men, do not understand themselves.

If, in ordinary practice, we are less respectful of a woman's understanding of herself than we are of a man's, social theories like Durkheim's, Freud's, Becker's, and Radcliffe-Brown's change that. Men and women get equal treatment. The theories look upon men as men are inclined, in ordinary life, to look upon women. According to the theories, men have no more understanding of the causes of their own behavior than women do. Without the aid of theory or therapy, men and women stand together in the dark.

In turning aside the subject's own explanation of her anger and looking for a nonrational or hidden cause of it, we remove her anger and interpret her behavior as a symptom of something, rather than as a reasonable response to the wrongful actions of others. By turning her explanations aside, we retreat from the strains of involvement, for we hide her attitudes from our view; and, if we turn enough of her explanations aside, we will no longer see her as rational or as the bearer of any attitudes that deserve our respect.

It is not surprising, then, that people should feel demeaned or at risk when their own explanations of their actions are judged to be false and are replaced by explanations in which their reasons are not cited as the causes of their actions. For when many of a person's own explanations are discounted, her actions lose their moral worth, and she loses her status as a person capable of rationally deliberating among differing ends – as an autonomous individual – and a subject of our morality.

For some liberals – for example, J. S. Mill – value-neutrality is intended to protect and promote the autonomy of the individual. On their liberal view, education should produce in children the desire and the ability to rationally deliberate among differing ways of life and to make practical and moral decisions on their own; and the state should encourage individual initiative and personal choice and resist all forms of paternalism.[62] Society's basic institutions, they believe, should be designed to ensure that individuals, so far as possible, have the opportunity to express their nature as free and equal rational beings.[63]

As I explained in chapter 1, the liberal sciences, like the state and the schools, are part of that design. Like other liberal institutions, they assume that deliberation among differing ends should be left to the individual to decide. However, as I have shown in this chapter, the standards of explanation common to the liberal sciences oppose the very idea of the autonomous individual. The standards take away what neutrality aims to protect: a community of free and equal rational beings legislating their own principles of conduct. In chapter 6, I explained how the standards for collecting data in the social sciences include devices for limiting the active presence of the subject in the practice of the science and, in particular, devices for weakening the will of the experimental or interview subject. The standards for explaining the behavior of the subject also include devices for limiting her active presence in the practice of the science. But whereas in collecting the data, the agency of the subject is limited or tightly controlled, in explaining the data, her agency is entirely eliminated, and she is no longer an individual with a conception of the good; but if the subjects of the social sciences have no conception of the good, their autonomy is no reason for the sciences to be neutral between the different conceptions of their subjects.

There is an incoherence in the ideals of the social sciences. On the one hand, the ideal of value-neutrality assumes that the subjects of the science are rational beings who choose between competing conceptions of the good and that, as rational beings, their choices are deserving of respect. On the other, the ideals of reliable and valid data and scientific explanation assume either that they are not rational beings or that their choices are not deserving of respect. What one ideal gives, the others take away. A coherent approach would either not include value-neutrality as a regulative ideal or not include the many devices for limiting the active presence of the subject in the social sciences.

Conclusion

What I have tried to show is that an approach to explanation common to a number of different social sciences is not consistent with a view of subjects assumed by many of our ordinary moral concepts. In particular, I have argued that if a subject's reasons are too seldom accepted as an explanation of her behavior, then we cannot adopt our ordinary moral

Also, if social science explanation is not consistent w/ theories of morality, why reject social sci. explanation?

attitudes toward her or view her as an appropriate bearer of moral responsibility. Whereas in other chapters, I have shown how particular practices in the social sciences favor one conception of the good over another, in this chapter, I have shown how the practice of explanation in the social sciences opposes the very idea that subjects have conceptions of the good that institutions, like the social sciences, should respect and neither condemn nor condone.

My claim was not that determinism and morality are incompatible, but that a particular form of misjudgment and morality are so. It is inconsistent to say, I argued, that someone is a moral subject yet mistaken in many of her judgments about the immediate causes of her own behavior. In short, the point of this chapter has been to defend a new version of incompatibilism – the thesis that discounting in the social sciences is incompatible with our ordinary or everyday psychology of participant explanation and with the groundwork of our moral philosophy – and to show that although the social sciences are founded on the liberal ideal of value-neutrality, the approach to explanation common to the social sciences is illiberal, for it does not recognize – let alone respect – the conception of the good of the subjects of the science and, far from encouraging or endorsing their autonomy, opposes the idea that they have any autonomy at all.

NOTES

1 Rawls, *Theory of Justice*, p. 3.
2 Ibid., p. 128.
3 See S. Lukes, *Marxism and Morality* (Oxford University Press, 1985), for a discussion of Marx's criticisms of these concepts. In some of his criticisms, Marx seems to suggest that all moral concepts are bogus and simply mask the reality of the social relations of production under capitalism; but I am persuaded by Lukes that Marx does not mean to call all moral concepts into doubt but only the juridical concepts favored by the many socialists of his day.
4 See A. Wood, *Karl Marx* (Routledge and Kegan Paul, 1981), pp. 136–40.
5 R. E. Nisbett and T. D. Wilson, "Telling More than we can Know: Verbal Reports on Mental Processes," *Psychological Review*, 84 (1977), p. 247. Nisbett and Wilson argue that accounts offered by subjects of the causes of their own judgments, as well as the causes of their behavior, are very often mistaken. My remarks are limited to judgments that people make about the causes of their own behavior.
6 I want to allow that our ideas about how to explain our behavior and about when such explanations are in order have a history. There is no reason to believe that the explanations that people offer of their behavior are everywhere

the same, or even that explanations are everywhere offered. That is, the practice of calling on and being called on by others to explain one's behavior may be a feature of our own time and place. I do not know, e.g., that our practice of seeing human beings as agents and as acting on the basis of reasons was also the practice of the serfs of thirteenth-century Europe or is now the practice of the Trobriand Islanders. Moreover, though I will contrast our ordinary practice with the practice of social science, I want to admit that our ordinary practice is affected by the practice of social science. We are influenced by expert opinion and may come to think about ourselves the way the experts do. If the experts maintain that you and I are utility-maximizers, we may increasingly become so. This fact alone, as Foucault argues, opposes the idea that the social sciences are morally neutral and that a theory in the social sciences can be positive without, at the same time, being critical. My point is merely that, at present, in my own part of the world, there is a contrast between the ordinary, garden variety explanations that people offer of their own behavior and the explanations that the social sciences offer, and that the garden variety are rational explanations.

7   Donald Davidson, in *Essays on Actions and Events* (Oxford University Press, 1980), essays 1–5, offers a subtle account of rational explanation. He argues that reasons can be causes and that rational explanations are a species of singular causal explanation. According to this view, a participant's rational explanation is false or inadequate if the reasons she cites do not cause her behavior, or cause it in just the right way. Social scientists who believe that only causes explain and that reasons are not causes, will discount or set aside as false a rational explanation, whether offered by the participant or an observer, as I explain later in this chapter.

8   For a more detailed discussion of this point, see D. Davidson, *Inquiries into Truth and Interpretation* (Oxford University Press, 1984), essays 9–11, and *Actions and Events,* essay 15. Davidson argues that to interpret a subject's behavior and attribute thoughts to her, we must assume that her judgments about her own thoughts are, for the most part, true. Davidson writes: "What operates as a constraint on the interpreter amounts to a bestowal of authority on the person interpreted; when he honestly expresses his motives, beliefs, intentions, and desires an interpreter must, if he wants to understand, interpret the speech in a way that makes sense not only of what the speaker says but also of what he believes and wants and does. Making such sense requires that causality and rationality go hand in hand in important cases: perception, intentional action and the indirect passions are examples. People are in general right about the mental causes of their emotions, intentions, and actions because as interpreters we interpret them so as to make them so. We must, if we are to interpret them at all" (*Actions and Events*, p. 290). On Davidson's view, to discount many of a participant's accounts is to lose our reasons for believing her to be an agent and for believing that we understand the contents of her thoughts or intentions. See also my paper "Davidson and Social Science," in *Truth and Interpretation: Perspectives on the Philosophy of Donald Davidson,* ed. E. Lepore (Basil Blackwell, 1986), pp. 272–304. For an opposing view of the

relation between rationality and charity, see P. Thagard and R. E. Nisbett, "Rationality and Charity," *Philosophy of Science*, 50 (1983), pp. 250–67.

9   B. Latane and J. M. Darley, *The Unresponsive Bystander: Why doesn't he Help?* (Appleton-Century-Crofts, 1970).

10 M. Storms and R. E. Nisbett, "Insomnia and the Attribution Process," *Journal of Personality and Social Psychology*, 16 (1970), pp. 319–28. See Nisbett and Wilson, "Telling More than we can Know," pp. 241–2 and 237–8, for a discussion of such studies of benighted subjects.

11 For a discussion of the compatibility of Marx's materialist explanations and the rational explanations that individual workers and capitalists might offer of their own behavior, see Wood, *Karl Marx*, pp. 101–22.

12 This idea belongs to G. H. von Wright, *Explanation and Understanding* (Cornell University Press, 1971), pp. 1–33.

13 E. Durkheim, *Suicide: A Study in Sociology* (Free Press, 1966). See Keat and Urry, *Social Theory as Science*, for a discussion of Durkheim's views on causal explanation.

14 Radcliffe-Brown, *Structure*.

15 G. Becker, *The Economic Approach to Human Behavior* (University of Chicago Press, 1976).

16 S. Freud, *Five Lectures on Psycho-Analysis*, tr. and ed. J. Strachey (Norton, 1977).

17 Quoted in P. Winch, *The Idea of a Social Science* (Routledge and Kegan Paul, 1958), p. 23.

18 Durkheim, *Suicide*, pp. 297–8.

19 Ibid., p. 306.

20 Davidson, *Inquiries*, p. 208.

21 On Durkheim's view, beliefs and desires do not explain an action, but they can help to define it. Only those actions that subjects perform in the belief that they will bring about their own death, e.g., count as suicide, according to Durkheim. Though there is no causal connection between the belief and the action, on Durkheim's view, there is a definitional one. See *Suicide*, p. 44.

22 See, e.g., Freud's remark in *The History of the Psychoanalytic Movement* that he came to realize that the causes of behavior are as hidden to normal persons as they are to his nervous patients (*The Basic Writings of Freud*, ed. A. A. Brill (Random House, 1938), p. 954).

23 Freud, *Five Lectures*, p. 27.

24 Ibid., p. 50. Freud, so far as I know, does not explain how satisfying one desire – e.g., the desire to draw birds in flight – satisfies another, different desire – e.g., a sexual desire. He seems to think that the fact that one desire is a symbol for the other explains how such displacement is possible; but it is hard to see how one's hunger for food, e.g., can be satisfied by satisfying a desire to draw sheaves of wheat, even if the sheaves are a symbol for food.

25 S. Freud, *Leonardo da Vinci and a Memory of his Childhood*, tr. and ed. J. Strachey (Norton, 1964), pp. 32–56.

26 Radcliffe-Brown, *Structure*, p. 144.

27 Ibid., p. 152.

28   Ibid., p. 143.
29   The idea that the "natives" have beliefs about nature radically different from the anthropologist's own is itself a reason for the anthropologist to believe that she has misinterpreted the natives' beliefs. See Davidson's remarks on the role of charity in the interpretation of belief in *Inquiries*, essays 9–11.
30   Radcliffe-Brown, *Structure*, p. 142.
31   Becker, *Economic Approach*, pp. 5–6.
32   Ibid., p. 14.
33   Ibid., p. 8.
34   Ibid., p. 206.
35   Ibid., p. 7.
36   Here Becker follows Milton Friedman, who argues in "Methodology," that a theory is to be judged only by its predictive power for the class of phenomena which it is intended to explain and not on the reality of its assumptions. See chapter 5 for a discussion of the different interpretations of rational choice theory in economics.
37   For a fuller discussion of this distinction, see chapter 5.
38   It might be reasonable to believe that it is a law of nature that whenever A, B, in the absence of any understanding of how A causes B to happen – e.g., that ingesting aspirin reduces pain – but my point is that an understanding of the causes of B can be a reason to doubt that it is a law of nature if, according to that understanding, C is the cause of B, and there is no lawlike relation between A and C. For a more complete discussion of causes and laws in economics, see chapter 5.
39   Preference, according to some economists, is revealed preference, and revealed preference is nothing more than the internal consistency of observed choice. So understood, preference is not a state of mind or a possible cause of a person's choices at all, and if a participant's choices are consistent and she explains that she is acting contrary to her own preferences, she must be mistaken.
40   Sen, "Rational Fools," pp. 96–7.
41   Insofar as the social sciences discount participant accounts; and, as I have tried to show, discounting is a widespread practice in the social sciences.
42   P. F. Strawson, *Freedom and Resentment and Other Essays* (Methuen, 1974), pp. 1–25.
43   See, e.g., A. K. Stout, "Free Will and Responsibility," in *Readings in Ethical Theory*, ed. W. Sellars and J. Hospers (Appleton-Century-Crofts, 1952), pp. 537–48.
44   My position is similar to that of the soft determinist who argues that it is not causal determinism that threatens moral responsibility but the denial that a subject's own reasons are the cause of her behavior. According to the soft determinist, subjects are responsible only if they are able to exercise causal control over their behavior, and such control is exercised when their behavior is caused by their intentions (rather than by external forces or internal compulsions). My position is not that a moral subject must have exercised causal control over a part of her behavior to be responsible for it, but that she must

be able to exercise causal control over a large part of her behavior before she is responsible for any part of it.

45 An objection: my argument assumes that a person is rational only if her reasons are causes of her behavior; but some philosophers maintain that our concepts of rationality and causality belong to separate schemes. A person is rational, on their view, if she has beliefs and desires that are practical reasons for some large part of her behavior; but if her beliefs and desires rationalize her behavior, they do not cause it, for reasons cannot be causes. See, e.g., A. I. Melden, *Free Action* (Routledge and Kegan Paul, 1964), and R. S. Peters, *The Concept of Motivation* (Routledge and Kegan Paul, 1958). For a criticism of the view that reasons cannot be causes, see Davidson, *Actions and Events*, essay 1.

The objection, I believe, is without merit, because rationality and causality cannot be separated in the way that these philosophers suppose. Someone whose arm moves because it is pushed may have intended her arm to move to call attention to herself. Her intention is a reason for her arm moving; but because the push and not the intention is the cause of the movement, the movement is not intentional, and if not intentional, her intention does not explain by rationalizing her movement.

46 Freud, *Five Lectures*, p. 53.

47 S. Freud, *The Standard Edition of the Complete Psychological Works of Sigmund Freud*, vol. 11, tr. and ed. J. Strachey (Hogarth Press, 1967), p. 225; emphasis original.

48 The question has been much debated as to whether Freud's theory of double consciousness undermines moral agency or opposes otherwise appropriate moral evaluation. Those who maintain that it does argue that Freud's subjects, being the victims of the unconscious processes of repression or sublimation, are sufficiently ignorant of what they are doing and why they are doing it as to be blameless for doing it or are so coerced by these mechanisms to act contrary to their conscious intentions that their behavior is involuntary and so not subject to blame. For a useful survey of this debate, see M. W. Martin, *Self-Deception and Morality* (University of Kansas Press, 1986). My argument combines ignorance and coercion: Freud's subjects, on my view, suffer a forced ignorance of what they are doing and why they are doing it, and being ignorant and without the means to learn the truth, they are unable to exercise causal control over their behavior.

49 J. S. Mill, *Utilitarianism*, ed. Oskzr Priest (Bobbs–Merrill Company, 1957), p. 10. Mill maintained that the quality, not merely the quantity, of satisfied desire is the measure of happiness. I ignore this here, for it does not affect the argument.

50 Mill, *On Logic*, pp. 24–36.

51 See Davidson, *Inquiries*, essays 9–11.

52 There are utilitarians who separate intentionality from moral worthiness. On their view, sentience, the ability to feel pleasure and pain, is all that is needed to be someone whose welfare matters. Utilitarians who believe that harm to animals is a moral concern on a par with harm to persons, and yet that the

behavior of animals is not intentional, do not assume, as I have suggested, that only the bearers of intentions are members of the moral community. There is some evidence that Mill himself thinks that the moral community includes "the whole sentient creation." See *Utilitarianism*, ch. 2, para. 10.

53 I. Kant, *Groundwork of the Metaphysics of Morals*, tr. H. J. Paton (Harper and Row, 1964), pp. 68–9.

54 Ibid., pp. 57–8.

55 Ibid., p. 76.

56 Strawson, *Freedom and Resentment*, pp. 8–9.

57 Ibid., p. 9.

58 Ibid., p. 11.

59 Ibid., p. 18.

60 M. Frye, *The Politics of Reality: Essays in Feminist Theory* (Crossing Press, 1983), pp. 84–94.

61 Ibid., p. 84.

62 Gutmann, *Democratic Education*, p. 59.

63 See chapter 1 for a discussion of the different reasons for the belief that our basic institutions should be neutral on issues of the good; valuing autonomy is only one.

9

The fact/value distinction

John Stuart Mill's call for neutrality in the social sciences is based on his belief that the languages of science and art are different. "Science is a collection of truths; art, a body of rules, or directions for conduct. The language of art is, Do this; Avoid that. Science takes cognisance of a phenomenon, and endeavours to discover its law; art proposes to itself an end, and looks out for means to effect it."[1] Like Hume before him, Mill assumes that no body of rules (art) entails or is entailed by any collection of truths (science). Most recent discussions of the role of values in the social sciences rest on Mill's assumption. Max Weber, in arguing for value-freedom in the social sciences, for example, takes it for granted that there can be a language of science – a collection of truths – that excludes all value-judgments, rules, or directions for conduct. For Weber, as I explain in chapter 2, a body of research or teaching in the social sciences is value-free if and only if it does not contain any "practical evaluations regarding the desirability or undesirability of social facts from ethical, cultural or other points of view."[2]

In the preceding chapters, I argued that, given the way data are collected and theorized in the social sciences, rules (values) cannot be excluded from these sciences, but I did not question Mill's assumption that there is a logical gap between the languages of science and art. My point was to show not that the social sciences cannot be value-free, Weber's ideal, but that they cannot be value-neutral – that is, neutral between competing conceptions of the good – the broader liberal idea.

My aim in this chapter is to show that Mill's assumption is mistaken and that value-freedom in the social sciences is not possible. First, I argue that proper attention to the open texture of meaning and the tie between meaning and collateral information shows that words cannot be purged of their evaluative content and that values cannot be eliminated from the language of the social sciences. Second, I argue that proper attention to the use of the language of the social sciences shows that whether speech expresses a fact or a value, a truth or a rule, is not simply a matter of the speaker's words but of how and where they are used and who is using them. A speaker can recommend or prescribe using any words, no matter how factual, and an act of speech performed with the language of any science can have the force of a directive for action.

The first argument is intended to show that there can be no language of science whose terms are free of all evaluative content, the second to show that value-freedom is a property not of the language used but of the use of the language; that the use of a language can be value-laden no matter what the evaluative content of its terms and that many of the uses of language in the social sciences have the force of a directive for action and are therefore, in Weber's sense, laden with value.

The naturalistic fallacy

The claim that facts and values are distinct is usually understood to be a claim about language. Sometimes it is understood to mean A:

A: There are in language two classes of expressions, expressions that describe facts and expressions that express values, and no member of the one class can be defined solely in terms of members of the other.

Sometimes it is understood to mean B:

B: There are in language two classes of expressions, expressions that describe facts and those that express values, and no statement that contains the one can be inferred from statements that contain only the other.

We might call A and B "heterogeneity principles." According to A and B, facts and values are entirely heterogeneous. Principles A and B are obviously related. Were value expressions definable by factual expressions, a statement that contains a value expression could be inferred from a statement containing only expressions of fact.[3]

The phrase "the naturalistic fallacy" is sometimes used to describe efforts to infer values from facts. The phrase was coined by G. E. Moore in *Principia Ethica*,[4] but Moore himself did not have A or B in mind at the time. Moore's claim was about defining a particular value expression – namely "good" – that "good" could not be defined in any other terms either evaluative or factual. On his view, "good" was a simple quality that could not be defined at all. Nevertheless, it is B that most writers have in mind when they talk of the heterogeneity of fact and value and say that reasoning from facts to values commits the naturalistic fallacy.

Many who accept B attempt to reduce all expressions of value to one value expression. Some economists, for example, attempt to reduce all expressions of value to the comparative "preferable." On this view, whenever anyone says "x is better or more valuable than y," she means that (to her) x is preferable to y. Alternatively, some philosophers attempt to reduce all expressions of value to "ought" or to an imperative expression. Whenever anyone says "x is better or more valuable than y," she means that x ought to be chosen over y. For these philosophers, B means that no "ought" can be inferred from "is," no imperative from a declarative statement. This seems to have been Karl Popper's point when he wrote:

> Perhaps the simplest and most important point about ethics is purely logical. I mean the impossibility to derive [sic] nontautological ethical rules – imperatives, principles of policy; aims; or however we describe them – from statements of facts. Only if this fundamental logical position is realized can we begin to formulate the real problems of moral philosophy, to appreciate their difficulty.[5]

and R. M. Hare's point when he wrote that no imperative conclusions can be validly drawn from premises that do not contain at least one imperative.

> The rule that an imperative cannot appear in the conclusion of a valid inference, unless there is at least one imperative in the premises, may be confirmed by an appeal to general logical considerations. For it is now generally regarded as true by definition that (to speak roughly at first) nothing can appear in the conclusion of a valid, deductive inference which is not, from their very meaning, implicit in the conjunction of the premises.[6]

But Hume seems to have been the first to state the ban on inferring "ought" from "is" when he wrote:

> For as this *ought*, or *ought not*, expresses some new relation or affirmation, it is necessary that it should be observed and explained: and at the same time, that a reason should be given, for what seems altogether inconceivable, how this new relation can be a deduction from others, which are entirely different from it.[7]

Hume's claim about "ought" and Hare's claim about imperatives are connected, for Hare argues that the function of "ought" is to tell people what to do. To say that a person ought to perform some action is to advance a universal imperative (an imperative that applies to all persons) that prescribes the doing of it. Hare believes that the languages of science and morals are heterogeneous, but also that the language of morals is the language of imperatives. He is committed to both heterogeneity and reduction. All evaluative statements are reducible to statements of what ought to be done, and they, in turn, are reducible to prescriptive or imperative statements. Thus, for Hare, the fact/value distinction is reducible to a distinction between descriptive and prescriptive expressions. On his view, to value anything positively is to tell or direct someone to choose it.

Thick ethical terms

One complication for Hare's view of the language of morals is that moral language includes expressions that differ in meaning and thus cannot all be reduced to a single expression "ought" or a single imperative. To say, for example, that an action is brutal, cowardly, or ungracious is, in each case, to evaluate it; but in each case it is also to say something different about the action. But if all that is meant by saying any of these things of the action is that it ought not to be done, then there is no difference in saying one of them rather than another. The variety and specificity of the language of morals is lost when every expression is equated with one or a few abstract moral terms.

To allow that our language contains many different moral terms and that the many cannot be reduced to a few raises the stakes for value-freedom. To make their science value-free, social scientists must free it of terms like "ought"; but they must free it of terms like "delinquent," "victim," "gang," "terrorist," "democrat," and "criminal" as well. These are called "thick ethical terms," for they express both what is and what ought to be, while terms like "ought" or "good" are called "thin ethical terms" and express only what ought to be. The problem for the reductionist view is that the language of thick ethical terms cannot be reduced to the language of thin ethical terms, and the problem for the defender of value-freedom is that many of the words that social scientists borrow from ordinary language to record or theorize their data are thick ethical terms.

Hare offers a way of dealing with both these problems. He maintains that thick ethical terms combine a descriptive and a prescriptive element. The prescriptive part is expressed by the all-purpose prescriptive term "ought" and is the same for each thick ethical term, while the descriptive part differs from term to term. Hare maintains that given any thick expression, it is possible to produce another expression that has the same descriptive content but no prescriptive content at all. In short, his view is that it is possible for a social science to foreswear thick ethical terms, terms like "democrat," "juvenile offender," "learning-disabled," "well-adjusted," "chemically dependent," "educated," or "victim," by isolating the factual component and introducing a term to stand for it alone.

As an example, imagine that the terms "education" and "brainwashing" have the same descriptive content – namely, the idea that something is or has been intentionally transmitted – but different evaluative content – namely, one positive the other negative. To call a philosophy degree "an education" is to approve of it, whereas to call it "brainwashing" is to disapprove. Because the terms "education" and "brainwashing" have an evaluative content, were social scientists to include them in their writings or teachings, the latter would not be value-free but value-laden. However, on Hare's view, social scientists can include a term that expresses the descriptive content of "education" or "brainwashing," and if there is no term already in the language, they can coin one.

Value-freedom calls for social scientists to free their work of the language of morals. This is harder than it might at first seem, for it requires that they refrain from using any term that has as part of its meaning any evaluative content, and since many of the words of our ordinary language have some evaluative content, it requires that they coin a new language. However, many natural scientists turned away from ordinary language long ago to use a technical language in their work, and many social scientists believe that advances in the social sciences will come only if they follow the lead of the natural sciences and replace ordinary terms with technical terms designed to be free of evaluative content.

Coining a new language

Hare's solution to the problem of thick ethical terms assumes that it is possible to separate the descriptive and prescriptive contents of a word and to introduce terms that will stand for the descriptive elements alone. It assumes that prescriptive elements can be removed from a language by limiting the meaning of terms to the meaning given by stipulative definition. However, there are a number of arguments against Hare's assumption and against his strategy of stipulative definition. I will offer two. The point behind them is the same: namely, that the meaning of a word is not limited by the intentions of whoever defines it. Specifically, coined terms acquire meaning in the course of their use, and the meaning they acquire includes elements not included in any stipulative definition. Consequently, even if such terms were free of evaluative content at the moment the social scientists coined them, the new, technical terms would acquire evaluative content when the scientists put them to use.

The first argument rests on Friedrich Waismann's notion of open texture.[8] When we define empirical terms, according to Waismann, we cannot foresee all the cases to which we might wish to apply them. For "every definition stretches into an open horizon. Try as we may, the situation will always remain the same: no definition of an empirical term will cover all possibilities."[9] When possibilities arise that are not clearly covered by our definition, we can decide to either leave them uncovered or clarify the definition to cover them.[10] If we decide to clarify the definition, we need to decide what to add. We can clarify the definition so that the term applies to the new cases or so that it doesn't. The choice is a matter of practical rather than theoretical reason. Which clarification is best is not a matter of which best fits the facts, since if each refinement covers the new cases, each fits the facts equally well, but a matter of which best serves our interests.

When we choose one clarification over others on the basis of our interests, those interests add evaluative content to the term. The definition includes the clarification but also the valuation – that is, our reasons for choosing it over the others. Consequently, even if no evaluative content was included in the stipulative definition of the term, the term will acquire such content in the course of its use; and so, in the course of using any newly coined social scientific language, the terms of the language acquire an evaluative meaning and become thick ethical terms.

As an example, imagine that political scientists coin the word "democratic" and attempt to fix its meaning with the following stipulative definition: "democratic" means chosen by popular election. Let's grant that, so defined, the term has descriptive but no prescriptive or evaluative content. The political scientists go on to use the term to describe or compare a number of governments. Initially they look at governments with universal suffrage, voting by secret ballot, multiparty elections, and high rates of voter participation. The definition guides their use of "democratic" reasonably well and enables them to decide whether these governments should be called "democratic."

In time, however, they observe governments in which only males vote, ballots are not secret, there are no opposition parties, or voter turnout is low. In such cases their definition of "democratic" does not give them enough guidance. It does not enable them to decide how to apply the term. It doesn't tell them whether to call a government with low rates of voter participation or no opposition parties "democratic" or not; for it is not clear whether the election in which such a government was chosen was a popular election. The descriptive content of "democratic" – the notion of a popular election – is too vague for the political scientist to know whether the term covers the newly observed governments.[11]

The original definition can be clarified and made more precise. But there are different ways to do this. Some will include elections with low rates of voter participation, and others will exclude them. The choice is the political scientists'. They can base their choice on any of their many interests, and those interests include the value they place on voter participation. If they believe that (given secret ballots and opposition parties or candidates) the greater the participation rate, the more legitimate the government, then they have a reason, in clarifying their definition of "democratic," to choose elements that enable them to separate governments elected by low from those elected by high voter turnout. If the value they assign to high turnouts is a reason for their choice, the value gives evaluative content to the meaning of "democratic."

The political scientists could decide to stick with their original, stipulative definition and leave the governments with low participation rates, no opposition parties, or no female franchise outside the reach of the term; but as they come across more and more of these governments, this decision becomes less and less acceptable, for it leaves more and more governments undescribed and limits the generality of any theory they construct using the terms of the newly coined language. The desire for more rather than less generality gives the scientists reason to describe more governments rather than fewer; but to describe more, they must use their coined terms beyond the use supported by their stipulative definitions and decide how to clarify their meanings. They must decide, for example, whether governments that exclude women ought to be called "democratic."[12] Such a decision is a matter of practical reason, for there are no "facts" that tell one way or another. If they decide to call these governments "democratic," their reasons must include a judgment about the ends they expect the decision to serve, and the judgment becomes part of the content of the term.

The judgment of ends can be a judgment of political or moral value, and, in my example, the judgment is of the political or moral value of sexual equality, high voter turnout, and opposition parties. My impression is that, as political science is actually practiced, decisions concerning the definition of key terms are often based on interests of the political scientist that are appropriately described as political, and in these cases the term acquires political content.

Proponents of value-neutrality, as I explain in chapter 2, draw a distinction between scientific and nonscientific values.[13] Valuing a theory or an ideal-type for its predictive or explanatory power or its usefulness in solving problems, they say, is a matter of scientific value; whereas valuing it for its power to increase economic or political equality or for its usefulness in opposing a political practice or form of economic organization is not. Valuing Marx's theory of history, for example, for its truth or predictive power is science, but valuing it for its usefulness in raising the consciousness of the working class is politics.

A political scientist, on this view, could base her choice of definitions or clarifications on her scientific rather than her political values. She could choose to clarify her definition of "democratic," for example, to exclude governments that exclude women, not because she believes that the governments are not legitimate but because she believes that the clarification will increase the predictive or explanatory power of the term. Though the term acquires evaluative content, it is scientific rather than political. Value-neutrality, the liberal would say, precludes basing a choice on political values but not on scientific ones. The argument from open texture is meant to show not that the social sciences cannot develop a technical language free of all political content but only that some evaluative content will accrue to the language during the course of its use and that, given the interests that guide research in the social sciences, the content will often be political.[14]

The second argument against ridding a language of thick ethical terms is based on W. V. O. Quine's idea that there is no distinction to be drawn between meaning and collateral information.[15] According to Quine, the meaning of a term used by a community to describe an object cannot be distinguished from the community's beliefs about the object. Whatever collateral information members of a language community share about an object they impart to the terms they use to describe it. If the collateral information includes an evaluation of the object, then members of the community impart the evaluation to the term. Consequently, even if the social scientist intends her coined term to have no evaluative content, the term absorbs the evaluative attitudes she has towards objects she uses the term to describe.[16]

To take an example, imagine that the term "female," as it is used in ordinary language to describe human beings, is a thick ethical term; it not only describes a person's sex but prescribes how she ought to look or behave – namely, feminine. Anxious to rid their work of value-laden language, sociologists decide to replace the term with a technical one. They intend their definition of the new term to include only the descriptive element of the old. The new term, they stipulate, means the sex of those human beings who have two X chromosomes. But the sociologists who use the new term believe that members of that sex ought to be

feminine. Coining the new term does not change their view. The values
they place on the subjects to whom they once applied the old term and
now apply the new one remain. Consequently, as they apply the new term
to these subjects, they impart their moral judgments.

If, as Quine argues, meaning cannot be distinguished from belief, then
there is no eliminating thick ethical terms from the language of the social
sciences; for as long as social scientists have beliefs about the moral
qualities of their subjects, those beliefs, like any others, are wedded to
their words. Weber exhorts his colleagues not to include their moral or
political values in their teaching or writing of social science, but he does
not exhort them to give them up. He is concerned that the social scientists' values not be included with their facts, but he is not concerned
that social scientists have moral or political values. However, if these
values are absorbed into the language of their science, then their teaching
and writing of social science will be value-laden even if they replace the
terms of ordinary language with new, technical terms coined with the
express intention of eliminating values from their science.

According to Quine's account, the speakers who coin the new terms
apply them to or withhold them from an object on the basis of all their
beliefs about the object, not simply on the basis of some of them – namely,
those that are a matter of meaning alone. Thus, even if we accept the
fact/value distinction and view some of the speakers' beliefs as factual
and others as evaluative, the distinction doesn't carry over to the terms
– some terms factual and others evaluative – because the terms are attached
to all the speakers' beliefs – both factual and evaluative – and not merely
to some.[17]

Pure and applied research

A distinction is often drawn between pure and applied research.[18] The
aim of pure research, it is said, is to discover and communicate the truth,
while the aim of applied research is to use the truth to direct or recommend a policy or program of action. Pure research, according to this
view, seeks scientific knowledge for its own sake, and though it can be
used for either good or evil, it is itself morally and politically neutral;
whereas applied research includes directives or recommendations and, as
a result, is not. Pure research can be abused – used for wrongful purposes
– but, apart from its uses or applications, it cannot be judged to be right
or wrong but only true or false. Science, according to this view, is
political only in its applications.

Some of the proponents of neutrality believe that scientists who limit themselves to pure research are not responsible for harm caused by those who use or apply their work.

> The ideal of science as neutral and apolitical translated into the assumption that, as long as one had concentrated solely on one's science, one was exempt from blame; indeed, in 1945 some German scholars considered it a form of resistance simply to have kept the flame of science alive. The quiet pursuit of science constituted a kind of "inner emigration" that separated one from the culpability of government actions.[19]

However, other proponents of neutrality allow that even if the research is neutral, scientists can be held responsible for the use of it by others. E. O. Wilson can be held responsible for the consequences of teaching that females are genetically disposed to care for the young and males are not, or Richard Herrnstein for teaching that intelligence is inherited or tied to race, even if the teaching does not contain any thick or thin ethical terms.[20] Herrnstein can be held responsible for the actions of those who use his teachings to defend tracking in primary or secondary school, even if he is silent on how his teachings ought to be applied to issues of educational policy.

We can criticize the speech of a psychologist who says that race determines IQ for inspiring or causing acts of racial harassment, even if he does not recommend or endorse such acts. The psychologist may say that he is only describing the "facts"; he is not recommending how members of one race ought to be treated by members of another. If his speech leads someone to do wrong, he is not responsible for that, he might argue, for his speech does not include any recommendations to anyone to do anything at all. "I only stated the facts," he might say; "the people to blame are those who recommended or engaged in the harassment." The truth of the matter, however, is that the circle of responsibility cannot be drawn so narrowly. It can include responsibility for the harassment caused by a speaker's saying what (he believes) *is* no less than the harassment caused by his saying what (he believes) ought to be.[21]

Nevertheless, a distinction can be drawn between whether the words used give the audience reason to act and whether the use of the words causes the audience to act. Value-freedom is meant to insure that the words do not give someone reason to act but not to insure that a use of the words won't cause her to act. Moreover, on the liberal view, the findings of pure research are not a reason for action, although their presentation can be a cause of action. Since the questions of responsibility and neutrality are separate, the fact that pure researchers are responsible for their findings does not show that their research is not neutral.

Speech acts as reasons and causes

The liberal's distinction between the findings and their use is problematic. Descriptions, in the appropriate context, can have an imperative force. The sociologist who tells his colleagues "You get much better data if you ask directed questions" may be saying that they ought to ask directed questions even though he did not use the word "ought." Even if the sentences that social scientists use were free of all thick and thin ethical terms, it is possible that, in some of the circumstances in which they use them, they are not merely declaring how things are but prescribing how they ought to be; for whether they are declaring or prescribing is not a function of the sentences alone but of their use of the sentences in a context.

Because a speaker can prescribe what ought to be even with words that are or appear to be value-free, her act of speech can direct another's actions even when she uses the language of science and avoids the language of morals – that is, avoids thick and thin ethical terms. A psychologist who says "Student Jones has an IQ below 95" to a teacher whose job the psychologist knows is to assign students with IQs below 100 to "slow classes," for example, is using "is" words but can be properly understood by the teacher to be saying that Jones ought to be assigned to a slow class. The psychologist foresees that her speech act will cause the teacher to assign the student to a slow class, because she knows that the teacher will understand her to be directing him to do so, and so to be offering him a reason to assign the student to that class.

Even if a science were free of all thick and thin ethical terms, a speaker who uses the terms of the science could still be saying or implying what ought to be. If there is a morally important difference between pure and applied research, it is not due to the language of the research but to how the language is used and the context in which the findings of the research are reported. Even if the language of science is a collection of truths, the use of the language and the expression of those truths can be art rather than science; for the act of expressing an "is" can be a judgment of the right or wrong thing to do.

In his paper "Logic and Conversation," Paul Grice explains how speakers can exploit the principles that govern the use of language to communicate information that is not part of the proposition expressed by the speakers' words.[22] His explanation depends on his theory of "implicatures," and his theory can be used to explain how social scientists can communicate what ought to be even if they say only what is.

Grice's theory rests on the distinction between the semantics and the pragmatics of a language. Semantics has to do with the meaning of expressions of a language independent of their use, pragmatics with the use of language to produce certain effects. It is a semantic fact about the conjunction "and" in English, for example, that the sentence "Sociology and psychology are liberal sciences" implies "Psychology is a liberal science"; while it is a pragmatic fact about the use of "or" in English that when a speaker uses the sentence "Either sociology or psychology is a liberal science," she implies that she doesn't know which of them is. Both are facts about implication in English, but the first implication is semantic, because it depends solely on the meaning of "and," whereas the second is pragmatic, because it depends both on the meaning of "or" and the use of "or" by a speaker to communicate some information to an audience on a certain occasion.

To take another example, I know that you know that I was a subject in one of Stanley Milgram's obedience experiments and that, along with the other subjects, was misinformed about the experiment and resent Milgram's failure to seek my informed consent.[23] I say to you, "Milgram is uncompromisingly committed to informed consent." In saying these words in this context, I am implying that he is not; but the implication is not carried by the meaning of my words, by the semantic facts, but by facts about the use of these words in a certain setting. You request a letter from me on Milgram's research ethics. In reply, I write, "Milgram knows a lot about social psychology." In writing these words in this context, I am implying that his ethics as a researcher are questionable; the implication is not a consequence of the meaning of the words I use but of the rules that govern my use of them.

Proponents of value-freedom assume that value-freedom is a semantic fact about an expression in a language. Sentence A is value-laden, they assume, if and only if either A is a value-judgment or there is a sentence B which is a value-judgment – for example, an imperative sentence – and A semantically implies B. But their assumption overlooks pragmatic facts about the use of an expression in a language. As I explain in the next section, Grice gives us reason to believe that value-freedom is as much a pragmatic fact about the use of an expression as a semantic fact about the expression itself. Sentence A is value-laden when used in context C, Grice would say, if there is a proposition p which is a value-judgment and A pragmatically implies p when used in C. In addition, John Austin, as I explain in the last section of this chapter, gives us reason to believe that value-freedom is *only* a pragmatic fact about the use of an expression and not a semantic fact about the language at all. On Austin's view, whether a social scientist's speech describes what is or prescribes what ought to be is a matter not of the meaning of her words but of their force when she uses them in a particular setting.

Grice

Grice offers an explanation of how the use of language can produce pragmatic implications. His explanation rests on the idea of community-wide norms of linguistic cooperation. There are, he maintains, conversational norms that all the users of a language assume that every other user observes unless there is good evidence to the contrary. He calls these "conversational maxims." As examples of conversational maxims, Grice offers the maxims of "quantity" (make your contribution as informative as is required for the current purposes of the talk exchange), "relation" (make your contributions appropriate to the immediate need of the talk exchange), and "quality" (make contributions that are genuine and not spurious).

Any speaker who cares about the goals of talk exchanges can be expected to have an interest in observing these maxims. One speaker concludes that another is implicating p in uttering A in context C on the basis of the following syllogism:

1 Unless the speaker is implicating p in uttering A in C, the speaker is not observing the conversational maxims.
2 The speaker is observing the maxims.
3 The speaker is implicating p in uttering p in C.

Grice calls the implications that rest on this form of reasoning "conversational implicatures." Grice's conversational implicatures are a species of pragmatic implication.

When I respond to your request for a letter testifying to Milgram's ethics by writing "Milgram knows a lot about social psychology," you should conclude that I am implicating that Milgram's ethics are questionable:

1 Unless he is implicating that Milgram's ethics are questionable in writing "Milgram knows a lot about social psychology" in response to a request for a letter about his ethics, Root is not observing the maxim of relation.

2   Root is observing the maxim of relation.
3   Root is implicating that Milgram's ethics are questionable.

Though I do not say that Milgram's ethics are questionable, I conversationally implicate it, for unless that is what I intend to communicate, I am not speaking to your question and not making my contribution as informative as is required for the current purpose of our talk exchange.

How does this apply to the speech of social scientists? Consider the earlier example of the psychologist and the teacher. The teacher, whose job it is to assign students with IQs below 100 to slow classes, asks the psychologist, who knows what the teacher's job is, for a recommendation concerning Jones. The psychologist says, "Student Jones has an IQ below 95." The teacher reasons as follows: either the psychologist is flouting the maxim of relevance or he is implicating that Jones ought to be assigned to a slow class; I have no evidence that she is flouting the maxim (other than the fact that her words do not themselves speak to my request); therefore, she is implicating that Jones ought to be assigned to a slow class. The example shows that there are occasions on which, in uttering a sentence in the language of a social science, a social scientist can conversationally implicate a proposition that is not included in the meaning of her words or in what she says using those words. Moreover, the proposition she implicates can be a directive for action and therefore a judgment that is value-laden.

According to Grice, there are two categories of conversational implicatures: particularized and generalized. In the case of a particularized conversational implicature, what is implicated is carried by what is said on a particular occasion in virtue of special features of the context. My implicating that Milgram's ethics are questionable, in saying that he knows a lot about social psychology, is particularized, for it depends on the context – namely, one in which I am replying to a request for a recommendation on his ethics. In the case of a generalized conversational implicature, what is implied is normally carried by what is said, and is carried independent of knowledge of any special features of context. The implicature that the speaker does not know which disjunct is true when she uses a disjunction is generalized, for it is carried in different contexts in which she might be using the disjunction.

There are contexts, as I have shown, in which the "scientific" speech of a social scientist carries particularized conversational implicatures and in which the implicatures are prescriptive or evaluative. In these contexts, when the social scientist says what is, she implicates what ought to be. Here "is" and "ought" are not entirely heterogeneous, and though the social scientist's words seem to be value-free, part of what she communicates with them is a judgment that is value-laden. Whether a social scientist's speech is value-laden is a matter not merely of the words she uses but also of the conversational maxims that are understood to guide her in her use of words.

Objection: advocates of value-freedom could grant that value-freedom is a matter not merely of what a speaker says but also of what she implicates by what she says and could still call on social scientists to free their teaching and writings of value; for they could require them to avoid every context in which their speech would implicate what ought to be or to cancel any such implicature when it is carried by their speech. According to Grice, an implicature is cancellable if it can be removed by adding a clause which states that the speaker is flouting the conversational maxims, and all conversational implicatures are cancellable. The psychologist, for example, would not implicate that the student ought to be assigned to a slow class if she added the words "I don't mean to make my contribution as informative as is required" to her speech. Alternatively, she would not implicate that the student ought to be assigned to a slow class if she refused to report his IQ if asked to recommend the class to which he ought to be assigned.

On Grice's view, what a speaker communicates is a matter not merely of what she says but of what she intends her audience to believe by what she says. Unless the psychologist intends that the teacher believe that he ought to assign Jones to a slow class, she does not communicate that he ought to be by reporting Jones's IQ. Consequently, even if a social scientist cannot always avoid judgments of value by sticking to the language of science, she can avoid them by informing her audience that, in using the language of science, she intends to communicate no more than what she literally says. Speech in the social sciences would be value-free, advocates of value-freedom could say, if every speaker spoke only in the language of science and always prefaced her remarks with a disclaimer that would cancel any implicature concerning what ought to be done.

Reply: words alone do not cancel. The psychologist, let us imagine, regularly reports to a teacher the IQ scores of his students and knows that part of the teacher's responsibility is to assign the students to classes on the basis of the scores. The psychologist prefaces all her reports with the disclaimer that she is not recommending a use for the reports. She says that it is no part of her intention that any student be assigned to any class on the basis of her report of his or her IQ. Nevertheless, she continues to report IQs, knowing that students will be assigned to classes on the basis of her reports. What are we to make of her disclaimers?

A person does not intend every known consequence of her actions. The psychologist knows that her descriptions will result in class assignments, but the teacher cannot conclude from that alone that the psychologist intends the assignments. On the other hand, he cannot conclude merely from her disclaimer that she does not intend the assignments either. Given that the psychologist continues to measure and report the IQs of the students and knows the role her reports play within an established educational practice, the teacher can reasonably conclude that the psychologist is not flouting the conversational maxims and, despite her disclaimers, is not canceling the conversational implicature carried by her words in the context of the practice. Even if, as Grice suggests, conversational implicatures can be cancelled, they cannot always be cancelled by a verbal disclaimer. The psychologist's involvement in the practice of tracking students by IQ is too deep for her statement of intentions to be a mark of her intentions.

Speech in the social sciences can be value-laden even if every speaker speaks only in the language of science and always prefaces her remarks with the comment that she does not endorse any action that anyone might undertake on the basis of her remarks. Psychologists who, in speeches to educators, say that by nature males are better at mathematics than females and have reason to expect that their speech will be understood as a reason to offer boys a different education from girls can be implicating that boys ought to be offered a different education, even though they deny that they are making any recommendations at all. Whether they are implicating anything about the treatment of boys or girls depends on the context in which they communicate their beliefs about sexual difference and on whether there is an established practice or institutional arrangement in which words like these play a regular role and are understood to be a reason for public policy.

In contexts in which a psychologist's speech implicates that boys and girls ought to be treated differently, it directs the audience to treat them differently and, for that reason, is value-laden. However, whether the speech so directs the audience is not a simple matter of the meaning of the words. The term "IQ" may be a thick ethical term, but the direction that the psychologist gives the teacher in using it, she would give, no matter what new or technical term were coined to replace it. As long as the practice of assigning students to classes on the basis of their scores on a psychological test is maintained and research on IQ scores and the testing of IQ is part of that practice, directions are given in reporting the scores, even if the psychologist uses "scientific terms" to report them.

The use of apparently value-free or nonjudgmental terms can make the psychologist's speech appear to be free of practical force. Parents think that when the psychologist tests their children and reports the results, she is silent on how the schools ought to treat them. Thinking that the *but there is a sense in which this is true*

psychologist is only reporting what is, they are not concerned by the testing or the reporting even if they do not desire slow classes for their children, because the report does not order slow classes. The psychologist's use of scientific and apparently nonprescriptive language can mislead parents, even if that is no part of her intention. By saying only what the IQs of their children are, she is likely to receive more cooperation from the parents than she would were she to use thick or thin ethical terms or to order classes for the children.

The effect of replacing thick ethical terms with new, scientific, apparently nonjudgmental terms can mislead rather than inform an audience. In a certain setting, a psychologist who says that a child is slow will be understood by her audience to be saying or implicating that something is wrong with him or something about how he should be treated. A psychologist who says that he is learning-disabled will seem to be saying or implying less; but if, in the contexts in which they are used, the words "slow" and "learning-disabled" carry the same directives to the schools or the helping professions, the language of social science may merely obscure the practice of the psychologists. As Murray Edelman writes in a paper entitled "The Political Language of the Helping Professions":

> Social scientists, and a large segment of the public, have grown sensitive and allergic to agitational political rhetoric and to the ambiguities of such labels as "democracy," "communist" and "law and order." The most fundamental and long-lasting influences upon political beliefs flow, however, from language that is not perceived as political at all, but nonetheless structures perceptions of status, authority, merit, deviance, and the causes of social problems.[24]

The less political the language of the social sciences is perceived to be, the less sensitive or allergic the subjects of the social sciences will be to the language when it is applied to them; but the effects on the subjects on the practical level of using the less political language may be the same as the effects of the more political language. However, to the extent that the subjects are pacified by the less political language, they are less likely to resist and more likely to accept or cooperate with the social scientist's practice.

Austin

According to Grice, there is more to the act of using words than the act of stating a fact. Speakers can imply as well as state using a declarative or indicative sentence. They can use words to imply that p without saying that p at all. Speakers can direct their audience to action without saying what they ought to do. The psychologist can direct the teacher to assign the student to a slow class without saying that the teacher ought to do so, and the sociobiologist can direct the policymaker to offer boys and girls a different education without saying how boys or girls ought to be educated.

According to John Austin, we do many more things with apparently descriptive words or factual language than lay out facts or describe what we believe to be the case.

> Besides the question that has been very much studied in the past as to what a certain word *means*, there is a further question distinct from this as to what was the *force*, as we may call it, of the utterance. We may be quite clear what "Shut the door" means but not yet at all clear on the further point as to whether as uttered at a certain time it was an order, an entreaty or whatnot. What we need besides the old doctrine about meanings is a new doctrine about all the possible forces of utterances.[25]

Austin believes that certain verbs – he called them "performatives" – are used not to state some matter of fact but to perform some social or quasi-legal action. The verbs "to promise," "to endorse," "to censure," or "to recommend" (in the first-person present indicative active) are used to promise, endorse, censure, or recommend rather than to report a promise, an endorsement, a censure, or a recommendation; that is, they make, rather than describe, a happening.

According to Austin, in saying "I christen" in the appropriate circumstances, a speaker is not describing a christening, but christening. "When I say 'I name this ship the *Queen Elizabeth*' I do not describe the christening ceremony, I actually perform the christening; and when I say 'I do' (sc. take this woman to be my lawful wedded wife), I am not reporting on a marriage, I am indulging in it."[26] Whether he does in fact christen the ship in using the words depends on the setting. Not anyone could christen a ship by saying some appropriate words.

> Suppose that you are just about to name the ship, you have been appointed to name it, and you are just about to bang the bottle against the stern; but at that very moment some low type comes up, snatches the bottle out of your hand, breaks it on the stern, shouts out "I name this ship the *Generalissimo Stalin*," and then for good measure kicks away the chocks. Well, we agree of course

on several things. We agree that the ship certainly isn't now named the *Generalissimo Stalin*, and we agree that it's an infernal shame and so on and so forth.[27]

But the right person in the right setting does name a ship and does not report that she is naming it in saying "I name this ship *Generalissimo Stalin*." Whatever the meaning of her words, their force is not the force of a description. She is not saying what is, but making what she believes ought to be.

Often speakers use words to promise, endorse, censure, or recommend, Austin points out, without using a performative verb. Speakers can perform the speech act of promising, endorsing, censuring, or recommending with any variety of words. By including a performative verb in her sentence, a speaker makes the act she is performing explicit, but the act can be performed without using a performative to announce it. The school psychologist, for example, can warn parents of the effect of her IQ tests by saying, "I warn you that they will be used to assign classes" or by merely saying "They will be used to assign classes."

An economist can endorse a decrease in the minimum wage not only by saying "I endorse an increase" but also by saying "A decrease would reduce unemployment." The first form of words seems to express a value-judgment, while the second does not; but what Austin teaches is that an act of endorsement can be performed with either form of words. Since performing an act of endorsement is making a judgment of value, a social scientist can, in using apparently value-free language, be making a value-judgment.

Whether speech in the social sciences is value-free is a matter not of what the words used mean but of what Austin calls the "illocutionary force" of the words.

> I explained the performance of an act in this new and second sense as the performance of an "illocutionary" act, i.e., performance of an act *in* saying something as opposed to performance of an act *of* saying something; I call the act performed an "illocution" and shall refer to the doctrine of the different types of function of language here in question as the doctrine of "illocutionary forces."[28]

Proponents of value-freedom assume that if the meaning of the words that social scientists use in their teachings and writing does not include any evaluative element, then the teaching or writing is positive rather than normative or prescriptive. But whether it is positive or normative is a matter of force rather than meaning. Whether a speaker makes a recommendation or gives her audience a directive in uttering a certain sentence in a certain context is, on Austin's view, not a matter of the meaning – what he calls the "locutionary force" of the sentence – but of the illocutionary act performed when the speaker uses the sentence in a context.

> We first distinguished a group of things we do in saying something, which together we summed up by saying we perform a locutionary act, which is roughly equivalent to uttering a certain sentence with a certain sense and reference, which again is roughly equivalent to "meaning" in the traditional sense. Second, we said that we also perform illocutionary acts such as informing, ordering, warning, undertaking, &c, i.e., utterances which have a certain (conventional) force.[29]

The meaning of the words helps to determine the illocutionary force of the speech, but the meaning can vary while the force stays the same. A speaker can make a recommendation with a sentence that contains a thick or a thin ethical term, but she can also make a recommendation with a sentence that does not contain any ethical terms.

Let's return to the case of the school psychologist whose responsibility it is to measure student IQs and the teacher whose responsibility it is to assign students to classes on the basis of the psychologist's measurements. The psychologist says, "In this school students with IQs below 100 are assigned to slow classes." Her sentence contains no ethical terms, and she appears to be saying what is rather than what ought to be. However, we need to consider the force of her words in the context in which she offers them. They can have the force of a recommendation or a command and not the force of a statement or a report. If they have the force of a recommendation or a command, then even if the words are value-free, her speech is not; for, in the circumstances, to speak those words to the teacher is to tell him what to do – namely, to assign students like Jones to a slow class.

Many theories in the social sciences have both a positive (descriptive) and a normative (prescriptive) side. The theory of the rational economic man in economics, for example, can be written as a description of how households or firms do behave or a recommendation of how they ought to. Most economists assume that if the sentences of their theory are indicatives, they describe behavior, and if imperatives, prescribe it. Since the sentences of predictive economics are indicative, economists assume that when they use these sentences, they are describing, rather than prescribing, the behavior of households or firms.[30] In saying "A firm lays off employees until the marginal cost of laying off one more employee is equal to the marginal benefit," economists seem to be (truly or falsely) describing or stating the facts; whereas in saying "Lay off employees until the marginal cost of laying off one more employee is equal to the marginal benefit!," they seem to be (rightly or wrongly) recommending or directing a firm to do something.

Austin would agree that a theory can have both a positive and a normative side. He would disagree, however, that the side a theory is showing is merely a matter of the words a speaker uses to express it. Describing or stating and recommending or directing are what speakers do with their words, not merely a matter of what their words mean. Economists can use the same words to recommend and to describe. Whether they are recommending or describing has to do with the illocutionary force of their words, and the illocutionary force is a matter of both meaning and context. If the context changes, the force of the economists' remarks can change, even if their words stay the same.

There are contexts in which an economist who says "A firm lays off employees until the marginal cost of laying off one more employee is equal to the marginal benefit" is not describing behavior but recommending or directing it. In such a context, the theory of the firm is showing its normative rather than its positive side. Given that the theory, in most contexts, does not truly describe the behavior of firms and that most economists know that it doesn't, the most reasonable or most charitable interpretation of the economists' act of speech, when they use the words of the theory, may be that they are prescribing rather then describing the behavior of firms. If so, when economists present their theory of the firm, what they do is normative even if the words they use are positive.

Conclusion

Both Austin and Grice offer an account of the pragmatics of language that opposes the traditional distinction between a language of facts and a language of values. According to the traditional distinction, whether a language expresses fact or value is a matter of the meaning of the words in the language. According to Austin and Grice, it is always a matter of the use by a speaker of the words of the language in a particular context and with a particular audience. If they are correct, then removing thin or even thick ethical terms from the language of the social sciences will not purchase value-freedom; for, in many of the contexts in which the new words are used, the speakers will be recommending or directing rather than stating or describing (à la Austin) or will be implying what

[handwritten margin notes: "really needs a distinction between real cultural authority -- as in the priests ability to marry -- and possible cultural influence, as in the feminist says"]

ought to be (à la Grice). Pure science or research cannot earn value-freedom by merely eliminating value-words; it must eliminate every use of words that has the force of a directive or implies that something ought to be done. The question is whether, in each of the settings in which research or teaching in the social sciences presently occurs, it is possible to use the language of the social sciences without directing or recommending that something ought to be done.

[handwritten margin notes: "having new wage will mean more money"]

In chapter 7, I explain how the practice of sorting and categorizing data collected from or about human subjects relies on practices within their own community of normalization. The community's practices provide the setting in which the scientist's practice goes on, and, in such a setting, the scientist's words often have the illocutionary force of a recommendation even if they are free of illocutionary verbs. Similar attention to other settings in which research and teaching in the social sciences occur should show that often when the researcher speaks, no matter what her words, she does more than describe how the social world is; she prescribes how it ought to be.

[handwritten note: "another V&S example that are too easy. What directive force is implied when a sociologist says 'the agenda is 70%'?"]

NOTES

1 Mill, *Essays*, pp. 123–4.
2 Weber, *Methodology*, p. 52.
3 Though B implies A, A does not imply B, for "Fa" could entail "Ga" even though "F" and "G" differ in meaning.
4 G. E. Moore, *Principia Ethica* (Cambridge University Press, 1966), pp. 5–8.
5 K. Popper, "What can Logic do for Philosophy?," *Proceedings of the Aristotelian Society*, supp. vol. 22 (1948), p. 154.
6 R. M. Hare, *The Language of Morals* (Oxford University Press, 1964), p. 32.
7 Hume, *Treatise*, p. 423.
8 F. Waismann, "Verifiability," in *Logic and Language*, ed. A. Flew, 1st and 2nd series (Doubleday, 1965), pp. 122–51.
9 Ibid., p. 129.
10 If the cases are left uncovered by the definition, then the term is neither true nor false of them: the semantic value of the term for these cases is undesignated.
11 The governments of South America offer a real example. Are Venezuela, Peru, Colombia, and Brazil democracies or not? Consider the following recent story from the *New York Times* (Dec. 6, 1992) : "Since 1989, when South America's last military dictator was toppled, the continent has been characterized as democratic throughout. But this political-science label papers over deep stains in a region where democracy is often new and far from consolidated. . . . Outwardly democratic, Venezuela's two major parties, led by Perez and Caldera, were built in the 1940s along authoritarian lines, with power restricted to small ruling circles. Party elites hand-pick judges and congressional

candidates. . . . Forty-four percent of Venezuelans responding to a poll last month said they would support a coup to remove Perez from office. But an overwhelming 93 percent also said that democracy is the best form of government for Venezuela. Playing to such sentiment, the military plotters have billed their revolts as bids to save democracy."

12 Many historians who write about Athens at the time of Socrates describe it as a democracy even though, as they themselves note, female citizens did not have the right to vote or any other political rights (except the right to pass the political rights of the fathers of their male children on to those children). Were these historians strong believers in women's equality, it is less likely that they would have chosen to call Athens "democratic." That is, I assume that the meaning of the term "democratic" for these historians includes positive evaluative content, and the fact that they believe that "democratic" is true of Athens rests on their own negative or ambivalent attitudes towards women.

13 See, e.g., Laudan, *Science and Values,* pp. xi–xiv.

14 I question the distinction between scientific and nonscientific values. The proponents of value-freedom, as I argue in chapter 2, must show that there is a reason why only judgments of scientific value should be included in a science. Weber's reasons for excluding judgments of value, I argue, are a reason for excluding scientific as well as nonscientific values; for his reasons are that all judgments of ultimate value (scientific and nonscientific alike) are irrational and that disputes over the judgments of science ought to be resolvable by reason.

15 W. V. O. Quine, *Word and Object* (MIT Press, 1960), pp. 37–42.

16 See D. Papineau, *For Science in the Social Sciences* (St Martin's Press, 1978), pp. 164–5, for a discussion of this process.

17 Hare's distinction between thick and thin ethical terms is based on a theory of meaning, opposed to Quine's, that assumes a real distinction between meaning and collateral information. In my argument against value-free terms, I assume, but do not show, that Quine's account of meaning is better than Hare's.

18 See, e.g., Beales, *Politics of Social Research.*

19 Proctor, *Racial Hygiene,* p. 293.

20 R. Herrnstein, *IQ in the Meritocracy* (Little Brown, 1973), and Wilson, "Human Decency is Animal."

21 Speech itself can be an act of harassment. Some sexual harassment policies include speech that portrays women as inviting or delighting in sexual violation or assault as a form of sexual harassment. It is not necessary to show that the speech causes men to assault women to show that it harms women. Speech that portrays members of one sex as inviting or delighting in sexual assault can also be seen as harassment.

22 G. P. Grice, "Logic and Conversation," in *The Logic of Grammar,* ed. D. Davidson and G. Harman (Wadsworth, 1975), pp. 64–78.

23 For a discussion of Milgram's research, see chapter 6.

24 Edelman, "Political Language," 45–6.

25 J. L. Austin, "Performative Utterances," in *Philosophical Papers* (Oxford University Press, 1961), p. 238.

26 Ibid., p. 222.

27 Ibid., pp. 226–7.
28 J. L. Austin, *How to Do Things with Words*, 2nd edition (Harvard University Press, 1975), pp. 99–100.
29 Ibid., p. 109.
30 Though, as I explain in chapter 5, the economists' words include ideal-types that do not describe how firms or households actually behave. At best the behavior approximates the type. Moreover, the sentences of neoclassical theory are, by now, known to have weak predictive power; as a result, when economists continue to advance them, there is reason to doubt that they intend to be describing the actual economic world.

10

Social science and perfectionism

As I explain in chapter 1, social scientists, in pursuing the liberal ideal of value-neutrality, seek a form of social research and educational practice that is acceptable to constituents with different and competing commitments. Value-neutrality is possible, they think, because science abstracts from the values that people attach to objects and events, including their own actions and institutions, to reveal facts about their underlying nature or character; and neutrality is desirable because, on the liberal view, questions of value are not rationally resolvable, the interests of social science are better served by avoiding values, and neutrality contributes to political and personal autonomy.

There is an alternative view of the social sciences, however, which eschews value-neutrality and does not attempt to separate facts from values, but rather seeks after the facts in ways which advance some set of substantive values or one conception of human perfection over another. On this alternative, perfectionist view, the social scientist is overtly partisan and openly chooses her methods or validates her findings on the basis of some moral or political commitment. The research is designed to advance these commitments, and they explicitly guide its conduct.

A perfectionist science is no better than the ideal of human perfection it is designed to advance. Nazi anthropology was perfectionist and was designed to show that Aryans were a superior people. Such a science is more dangerous and more objectionable than a liberal science that forbids talk of superiority. No case can be made for perfectionism as a general approach to the social sciences, for some such approaches are contemptible, while others are admirable. The question is not whether to settle for perfectionist science but what conception of the good we want our science to be advancing. On the perfectionist view, the quality of some teaching and research in the social sciences is measured at least partly by the quality of the moral or political reasons for undertaking it. The poor moral reasoning that led Nazi researchers to pursue their theories of racial limits is as much a measure of the quality of their research, on this view, as their misuse of statistical reasoning or poor techniques of data collection.[1]

Many recent perfectionist alternatives to the liberal sciences are communitarian. The scientists attempt to promote a substantive conception of the good life based on the way of life or shared ends of a particular community. Research and teaching in the science is designed to advance these ends, and the community has a voice or a hand in how the research or teaching is conducted. To the extent that I can identify with the community's values, I can support their science. Communitarian research includes devices for increasing (rather than limiting) the active presence of the subjects in the conduct of the research and aims more at helping the subjects to learn about themselves than at finding theories or models by which others can predict or explain their behavior.[2]

Communitarian approaches to the social sciences have a long history, extending back to Engels's work with the working classes in Manchester, Marx's idea of the proletariat as a vanguard class, and the efforts of members of the Frankfurt school to offer a social science that ties theory to practice, and forward to recent feminist research in the social sciences. Value-neutrality is not an ideal for feminists currently working in the social sciences any more than it was for Marx; feminist research is openly partisan and seeks to advance the values of a community of women, just as Marx's research was partisan towards the working class.[3] "The postulate of *value-free* research, of neutrality and indifference towards the research objects, has to be replaced by *conscious partiality*, which is achieved through partial identification with the research objects."[4]

In this chapter, I will consider three examples of the communitarian approach – critical theory, participatory research, and feminist social science – and explain how they are alternatives to the traditional, liberal approach to the social sciences. My aim is to show how social research that is openly tied to the perspectives and politics of a particular community is possible and the ways in which it can be desirable.

Communitarian social science is not the only perfectionist alternative to the liberal sciences, but it is especially attractive because it places the research directly in the service of the subjects of the science. Whereas liberals would be pleased if their science did some good to the communities they chose to study, communitarians would object to their science if it didn't. My impression is that liberal research often takes more from its subjects than it returns to them; but the important methodological point is that, on the liberal view, the value of the research does not depend at all on the balance sheet – on who receives more, the social scientist or her subjects – whereas on the communitarian view, in measuring the quality of the research, the balance sheet matters.[5]

Communitarian approaches are not all equal, and many raise serious methodological questions. One aim of this chapter is to raise and answer some of these questions. Of the various communitarian approaches, I find participatory research most attractive, for it helps the subjects to invent new kinds and to use them to sort the facts and features of their lives. Where there are imbalances of power or authority within a community, a program or campaign to address the problem usually requires new categories or kinds, for many of the old ones help to sustain the status quo. The examples of participatory research described in this chapter all include the invention of kinds as part of a program to alter the balance of power and increase the authority of the subjects.

Critical theory

Jürgen Habermas is a prominent, contemporary proponent of critical theory. In his book *Knowledge and Human Interests,* he maintains that there are three different ways to study social life and that each is designed to serve a different human interest.[6] The most familiar is the approach of the natural sciences, or what Habermas calls the "empirical-analytic sciences." According to him, the empirical-analytic sciences are designed to serve technical interests and, in particular, an interest in predicting and controlling natural events. Physics and chemistry are the paradigms, and, on Habermas's view, many social sciences – those I have been calling the "liberal sciences" – attempt to emulate them. They embrace the ideals of neutrality and objectivity and seek general laws with which to predict or control events in the social world.

A second, different approach to the study of social life is offered by the humanities or what Habermas calls the "historical-hermeneutic sciences." Their aim is to interpret history, language, and works of art and literature – texts or artifacts that carry meaning. They serve practical interests and, in particular, an interest in developing and maintaining the mutual understanding and shared meanings necessary for a common culture and a shared social life.

The third approach is displayed in the theories of Marx and Freud, or what Habermas calls the "critical sciences." They are concerned not with prediction or interpretation but with criticism and are designed to serve the emancipatory interests of empowering or liberating exploited or oppressed people by offering them a critique of their political or economic condition.

Habermas's principal thesis is that critique, the product of the critical sciences, is a distinctive form of knowledge with its own methods, standards of reasoning, and ideal of justification. He calls each of the three different approaches – namely, the empirical-analytic, the hermeneutical, and the critical – "science," because he believes that each offers something that can be properly called "knowledge" and sees science as any disciplined activity whose aim is the acquisition of knowledge. That is, he opposes the idea shared by most researchers in the liberal sciences that the empirical-analytic approach is the only one that deserves the honorific title "science" or whose results deserve the honorific term "knowledge."

A critical science of society, as Habermas sees it, is different from an empirical-analytic science in a number of important ways: in aim, structure, and justification.[7] The aim of empirical science is to present or describe the world as it is and discover the means to predict how it will be and ideally to control it: "Theories of the empirical sciences disclose reality subject to the constitutive interest in the possible securing and expansion, through information, of feedback-monitored action. This is the cognitive interest in technical control over objectified processes."[8] The aim of a critical science, on the other hand, is to show what is wrong with the world as it is and help to improve it. The critical sciences borrow from Marx the idea that the proper aim of social theory is the "relentless criticism of all existing conditions of the time." As Habermas explains:

> The systematic sciences of social action, that is economics, sociology, and political science, have the goal, as do the empirical-analytic sciences, of producing nomological knowledge. A critical social science, however, will not remain satisfied with this. It is concerned with going beyond this goal to determine when theoretical statements grasp invariant regularities of social action as such and when they express ideologically frozen relations of dependence that can in principle be transformed.[9]

While an empirical-analytic science is designed to reveal the facts of social, economic, or political life, a critical science is designed to reveal how those facts oppress or severely limit the freedom of the members of some groups – for example, women, people of color, or the working class – and to lead the members to act to improve their economic or political prospects.

While the empirical-analytic sciences are limited to questions of means – how to cause a given effect – a critical science is centrally concerned with questions of ends – whether an effect is morally or politically desirable. The aim of an empirical science is to supply one of the premises of the policy syllogism, and the aim of a critique is to supply both.[10] The rationality assumed by an empirical science is instrumental rationality, or the rationality of means, whereas that assumed by a critical science is political rationality, or the rationality of ends.[11]

An empirical-analytic science contains statements about the causal structure of the world and the data against which those statements are to be tested.

> In the empirical sciences the frame of reference . . . establishes rules both for the construction of theories and for their critical testing. Theories comprise hypothetico-deductive connections of propositions, which permit the deduction of lawlike hypotheses with empirical content. The latter can be interpreted as statements about the covariance of observable events; given a set of initial conditions, they make predictions possible.[12]

A critical science, by contrast, contains statements about how subjects view that world and how the views are ideological – that is, false – but function to legitimate a form of economic or political life which disadvantages many of the people who hold them.[13] A critical science is called "ideology critique," for it is critical of the view of the subjects; indeed, the very act of calling a view "ideological" is an act of criticism, since it says that the view is false but serves a politically undesirable purpose.

Critical theories and the ideal of partisanship

Critical theories are perfectionist, for they are designed not to be value-neutral but partisan. Value-neutrality is not an ideal for a critical theory, but part of the ideology that the theory is designed to criticize. Critical theories are always critical for a particular community, and the values they seek to advance are the values of that community. In that respect, critical theories are communitarian.

One example of a critical science is Marx's theory of history, which is critical for the working class. He theorizes that the beliefs of capitalists and proletarians about private ownership of the means of production are false but have the effect of legitimating the roles of capitalists and proletarians and giving members of both classes a reason to accept and conform to them. The aim of the theory is to reveal to members of the working class how capitalist ownership of the means of production exploits them and to offer them a reason to resist their exploitation.

Some feminist theorists borrow from Marx's theory of history but offer a theory that is critical for women rather than the working class.[14] They theorize that our common beliefs about the sexual division of labor are false but have the effect of legitimating traditional sex roles and giving men and women reason to accept and conform to them. Their aim is to reveal to women how the sexual division of labor exploits them and to motivate women to resist the traditional roles. While economic class is the critical category for Marx and sex the critical category for feminists, they share the idea that a theory of a society should focus on exploitation and oppression – the domination of one group of people by another – and explain how the society's laws, politics, economics, religion, and culture enforce them.

A critical theory does not aim merely to describe or explain exploitation and oppression but, in addition, to relieve them. The theory is intended to emancipate the members of the oppressed group by making them aware of the forces allied against them; for it is assumed that if they knew the truth about their situation, they would have a reason to change it. The reasoning seems to be this: subjects accept a role that is oppressive or harmful to their interests because of a mistaken belief that it is fair or harmless; a critical theory shows that the belief is ideological and thereby reveals the harm; revealing the harm does not eliminate the role but does offer the subjects a reason to oppose it.

For critical theorists, the standard for choosing or accepting a social theory is the reflective acceptability of the theory by members of the community for whom the theory is critical. They are the intended audience for the theory and the final judges of whether the theory is acceptable. Nancy Hartsock, who borrows from Marx but offers a theory critical for women, writes: "I suggest that, like the lives of proletarians according to Marxian theory, women's lives make available a particular and privileged vantage point on male supremacy, a vantage point that can ground a powerful critique of the phallocratic institutions and ideology that constitute the capitalist form of patriarchy."[15] Unless the subjects – the women or the proletarians – accept the judgments of value and ideas about oppression expressed in the theory, after thorough consideration in conditions of full information and full freedom, the theory is not acceptable.

A critical theory addressed to the proletariat or to women is acceptable only if, after appropriate discussion and reflection, it is accepted by them. The value-judgments of those who occupy the privileged standpoint are included not as data but as a source of validation, and, as a result, the theories are not value-neutral but partisan to the values of the subjects who are given the authority to validate them. For feminists like Hartsock, as for Marx and other critical theorists, politically value-laden research produces more complete and less distorted social analyses than research that attempts to be value-neutral.

Privileging the subject

In chapter 8, I explain how little privilege the subject enjoys within the liberal sciences. Theories must fit the facts, and though the subjects are the facts, they have no say in deciding whether a theory fits them. Critical theories give the subjects a say. They act as informants – like bilingual informants for a linguist trying to translate the informant's language. The informants are allowed to judge the correctness of the translation, and the subjects are allowed to judge the correctness or validity of the theory.

The burden of a critical theory is to explain why the subjects' authority is deserved. Why should the subjects have a say as to whether the theory fits them, and why is their attitude toward the theory even relevant? Critical theorists give a number of different answers to these questions. Some give practical or pragmatic answers. The aim of their theory, they say, is to emancipate the subject, to empower her and help her to escape the social roles that exploit or oppress her. The theory emancipates a subject by removing her reasons for accepting or conforming to these roles. To succeed, the subject needs to be convinced that her reasons are not good reasons but ideological reasons, and she will not be convinced unless she accepts the view of her world offered by the theory. In other words, acceptance by the subject is relevant because the aim or end of the theory is to get the subject to do something – resist namely – and her accepting the theory is the means to secure her resistance.

Habermas cites Freud's theory of psychoanalysis in explaining the authority owed the subject.[16] The aim of psychoanalysis, he explains, is not principally to describe or diagnose the client's or analysand's neurotic condition but to cure it; but, in order to cure the condition, the analysand must be brought to accept the analyst's theory or interpretation of her condition. In other words, the basis of the analysand's authority is practical; granting her the authority to validate or invalidate the theory is a means of effecting a cure, and effecting a cure is the aim of the theory.

Freud's theory is a critical but not a social theory; for it is critical for an individual – a particular neurotic person – and not for a socially exploited or oppressed class – for example, women or the proletariat.[17] Nevertheless, Habermas believes that the logic behind Freud's psychological theory and Marx's social theory is the same. The aim of Marx's social theory, on his view, is to cure the social or political ills of the members of the working class, not merely to describe or diagnose them, and in order to cure the ills, the members must be brought to accept the theory.

The problem with critical theory

The practical or pragmatic defense of critical theories is problematic, for it seems to ignore the question of truth; yet even a critical theory, it would seem, must be tested by the truth. Even if a subject changes her mental condition by accepting a theory like Freud's, the change is a cure only if the diagnosis of her original condition was true; that is, only if she really was psychoneurotic. The theory must not only lead to a change, but the change must be an improvement. Whether the change is an improvement, however, depends on whether the theory's account of the original condition was true. The workers of the world must be oppressed in order for a critical theory to free them; but whether they are oppressed is a question of whether the theory's account of their condition is true.

The critical theorist ties the theory to the practice. The test of a theory is a matter of what is done with it. The correct or best theory, she says, is the one that leads to the most successful practice. However, whether a practice is successful is itself a matter of whether the theory offers a true description of the condition of its subjects. As a result, practice does not offer a test of a theory separate from testing the theory's truth but only a test that assumes or relies on the theory's being true.

Critical theorists do address the question of truth. Hartsock argues, for example, that under the proper circumstances, the fact that the subjects accept the theory is evidence of its truth; for the subjects' reflective judgments about whether their own beliefs are ideological are more likely to be true than the judgments of any so-called disinterested outsider or anyone who is exploiting her.[18] According to Hartsock, material life is expressed in one's class position and limits the understanding one can have – whether proletarian or capitalist – of the deployment of power within the society. But the material life of the proletarians, Hartsock explains, limits their understanding of the inequality of power in capitalist society less; for the interests of the capitalist class are better served by misunderstanding the inequalities of power than are the interests of the proletarians. Their interests do not depend on the oppression of another class, while the interests of the capitalists do.[19]

Hartsock's explanation, however, relies on a number of very contested assumptions – for example, that an individual's interpretations and interests are a product of her class position or sex and that whether her interpretations are true is a matter of whether a true interpretation would better serve her interests than a false one – and assumptions like these would seem to be for an empirical-analytic rather than a critical science to secure. If so, Hartsock has not shown that the methods for justifying a critical theory and an empirical theory are different, but rather that a critical theory is acceptable only if, like an empirical theory, it fits with the facts about a subject's social position and interests.

The problem facing Hartsock and other critical theorists can be put another way. A critical theory is acceptable only if its subjects' interpretations or beliefs are, in fact, ideological; but the question of whether they are ideological would seem to be a question for an empirical-analytic rather than a critical science and not one over which the subjects can be simply assumed to have reliable insight or authority. Though critical theorists claim that justification is different for a critical than for an empirical science, their theories seem to belie it, for they rely on many assumptions that seem to require traditional, empirical justification.

Similar objections can be raised against Habermas's account of the difference between an empirical and a critical science. Knowledge, he maintains, inheres in interests and can only be measured or tested in light of those interests. "[Interests] determine the aspect under which reality can be objectified and thus made accessible to experience."[20] It is an illusion – he calls it the "objectivist illusion" – that the universe can be understood or known as a collection of facts independent of the interests of the knower.[21] Each science is organized within its own framework of interests (Habermas calls them "knowledge-constitutive interests"), and validity in the science is relative to the framework. No object is simply an object of knowledge; rather, it is an object of knowledge from a certain viewpoint or in the context of some human interest.[22]

In the empirical-analytic sciences, nature is an object of knowledge relative to an interest in technical prediction or control; whereas in the historical-hermeneutical sciences, the expressions of culture (Habermas calls them "meaning structures") are the objects of knowledge relative to an interest in developing or maintaining mutual understanding. In the critical sciences, culture again is the object, but now the context is an interest in human freedom. The validity of a critical theory, Habermas argues, cannot be measured by the knowledge-constitutive interests of the empirical-analytic sciences any more than the knowledge-constitutive interests of the critical sciences can measure the validity of a theory in the empirical-analytic sciences.

Habermas's account rests on two ideas: that knowledge is always connected to interest and that the interest is not always an interest in the truth, or what the truth is varies with the knowledge-constitutive interests of the science. But even if Habermas is right that the object of knowledge is not always truth or that truth is relative to a science or to human interests, critical theories include judgments – namely, judgments about the deployment of power or the subordination of one class by another – whose truth would seem to be a matter for the empirical-analytic sciences. That is, the theory relies on the judgment that some group of people is oppressed. The question of whether it is oppressed is not a purely empirical question; but neither is it a purely critical one to be settled by a critique of ideology. Knowing whether the group is oppressed depends on knowing some facts about political and economic power that seem to fall within the empirical-analytic sciences.[23]

But, more to the point of this chapter, even if critical theories do offer a distinctive approach to research in the social sciences, they do not offer a fully communitarian one, for they do not abandon the ideals of expertise of the liberal sciences; though a critical science is supposed to transfer authority from the expert or theorist to her subjects, theorists like Marx and Freud hold on to their authority; for in treating their subjects as deluded, benighted, self-deceived, or suffering from false consciousness, they give them little or no say in how the research is to be conducted. Moreover, the subjects' say on whether the theory of working-class oppression or sexual repression is acceptable is won only after appropriate discussion and reflection, and Marx and Freud alone decide whether the discussion and reflection are appropriate.

Many of their subjects resist the claim that they are self-deceived or benighted. From their vantage point, the claim is perverse or foolish, but Marx and Freud persist; they see the resistance as a reason for more discussion and reflection rather than as a reason to revise their theory. They offer a program of discussion and reflection to bring the subjects to see the truth and overcome their illusions. Freud offers a program of psychotherapy to remove the scales from his clients' eyes, while Marx offers political training and consciousness raising for the working class. But are they offering discussion and reflection or brainwashing? The programs correct rather than impair the vision of the subjects only if the subjects are benighted before, rather than after, the treatment or the training. Of course, Marx and Freud believe that their subjects are benighted before, but this belief is not one that the subjects are given any authority to question. No matter how firm their resistance or opposition to the research, and, in particular, to the standards of appropriate discussion and reflection, the subjects' resistance is discounted, and Marx and Freud alone decide when the views of their subjects should be taken seriously. Supporters of Marx and Freud would reply that those decisions are themselves subject to the test of reflective acceptability, but this does not answer the question of who wears the trousers but only forestalls it. Marx and Freud cannot both distrust their subjects – as their theories give them reason to do – and trust them to know whether the distrust is justified.

Participatory research

There are other openly partisan approaches to the social sciences that do more to transfer trust and authority from the experts to the subjects of research. A common umbrella name for these approaches is "participatory research."[24] Participatory research is a form of schooling. The aim is for the subjects to learn to do research and learn the economics, politics, and sociology of their community by researching them for themselves. Collecting and sorting data, formulating and testing hypotheses, or advancing predictions or explanations become lessons, and the benefits of the research extend beyond the findings to include the skills acquired by the subjects in helping to plan and carry out the research.

All research aims to make someone wiser, but participatory research differs from liberal research in specifically aiming to make the participant subjects wiser. As I explain in chapter 6, the liberal protocols for collecting data in the social sciences often limit the interviewer's responses to a respondent's questions and limit how much the experimenter can inform the experimental subject of the nature of the experiment. The interviews and experiments are not designed to educate the subject, and the methods used to assure that the data are reliable and valid often require that little information and even some disinformation be passed on to her.

Any increase in the store of knowledge resulting from the research is from the findings rather than the conduct of the research and is usually for an audience that doesn't include the experimental or interview subjects. The liberal sciences present their findings to a relatively select audience in specialized publications and classrooms and write them in an academic or professional language of experts. Moreover, the research is often pitched to those who fund or pay for it, and this group seldom includes those whose lives the research is designed to document or explore.

According to the ideals of participatory research, the primary recipients and users of the research should be the participant subjects, and the research should be designed to assure that they are the people whom the research makes wiser. They should learn both from their role as participants in the research and from the findings of their research. This requires that the content, form, and aim of the research be defined in terms of their interests and understanding and that they be given authority over how the research is to be conducted.

Participatory research has been used in East Africa, South Asia, and South America and in poor or underdeveloped regions of the United States as an alternative to liberal research which, like many traditional economic development programs, ignores the perspective of the local people and substitutes the views of the researcher or development official for those of the inhabitants of the region. In 1977, supporters of participatory research organized the Participatory Research Network and worked with the International Council of Adult Education to further the idea of people as experts and research as a form of community-based adult education.

For example, in the United States, participatory research is part of the program of the Appalachian Alliance, a coalition of community groups attempting to influence land-ownership policies in Appalachia.[25] In 1978, a group of over 60 citizens and scholars, under the auspices of the Alliance, conducted a research project on land ownership in 80 counties in 6 Appalachian states: West Virginia, Virginia, Tennessee, North Carolina, Alabama, and Kentucky. They collected ownership and tax data from county courthouses using publicly available tax records and used the data to establish the patterns of land ownership in the region and reveal the impact of the patterns on the rural communities.

Rather than calling in experts to study the question of ownership patterns, the Alliance sought to organize groups of people from the community to study the patterns and document their impact for themselves. Their aim was as much to develop the skills of the people to do research on the economics of the region as to find out who owned the land.

> From the beginning, it was hoped that the land ownership study would provide comprehensive information that would be useful to local groups and which would influence regional and national policies on land-related questions. Yet, also from the beginning, there were other equally important goals:
>
> – to provide a model for citizens doing their own research, growing out of their own local needs and concerns, rather than from professional consulting firms doing research based on needs and interests of governmental agencies;
>
> – through the research process, to train local citizens and groups in obtaining information they need;
>
> – through the research process, to develop a network of individuals and groups who would be concerned with land-related issues and

who would be committed to using the results of the study for constructive action;

– using the results of the research process, to begin to educate and to mobilize a broader constituency of local groups for action on land-related questions in their own communities, as well as at the state and regional level.[26]

One aim of the research was to discover and document the truth: to find out who owned the land and how the ownership affected its use and contributed to regional poverty. Such a goal could have been achieved by liberal science. The other aims, however, could not have been; for they required that the research be openly partisan and, in particular, that it promote land reform.

Feminist social science

Feminist research in the social sciences usually attempts to erase the line between the researcher and her subject.[27] Some feminist social science is grounded in critical theory – a theory that is critical for women – while other feminist research parallels one or another form of participatory research. Common to all of them is the idea that the research and teaching about society should promote the shared ends of some community of women. A research project in Cologne, West Germany, in 1976–7, for example, grew out of an effort to draw attention to and help address the problem of wife battering.[28] The research was part of a campaign to create a shelter for battered women. The campaign did not start with an explicit interest in research, but the need to document the seriousness and extent of the problem led a group of women who were campaigning for the shelter to survey wife beating in Cologne. Such surveys are usually prepared by professional social scientists using standard interviewing techniques or official records, but in this case the women were led to develop their own methods for proving the need for the shelter because of the cost of professional research, the absence of records, and their desire to increase their own power and authority on questions concerning the safety of women.

The group established the need for a shelter by organizing street actions and conducting interviews with women and men who were attracted to them. The actions and interviews were reported by the press. The continuing publicity brought women in search of shelter to members of the group, and members sheltered some of them in their own homes. In using their own homes as shelters, they called more public attention to the problem of wife battering and increased the pressure on the municipal authorities to act. The municipal authorities began to document cases of battering, and in time there were statistics to show that many women were in need of protection.[29] Finally, the Social Welfare Department was convinced or pressured into admitting that there was a problem of wife battering in Cologne and that the city should fund a shelter.

The research on battering and on patterns of land ownership challenges the assumption (at the core of the liberal approach) that in research, labor should be divided, and control of the work turned over to experts. It also challenges the idea that research should always precede and stand apart from political action, for in Appalachia and Cologne, research and a campaign for political change were intentionally run together. The efforts to learn about the problems of land ownership and wife battering were made part of a campaign to solve them. The Alliance and the Cologne group, a liberal critic might say, acted before they knew what to do; but, on the communitarian view, it could be said that they came to know what to do by doing it.

In Cologne, for example, the group could not have known the extent of wife battering before setting out to campaign for a shelter, because wife battering was not yet either a privately or a publicly recognized kind of conduct within the community. In 1976–7, many women who were struck by their husbands would not have seen the striking as battering, and city officials would not have counted it as battering or as a matter of public or state interest had the women come to them with a complaint. The campaign and the research by the Cologne group did not generate data in the usual sense of evidence that independent reviewers could use to validate claims of wife battering and domestic abuse. Rather, they changed the nature or status of the violence against women by establishing a practice within which the husbands' behavior would be seen as abusive and criminal rather than as a show of temper, a fit of pique, a lovers' quarrel, a domestic squabble, or a matter of family discipline. The campaign against wife battering was needed to invent the kind, and until the kind was invented, it was not possible to sort the behavior of husbands towards their wives in Cologne as cases of wife battering.

As I explain in chapter 7, through their own efforts alone, social scientists – experts trained in survey research – cannot invent kinds like wife battering; but without the invention of the kind, they cannot measure the frequency of the behavior. The wives had to see themselves and be seen by others in the community as sharing an important trait and as having been subjected to the same kind of mistreatment; but only through participatory research and their participation in the research could the facts of wife battering be discovered, because only through such shared effort could the kind have been invented.

Theory and practice

Participatory research and feminist social science are not merely a form of investigation or a search for facts; they are also a form of political action – a practice.[30] They are conducted not only to advance knowledge but to promote social change. The study of land ownership organized by the Appalachian Alliance was designed to discover the pattern of ownership but equally to mobilize the citizens to work for land reform in their own communities. The training, data gathering, devising of the case studies, and networking were designed to arouse and organize the subjects into an interest group to oppose current governmental policies as well as to equip them with the knowledge and understanding needed to give their opposition intellectual authority.

The liberal sciences, by contrast, aim to keep theory separate from practice; for practice is always partisan, and, on the liberal view, theory should be value-neutral. The liberal sciences aim to provide knowledge but not to favor the use or application of the knowledge to support one social practice rather than another. On the liberal view, every practice is served equally well by valid scientific theories and reliable scientific knowledge.

The liberal sciences accept the Baconian edict that those who best obey nature will in the end best command it, or, in other words, that an interest in practice is best served by a refusal to allow that interest to shape or influence the content or form of theory.[31] According to the edict, in the long run, the most effective strategy for improving or bettering anyone's condition is by not allowing one's interest in improvement to influence one's understanding of the nature of the condition.

Participatory research rejects Bacon's edict and aims at a social theory based on a social practice.[32] As John Gaventa and Billy D. Horton explain the participatory approach:

> Most of the premises of participatory research are not particularly new. Rather, it is the combination of research and action into a strategy for radical social change that should appeal to progressive social scientists. Most of us, including those who have Marxist leanings, have proven ourselves fairly incompetent at combining theory and practice in our own careers. While the participatory research approach has some weaknesses and occasionally falls victim to its own illusions, it nevertheless provides us with one example of an attempt to integrate theory and practice. For that reason alone it deserves our serious attention.[33]

The approach integrates theory and practice, for one important test of the research is how successful it is as a form of education and community organizing. However accurate the research findings, the research is not good as research, according to the participatory ideal, unless the practice – the act of carrying out the study – trains, organizes, informs, authorizes, politicizes, and improves the prospects, of the research subjects.

Though liberal research aims to keep theory separate from practice, it does not do so; for, as I have argued throughout this book, however earnestly the liberal sciences attempt to be value-neutral, they are always partisan. Being partisan, they serve interests other than truth, and the form of their research and the content of their findings serve the interests of some communities better than others. As a rule, the interests best served are not those of their subjects and, in particular, not those of their participant subjects. Since, as I explain in chapter 1, much of the partisanship is institutional, it often goes unnoticed or unintended. Often the partisanship is in the kinds or categories (see chapter 7) the scientists use to sort their data or in the way they distinguish between conditions that are fixed and conditions that are variable (see chapter 4) or choose their *ceteris paribus* conditions and separate causes from mere correlations (see chapter 5).

Traditional, liberal research in sociology is based on kinds like occupation, marital status, wealth, income, educational level, religious affiliation, stage of life, criminal record, citizenship, and level of political participation, and the existence and continuation of these kinds rely on their application in the criminal justice system, schools, churches, and clinics. Liberal sociologists believe that their theories of sexual deviance, inner-city crime, teenage suicide, or domestic violence are independent of their applications, but they are not, for (as I explain in chapter 7) the kinds are not discovered but invented, and invented in the courts, prisons, schools, churches, and clinics in which the sociologists' theories are applied.

If the social sciences cannot be neutral, the question is for whom, not whether, they should be partisan. The question is not whether a theory is separate from practice, but on whose practice it should rely or whose practice it should serve. Before the campaign for the shelter, there was no practice in the Social Welfare Department or criminal justice community in Cologne of sorting women as battered wives. In order to conduct research or offer a theory on wife battering, the practice of identifying and counting cases of wife battering had to begin. Women who were struck by their husbands had to treat the striking as battering, and public officials had to treat the behavior as more than a private affair and as something other than a husband's conjugal right.

Researchers who, in the name of value-neutrality, would have waited until the officials in Cologne made wife battering a kind, could not have discovered the truths about wife battering in their city, because they could not have conducted the campaign through which the kind was invented. The question is not whether research on domestic abuse in Cologne should be value-neutral, but whose values the research should favor, and only if the values of the wives are favored over those of the city officials will the research document the problem of wife battering in the city.

The degree and range of participation

Research is collaborative or participatory when those directly affected by it – the participant subjects – have a say in how it is conducted and a hand in conducting it, including a voice or hand in deciding which problems should be studied, what methods should be used to study them, whether the findings are valid or acceptable, and how the findings are to be used or implemented.[34] Participation varies in degree: at one extreme, the subjects are merely informed; at the other, they are given full say. The greater the subjects' influence, the more real their participation. Participation also varies in range: at one extreme, the subjects speak to one decision; at the other, they speak to all decisions. The wider the influence of the subjects – the more far-reaching their voice – the more real their participation, and the more the approach differs from the liberal approach to research in the social sciences.

With the participatory approach, the choice or identification of the problem is always taken over by the research subjects. As I note in chapter 2, many feminist critics of the liberal sciences maintain that research on women is often more relevant to the interests of men than women, or more relevant to an interest in maintaining women's subordination than increasing their power or status. They call for research on women that is relevant to women by giving women the say over what questions the research will ask and how the questions will be answered; moreover, most feminist research on women is also research for and by the women who are the subjects.[35]

In research carried out in Vancouver in 1976–7 within the Vancouver Women's Health Collective, for example, members of the collective, rather than the social scientists who worked with them, decided what needed to be known and how the knowledge should be acquired.[36] The findings were relevant to the interests of the collective, because the members decided what questions to ask and chose the methods to use in answering them. The findings were useful to them, because the answers were expressed in the members' own language.

The study would have been different had it been conducted to serve a broader or more scientific interest. The members of the collective would have been data sources, the collective would have been one of many medical facilities studied, and the need to compare the different facilities would have required questions that would have had less bearing on the way in which the members thought about the collective or on the problems faced in the course of their own practice. Liberal scientists hoping to inform public policy would want to know how the costs or quality of care compared with those in more traditional clinics. They would use the Vancouver Women's Health Collective to acquire this knowledge; but unless members of the collective had an interest in how their clinic compares on these measures of cost or quality or in the other clinics included in the study, the knowledge would not contribute to the collective.

The liberal scientists would be interested in producing general, abstract findings applicable to the many different facilities included in their study. Whereas the participatory research conducted in the collective aimed at producing a practical theory of the local situation – that is, findings that the members of the collective see as useful in solving what they see as their problems – the liberal research would aim at producing a broader theory of the general situation of health facilities that could be useful in solving what the researchers or makers of public policy see as problems in the delivery of health care or health care to women.

Some participatory research gives the subjects a say in choosing or developing the research methods, while some leaves that choice to the experts. Some participatory research employs traditional quantitative or qualitative social science methods, while some, like the Cologne study, uses methods that seem hardly scientific at all. In the study of land ownership sponsored by the Appalachian Alliance, the citizen-researchers were trained to follow traditional methods. The decision to use traditional methods of collecting, sorting, and analyzing the data seems to have been strategic. The findings of the study had to be credible to members of the Appalachian Regional Commission, a government agency concerned with Appalachian development, given that the alliance wanted to influence the Commission's policies and saw the study as a means to do so. The less traditional the research methods, the less credible the findings would have been in the eyes of the Commission.[37]

The less traditional the methods used by the subjects in their research, the more risk that the research will not look scientific and the less likely the findings will be taken by public officials or their professional staff to be authoritative or trustworthy. Given these risks, the subjects may well decide not to turn their backs on the traditional notions of objectivity, reliable and valid data, replicated findings, testability, and confirmation that are identified with the liberal sciences; but, according to the communitarian ideal, the choice should be their own.

Some members of the Participatory Research Network turn their backs on traditional methods and speak in the language of relativism; knowledge or truth, they say, is always relative to a group or to a group's interests.[38] They define participatory research as "a research process in which the community participates in the analysis of its own reality"[39] and write: "Participatory research adopts a relativist approach and, therefore, emphasizes the relevance of values and ideologies in the process of producing knowledge."[40] Some members advocate a class analysis and the methods of Marxism. However, many examples of participatory research – for example, the Appalachian land-ownership study – are not based on a Marxist class analysis, and the methods adopted by subjects to conduct their own studies seem more those of the empirical-analytic than the critical sciences. While some of the advocates of participatory research maintain that a critical theory is central to the process, others maintain that participatory research should embrace a variety of analytic approaches.[41] In general, advocates do research with varying degrees of citizen participation, inspired by a variety of political ideals and guided by different standards of good or appropriate research method.

The differences between participatory research and traditional research in the social sciences, both pure and applied, are summarized in table 1. The table summarizes the variety of ways in which participatory research, unlike traditional pure or applied research, enlightens the research subject and helps to increase her authority and power. Whatever the standards by which the findings (the theory coming from the research) are assessed or evaluated, the research is conducted so that it arrives at the findings by means of an educational and political practice.

Perfectionism and the liberal university and state

Much of the support for research in the social sciences comes from universities and the state. A liberal university or government can support a liberal but not a perfectionist science. If a science is openly partisan and supported by university or government funds or facilities, then the university or government would be openly partisan and violate the ideal of neutrality. As a result, were the social sciences to preach the ideals of perfectionism, the liberal university and liberal state could not openly support them.

Neo-conservative critics of recent changes in the university – critics of

[handwritten margin note: – doesn't distinguish between "truth-seeking" science + "ideological" science –]

Table 1 Major differences between liberal and participatory research

	Pure research	Applied research	Participatory research
Principal goal of the research	Abstract general knowledge (not specific to a time, place, or interest)	Solutions to a problem faced by a client as diagnosed by an expert	Education of the subjects (theoretical or participant subject) of the theory and social change
Who learns from the research in the first instance	The social science community (usually other social scientists with the same research interests)	The client (usually the government or business)	The subjects
Likelihood that those supplying the data use the findings	Very low	Low	High
Relations between researcher and subject	Theoretician to the object of the theory	Expert to a client	Colleague to colleague

Source: Adapted from a table in Elden, "Sharing the Research Work," p. 263

multiculturalism and efforts to revise the canon – complain that university education is becoming illiberal. As I have argued in this book, education in the social sciences, though aiming to be liberal, is always illiberal and partisan. The changes in teaching and research opposed by the neo-conservatives make education more partisan in word but no more partisan in deed than before. Though all universities are institutionally, if not overtly, partisan, the values they favor are many and often in conflict. The conception of the good favored by one research or teaching program – for example, in economics – is likely to be different from the conception favored by another – for example, in women's studies – and though there is partisanship everywhere, in most universities, it is not everywhere the same. Conservative critics like Allan Bloom are not opposed to a university that favors some conception of the good but only to those programs that do not favor their conception.[42]

Social scientists who depend on liberal universities or governments to support their research have a vested interest in preaching a liberal over a perfectionist approach to their science. They can justify the grants, salary, equipment, and office and laboratory space provided them only if they can say that their research is nonpartisan. As a result, the issue for them is not merely what goals or methods are appropriate for science but also what goals or methods will support the present relationship between the science and its clients and benefactors. Social scientists have practical reasons for claiming the ideal of value-neutrality in spite of arguments, like those in this book, that such an ideal is inappropriate or impossible.

In the first chapter, I explain how the philosophy of the liberal state and the ideals underlying liberal schooling are related to the liberal philosophy of the social sciences. The sciences are designed to produce information and knowledge that supports the government and the schools without promoting or favoring the life plans or projects of some citizens or students over those of others. My present point about state and university support for science extends the explanation. Value-neutrality is necessary for the sciences to receive aid from a liberal state. Unless the sciences hide their partisanship, support from the state or the schools will look partisan and be seen to violate the state's own liberal ideals.

The liberal approach to research pretends to be nonpartisan but not to be democratic. Liberal research is research by disinterested experts. The subjects cannot be given a say in the research because they are not experts and are not disinterested. Perfectionist approaches can also be undemocratic. The substantive conception of the good that drives the science may not reflect the conceptions of the subjects but only those of the researchers or their clients. However, the perfectionism of participatory research is meant to be democratic. Partisanship is to be blended with democracy. The research should favor the subjects' conception of perfection and allow their conception to govern the practice. While liberal research is based on an ideal of inequality, participatory research is based on an ideal of equality between the researcher and her subjects.

Liberal government and liberal schools may or may not be democratic. As a political philosophy, liberalism permits citizens or students (or parents) to have a voice in how the government or the schools are run but does not require it. However, as a philosophy of science, liberalism supports the rule of experts and the idea that on questions of means – for example, the content of the curriculum or the organization of the criminal justice system – the popular voice should be limited. The liberal sciences support a division of labor in public life between popular and professional authority and a limit on popular authority to the most general issues of policy – to questions of ultimate ends. The democratic ideals of participatory research, by contrast, support no limits on popular authority and encourage citizens to participate in areas of public life previously reserved for experts.

Conclusion

My aim in this chapter has been to describe some alternatives to the traditional approach to research in the social sciences. The alternatives have at least one thing in common: namely, that they do not aim to be value-neutral but partisan. Critical theories are partisan toward those for whom they aim to be critical. Participatory research and feminist social science are openly partisan toward the participant subject. The research aims to increase the authority and power of those subjects through education and political action.

My aim in discussing communitarian approaches here and liberal approaches in the earlier chapters is to describe not only how social science is done but how it could be done differently. The different ways of doing social science each raise questions of their own; but, unlike the liberal approach, they each have the advantage of being open and deliberate in their partisanship and ties to practice. If the social sciences cannot be liberal, the question that those working in the social sciences should consider is why they should not be openly perfectionist and, in particular, why they should not be communitarian. I hope that my discussion of communitarian approaches has been interesting and attractive enough to make them a central topic of future work in the philosophy of the social sciences.

NOTES

1   See chapter 3 for a discussion of limit theories in the social sciences and chapter 6 for a discussion of the quality of the data collected by Nazi researchers in the biomedical sciences.

2   With communitarian research, the values of the researcher and her subjects should be the same or at least in harmony, since, in doing the research, the researcher and her subjects will be acting as advocates. With liberal research, the values of the researcher and her subjects can be different or even in conflict, as, e.g., with liberal research on crime, street gangs, labor relations, unemployment, the welfare system, or sexual deviance.

3   See A. Bookman and S. Morgan (eds), *Women and the Politics of Empowerment* (Temple University Press, 1988), and D. E. Smith, *The Everyday World as Problematic: A Feminist Sociology* (Northeastern University Press, 1987), for a discussion and examples of feminist approaches to the social sciences.

4   M. Mies, "Towards a Methodology for Feminist Research," in *Theories of Women's Studies*, ed. G. Bowles and R. D. Klein (Routledge and Kegan Paul, 1983), pp. 128–36; emphasis original.

5   See the discussion of Milgram's research in chapter 6 for an illustration of this point.

6 Habermas, *Knowledge and Human Interests*, pp. 301–17.
7 My account of critical theory relies on Raymond Geuss's discussion in *The Idea of Critical Theory: Habermas and the Frankfurt School* (Cambridge University Press, 1981).
8 Habermas, *Knowledge and Human Interests*, p. 309.
9 Ibid., p. 310.
10 See chapter 5 for a discussion of the policy syllogism.
11 Weber and many of the proponents of the liberal approach, especially in economics, deny that there is a political rationality or a rationality of ends.
12 Habermas, *Knowledge and Human Interests*, p. 308.
13 See chapter 4 for a discussion of the concept of ideology.
14 Nancy C. M. Hartsock, in her book *Money, Sex and Power: Toward a Feminist Historical Materialism* (Longman, 1983), pp. 133–9, maintains that an adequate theory of power requires a different epistemological base than that on which empirical-analytic theory depends, and that the standpoint of the oppressed is the standpoint from which such a theory can be constructed and validated. She believes that the standpoint of the proletariat is the standpoint from which a theory of domination by class is to be constructed and the standpoint of women the standpoint for a theory of domination by sex.
15 Ibid., p. 231.
16 See Habermas, *Knowlede and Human Interests*, pp. 214–45.
17 Though it aims to emancipate a subject, the subject is to be emancipated from a psychological rather than a social condition. Freud's subjects are not oppressed by the law, religion, or the economy and do not suffer as a result of their race, class position, or sex but are repressed by a mechanism inside their heads and suffer as a result of a conflict between their libidinal desires and their acceptance of cultural taboos. Cure comes through personal therapy and not, as with Marx's theory or Hartsock's theory, through collective political action. Freud's theory is socially conservative in ways that critical theories are not, for the aim of his theory is to transform not the social conditions or social regulations (reflected in the superego) but the individual – cure her of her neuroses – by giving her knowledge of herself (knowledge of the desires hidden in the id by the ego) that will disarm the mechanisms of repression or sublimation.
18 Hartsock, *Money, Sex and Power*, pp. 123–39.
19 Ibid., p. 135.
20 J. Habermas, *Theory and Practice*, tr. J. Vietrel (Beacon Press, 1973), p. 9.
21 Habermas, *Knowledge and Human Interests*, p. 304.
22 Ibid., p. 286.
23 Facts like who owns the means of production and how the law favors capital over wage labor.
24 For a useful discussion of the nature of participatory research, see the special issue, vol. 14 (1981), of the journal *Convergence*. Participatory research springs from a number of different but overlapping sources. It was inspired by Marx's writings on social change, but also by a broader populist tradition that sees ordinary people as a source of wisdom and as the primary agents of social change (see M. A. Rahman, "The Theoretical Standpoint of PAR,"

in *Action and Knowledge: Breaking the Monopoly with Participatory Action-Research*, ed. O. Fals-Bordo and M. A. Rahman (Apex Press, 1991), pp. 13–23). It draws on Kurt Lewin's idea that causal inferences about the actions of human subjects are most likely to be true if the subjects participate in building and testing them (see W. F. Whyte, D. J. Greenwood and P. Lazes, "Participatory Action Research," *American Behavioral Scientist*, 32 (1989), pp. 513–51) and on criticisms of traditional programs of international development to the effect that they foster dependency and prevent people from taking initiatives to meet their own needs and that fit their own culture, tradition, and circumstances (see M. A. Rahman, "Glimpses of the 'Other Africa'," in *Action and Knowledge*, pp. 101–3). Finally, some proponents of participatory research have been inspired by the adult literacy programs of Paulo Freire, who believes that poor and oppressed people can best learn to read and write if their learning is part of a political struggle and a campaign to empower them (see P. Freire, *The Pedagogy of the Oppressed* (Seabury Press, 1970)).

25   The example is taken from J. Gaventa and B. D. Horton, "A Citizens' Research Project in Appalachia, USA," *Convergence*, 14 (1981), pp. 30–41, and P. D. Beaver, "Participatory Research on Land Ownership in Rural Appalachia," in *Communities in Economic Crisis: Appalachia and the South*, ed. J. Gaventa, B. E. Smith and A. Willingham (Temple University Press), 1990, pp. 227–41.

26   Gaventa and Horton, "Citizens' Research Project," p. 32.

27   See chapter 4 for a discussion of Ann Oakley's research in sociology on first-time pregnant single women as an example.

28   This example is based on an account by M. Mies in her paper "Towards a Methodology."

29   In 1976–7, Cologne, like most cities in the United States, did not take domestic violence seriously. The law enforcement community did not treat wife battering as a form of assault and saw violence against women by their husbands as part of the private rather than the public realm. As a result, cases of wife battering were seldom reported to, or recorded by, the police. To use the language of chapter 7, the kind or category "wife battering" had not yet been invented by the law enforcement community and, as a result, was not there for sociologists to discover.

30   B. L. Hall, "The Democratization of Research in Adult and Non-Formal Education," in *Human Inquiry: A Sourcebook of New Paradigm Research*, ed. P. Reason and J. Rowan (John Wiley and Sons, 1981), p. 455.

31   For a defense of the edict, see A. O'Hear, *An Introduction to the Philosophy of Science* (Clarendon Press, 1989), pp. 223–32.

32   See B. L. Hall, "Participatory Research, Popular Knowledge and Power: A Personal Reflection," *Convergence*, 14 (1981), p. 7.

33   Gaventa and Horton, "Citizens' Research Project," p. 40.

34   M. Elden, "Sharing the Research Work: Participative Research and its Role Demands," in *Human Inquiry: A Sourcebook of New Paradigm Research*, ed. Reason and Rowan (John Wiley and Sons, 1981), p. 258.

35   See L. Stanley and S. Wise, *Breaking Out: Feminist Consciousness and Feminist Research* (Routledge and Kegan Paul, 1983), pp. 150–75.

36 See N. Kleiber and L. Light, *Caring for Ourselves* (University of British Columbia Press, 1978).

37 Gaventa and Horton, "Citizens' Research Project," p. 36. However, the organizers of the study seem to have agreed with the Commission and to have thought that credible and accurate findings come by following more or less traditional methods of collecting and analyzing data, not by leaving the choice of methods up to untrained citizens.

38 Here they seem to see eye to eye with Habermas.

39 F. Vio Grossi, "Socio-Political Implications of Participatory Research," *Convergence*, 14 (1981), p. 43.

40 Ibid., p. 44.

41 See Hall, "Participatory Research," p. 12.

42 A. Bloom, *The Closing of the American Mind*, Simon and Schuster, 1987, pp. 243–382.

Bibliography

Abbott, Andrew, *The System of Professions: An Essay on the Division of Labor*, University of Chicago Press, 1988.

Ackerman, Bruce A., *Social Justice in the Liberal State*, Yale University Press, 1980.

Adair, John G., Dushenko, Terrance W. and Lindsay, R. C. L., "Ethical Regulations and their Impact on Research Practice," *American Psychologist*, 40 (1985), pp. 59–72.

Alchian, Arman, "Uncertainty, Evolution and Economic Theory," *Journal of Political Economy*, 58 (1950), pp. 211–22.

Almond, Gabriel A., *Political Development: Essays in Heuristic Theory*, Little Brown and Company, 1970.

Anscombe, G. E. M., "On Brute Fact," *Analysis*, 18 (1958), pp. 69–71.

Aries, Philippe, *Centuries of Childhood: A Social History of Family Life*, tr. Robert Baldick, Alfred Knopf, 1962.

Arrow, Kenneth, *The Limits of Organization*, Norton, 1974.

Austin, John L., *How to Do Things with Words*, 2nd edn, Harvard University Press, 1975.

Austin, John L., "Performative Utterances," in *Philosophical Papers*, Oxford University Press, 1961, pp. 220–39.

Barash, David, *Sociobiology and Behavior*, Elsevier, 1977.

Barry, Brian, *Political Argument*, Routledge and Kegan Paul, 1965.

Barry, Norman, *Welfare*, University of Minnesota Press, 1990.

Beales, Ralph L., *Politics of Social Research: An Inquiry into the Ethics and Responsibility of Social Scientists*, Aldine, 1969.

Beaver, Patricia D., "Participatory Research on Land Ownership in Rural Appalachia," in *Communities in Economic Crisis: Appalachia and the South*, ed. John Gaventa, Barbara Ellen Smith and Alex Willingham, Temple University Press, 1990, pp. 227–41.

Becker, Gary, *The Economic Approach to Human Behavior*, University of Chicago Press, 1976.

Bellah, Robert N., Madsen, Richard, Sullivan, William M., Swidler, Ann and Tipton, Steven M., *Habits of the Heart: Individualism and Commitment in American Life*, University of California Press, 1985.

Berlin, Isaiah, "Two Concepts of Liberty," in *Four Essays on Liberty*, Oxford University Press, 1969, pp. 118–72.

Bloom, Allan, *The Closing of the American Mind*, Simon and Schuster, 1987.

Bok, Sissela, *Lying: Moral Choices in Public and Private Life*, Pantheon, 1978.

Bookman, Ann and Morgan, Sandra (eds), *Women and the Politics of Empowerment*, Temple University Press, 1988.

Bramson, Leon, *The Political Context of Sociology*, Princeton University Press, 1961.

Chomsky, Noam, *Aspects of the Theory of Syntax*, MIT Press, 1965.

Cohen, G. A., *Marx's Theory of History: A Defense*, Princeton University Press, 1978.

Collard, David, *Altruism and Economy: A Study in Non-Selfish Economics*, Oxford University Press, 1978.

Connerton, Paul (ed.), *Critical Sociology*, Penguin, 1976.

D' Souza, Dinesh, "Illiberal Education," *Atlantic*, 267 (1991), pp. 51–79.

Davidson, Donald, *Essays on Actions and Events*, Oxford University Press, 1980.

Davidson, Donald, *Inquiries into Truth and Interpretation*, Oxford University Press, 1984.

Dawkins, Richard, *The Selfish Gene*, Oxford University Press, 1976.

Devlin, Patrick, *The Enforcement of Morals*, Oxford University Press, 1965.

Dewey, John, *Democracy and Education*, Free Press, 1966.

Diener, Edward, and Crandall, Rick, *Ethics in Social and Behavioral Research*, University of Chicago Press, 1978.

Dreyfus, Hubert L. and Rabinow, Paul, *Michel Foucault: Beyond Structuralism and Hermeneutics*, 2nd edn, University of Chicago Press, 1983.

Durham, William H., "Toward a Coevolutionary Theory of Human Biology and Culture," in *Evolutionary Biology and Human Social Behavior: An Anthropological Perspective*, ed. Napoleon A. Chagnon and William Irons, Duxbury Press, 1979, pp. 39–58.

Durkheim, Emile, *Divisions of Labor in Society*, tr. George Simpson, Macmillan, 1933.

Durkheim, Emile, *Suicide: A Study in Sociology*, Free Press, 1966.

Dworkin, Ronald, *A Matter of Principle*, Harvard University Press, 1985.

Eagleton, Terry, *Ideology: An Introduction*, Verso, 1991.

Edelman, Murray, "The Political Language of the Helping Professions," in *Language and Politics*, ed. Michael Shapiro, New York University Press, 1984, pp. 44–60.

Edgeworth, Frank Y., *Mathematical Physics: An Essay on the Application of Mathematics to the Moral Sciences*, London School of Economics and Political Science, 1932.

Elden, Max, "Sharing the Research Work: Participative Research and its Role Demands," in *Human Inquiry: A Sourcebook of New Paradigm Research*, ed. Peter Reason and John Rowan, John Wiley and Sons, 1981, pp. 253–66.

Elster, Jon, *Ulysses and the Sirens: Studies in Rationality and Irrationality*, Cambridge University Press, 1979.

Foucault, Michel, *Discipline and Punish: The Birth of the Prison*, tr. Alan Sheridan, Random House, 1979.

Foucault, Michel, *The History of Sexuality*, vol. 1, tr. Robert Hurley, Vintage Books, 1980.

Freire, Paul, *The Pedagogy of the Oppressed*, Seabury Press, 1970.

Freud, Sigmund, *The Basic Writings of Freud*, ed. A. A. Brill, Random House, 1938.

Freud, Sigmund, *Five Lectures on Psycho-Analysis*, tr. and ed. James Strachey, Norton, 1977.

Freud, Sigmund, *Leonardo da Vinci and a Memory of his Childhood*, tr. and ed. James Strachey, Norton, 1964, pp. 32–56.

Freud, Sigmund, *The Standard Edition of the Complete Psychological Works of Sigmund Freud*, vol. 11, tr. and ed. James Strachey, Hogarth Press, 1967.

Friedman, Milton, *Capitalism and Freedom*, University of Chicago Press, 1982.

Friedman, Milton, "The Methodology of Positive Economics," in *The Philosophy of Economics*, ed. Daniel Hausman, Cambridge University Press, 1984, pp. 210–44.

Frye, Marilyn, *The Politics of Reality: Essays in Feminist Theory*, Crossing Press, 1983.

Garfinkel, Alan, *Forms of Explanation*, Yale University Press, 1981.

Gaventa, John and Horton, Billy D., "A Citizens' Research Project in Appalachia, USA," *Convergence*, 14 (1981), pp. 30–41.

Geertz, Clifford, *The Interpretation of Cultures*, Basic Books, 1973.

Geuss, Raymond, *The Idea of Critical Theory: Habermas and the Frankfurt School*, Cambridge University Press, 1981.

Gilligan, Carol, "Do the Social Sciences have an Adequate Theory of Moral Development?," in *Social Science as Moral Inquiry*, ed. Norma Haan, Robert N. Bellah, Paul Rabinow and William M. Sullivan, Columbia University Press, 1983, pp. 33–51.

Gould, Stephen J., "Caring Groups and Selfish Genes," in *Conceptual Issues in Evolutionary Biology*, ed. Elliot Sober, MIT Press, 1984, pp. 119–24.

Gould, Stephen J., *The Mismeasure of Man*, Norton, 1981.

Gray, John, *Liberalism*, University of Minnesota Press, 1986.

Gregg, Dorothy and Williams, Elgin, "The Dismal Science of Functionalism," *American Anthropologist*, 50 (1948), pp. 320–3.

Grice, G. P., "Logic and Conversation," in *The Logic of Grammar*, ed. Donald Davidson and Gilbert Harman, Wadsworth, 1975, pp. 64–78.

Gutmann, Amy, "Communitarian Critics of Liberalism," *Philosophy and Public Affairs*, 14 (1985), pp. 308–21.

Gutmann, Amy, *Democratic Education*, Princeton University Press, 1987.

Habermas, Jürgen, *Knowledge and Human Interests*, tr. Jeremy J. Shapiro, Beacon Press, 1971.

Habermas, Jürgen, *Theory and Practice*, tr. J. Vietrel, Beacon Press, 1973.

Hacking, Ian, "Five Parables," in *Philosophy in History*, ed. Richard Rorty, J. B. Scheewind and Quentin Skinner, Cambridge University Press, 1984, pp. 103–24.

Hacking, Ian, "The Making and Molding of Child Abuse," *Critical Inquiry*, 17 (1991), pp. 838–67.

Hacking, Ian, "Making Up People," in *Reconstructing Individualism*, ed. T. Heller, M. Sosna and D. Wellbery, Stanford University Press, 1986, pp. 222–37.

Hall, Budd L., "The Democratization of Research in Adult and Non-Formal Education," in *Human Inquiry: A Sourcebook of New Paradigm Research*, ed. Peter Reason and John Rowan, John Wiley and Sons, 1981, pp. 447–56.

Hall, Budd L., "Participatory Research, Popular Knowledge and Power: A Personal Reflection," *Convergence*, 14 (1981), pp. 6–19.

Harding, Sandra, *Feminism and Methodology*, Indiana University Press, 1987.

Hare, R. M., *The Language of Morals*, Oxford University Press, 1964.

Harsanyi, John C., "Individualistic and Functionalistic Explanations in the Light of Game Theory: The Example of Social Status," in *Problems in Philosophy of Science*, ed. Imre Lakatos and Alan Musgrave, North-Holland Publishing Co., 1968, pp. 305–21.

Hartsock, Nancy C. M., *Money, Sex and Power: Toward a Feminist Historical Materialism*, Longman, 1983.

Hempel, Carl G., *The Philosophy of Natural Science*, Prentice-Hall, 1966.

Herlihy, David, "Medieval Children," In *The Walter Prescott Webb Memorial Lectures: Essays on Medieval Civilization*, University of Texas Press, 1978, pp. 109–42.

Herrnstein, Richard, *IQ in the Meritocracy*, Little Brown, 1973.

Hesse, Mary, *Revolution and Reconstruction in Science*, Harvester Press, 1980.

Hicks, John, *Value and Capital*, Oxford University Press, 1939.

Hills, Stuart (ed.), *Corporate Violence*, Rowan and Littlefield, 1987.

Hume, David, *Treatise of Human Nature*, Doubleday, 1961.

Hutchinson, T. W., *"Positive" Economics and Policy Objectives*, Allen and Unwin, 1964.

Kahneman, Daniel, Knetsch, Jack L. and Thaler, Richard H., "Fairness and the Assumptions of Economics," *Journal of Business*, 59 (1986), pp. 285–300.

Kant, Immanuel, *Groundwork of the Metaphysics of Morals*, tr. H. J. Paton, Harper and Row, 1964.

Kasler, Dirk, *Max Weber: An Introduction to his Life and Work*, University of Chicago Press, 1988.

Keat, Russell and Urry, John, *Social Theory as Science*, Routledge and Kegan Paul, 1975.

Kelman, Herbert, "Human Use of Human Subjects: The Problem of Deception in Social Psychological Experiments," *Psychological Bulletin*, 67 (1967), pp. 1–11.

Kessler, Suzanne J. and McKenna, Wendy, *Gender: An Ethnomethodological Approach*, University of Chicago Press, 1978, pp. 42–80.

Keynes, John Neville, *The Scope and Method of Political Economy*, Kelly and Millman, 1955.

Kidder, Louise H., *Sellitz Wrightman and Cook's Research Methods in Social Relations*, 4th edn, Holt, Rinehart and Winston, 1981.

Kimmel, Allan J., *Ethics and Values in Applied Social Research*, Sage, 1988.

Klappholz, Kurt, "Value Judgments and Economics," in *The Philosophy of Economics*, ed. Daniel M. Hausman, Cambridge University Press, 1984, pp. 276–92.

Kleiber, Nancy and Light, Linda, *Caring for Ourselves*, University of British Columbia Press, 1978.

Kohlberg, Lawrence, "From Is to Ought: How to Commit the Naturalistic Fallacy and Get Away with it in the Study of Moral Development," in *Cognitive Development and Epistemology*, ed. Theodore Michel, Academic Press, 1971, pp. 151–235.

Kohlberg, Lawrence, "Moral Stages and Moralization: The Cognitive Development Approach," in *Moral Development and Behavior: Theory, Research and Social Issues*, ed. Thomas Lickona, Holt, Rinehart and Winston, 1976, pp. 31–53.

Laslett, B. and Rapoport, R., "Collaborative Interviewing and Interactive Research," *Journal of Marriage and the Family*, 37 (1975), pp. 968–77.

Latane, Bibb and Darley, John M., *The Unresponsive Bystander: Why doesn't he Help?*, Appleton-Century-Crofts, 1970.

Laudan, Larry, *Science and Values: The Aims of Science and their Role in Scientific Debate*, University of California Press, 1984.

Leibenstein, Harvey, *Beyond Economic Man*, Harvard University Press, 1980.

Levine, Robert J., *Ethics and Regulation of Clinical Research*, 2nd edn, Yale University Press, 1988.

Lewontin, Richard C., "Adaptation," in *Conceptual Issues in Evolutionary Biology*, ed. Elliot Sober, MIT Press, 1984, pp. 235–51.

Lukes, Steven, *Marxism and Morality*, Oxford University Press, 1985.

Lumsden, Charles and Wilson, Edward O., *Genes, Mind and Culture*, Harvard University Press, 1981.

Lundberg, George, *Can Science Save Us?*, Longmans, Green and Co., 1947.

Mackie, J. L., *Hume's Moral Theory*, Routledge and Kegan Paul, 1980.

Malinowski, Bronislaw, *The Sexual Lives of Savages in North-Western Melanesia*, 3rd edn, Routledge and Kegan Paul, 1948.

Martin, Mike W., *Self-Deception and Morality*, University of Kansas Press, 1986.

Marx, Karl, *Karl Marx's Selected Writings*, ed. David McLellan, Oxford University Press, 1977.

Mead, George Herbert, "Scientific Methods and Moral Sciences," in *Selected Writings*, ed. Andrew J. Reck, University of Chicago Press, 1964, pp. 248–66.

Melden, A. I., *Free Action*, Routledge and Kegan Paul, 1964.

Merton, Robert K., *The Sociology of Science*, University of Chicago Press, 1973.

Mies, Maria, "Towards a Methodology for Feminist Research," in *Theories of Women's Studies*, ed. Gloria Bowles and Renate Duelli Klein, Routledge and Kegan Paul, 1983, pp. 117–36.

Milgram, Stanley, *Obedience to Authority*, Harper and Row, 1974.

Mill, John Stuart, *Essays on some Unsettled Questions of Political Economy*, Longmans, Green, Reader and Dyer, 1874.

Mill, John Stuart, *On Liberty*, ed. Elizabeth Rapaport, Hackett Publishing Company, 1978.

Mill, John Stuart, *On the Logic of the Moral Sciences*, Bobbs–Merrill Company, 1965.

Mill, John Stuart, *Utilitarianism*, ed. Oskar Priest, Bobbs–Merrill Company, 1957.

Moore, G. E., *Principia Ethica*, Cambridge University Press, 1966.

Nisbett, Richard E. and Wilson, Timothy De Camp, "Telling More than we can Know: Verbal Reports on Mental Processes," *Psychological Review*, 84 (1977), pp. 231–59.

O'Hear, Anthony, *An Introduction to the Philosophy of Science*, Clarendon Press, 1989.

Oakley, Ann, "Interviewing Women: A Contradiction in Terms," in *Doing Feminist Research*, ed. Helen Roberts, Routledge and Kegan Paul, 1981, pp. 30–61.

Papineau, David, *For Science in the Social Sciences*, St Martin's Press, 1978.

Patemen, Carole, *The Sexual Contract*, Stanford University Press, 1988.

Peters, R. S., *The Concept of Motivation*, Routledge and Kegan Paul, 1958.

Piaget, Jean, *Moral Judgment of the Child*, Free Press, 1932.

Pigou, Arthur C., *Unemployment*, Home University Library, 1913.

Plato, *Republic*, tr. G. M. A. Grube, Hackett Publishing Company, 1974.

Pollock, Friedrich, "Empirical Research into Public Opinion," in *Critical Sociology*, ed. Paul Connerton, Penguin, 1976, pp. 225–36.

Popper, Karl, "What can Logic do for Philosophy?," *Proceedings of the Aristotelian Society*, supp. vol. 22 (1948), pp. 141–54.

Proctor, Robert, *Racial Hygiene: A History of Nazi Medicine*, Harvard University Press, 1988.

Quine, W. V. O., *Word and Object*, MIT Press, 1960.

Radcliffe-Brown, A. R., *Structure and Function in Primitive Society*, Free Press, 1952.

Rahman, Muhammad Anisur, "Glimpses of the 'Other Africa'," in *Action and Knowledge: Breaking the Monopoly with Participatory Action-Research*, ed. Orlando Fals-Bordo and Muhammad Anisur Rahman, Apex Press, 1991, pp. 84–108.

Rahman, Muhammad Anisur, "The Theoretical Standpoint of PAR," in *Action and Knowledge: Breaking the Monopoly with Participatory Action-Research*, ed. Orlando Fals-Bordo and Muhammad Anisur Rahman, Apex Press, 1991, pp. 13–23.

Rawls, John, *A Theory of Justice*, Harvard University Press, 1971.

Reznek, Lawrie, *The Nature of Disease*, Routledge and Kegan Paul, 1987.

Richardson, Stephen A., Dohrenwend, Barbara Snell and Klein, David, *Interviewing: Its Forms and Functions*, Basic Books, 1965.

Robbins, Lionel, *An Essay on the Nature and Significance of Economic Science*, 2nd edn, Macmillan and Co., 1952.

Root, Michael, "Davidson and Social Science," in *Truth and Interpretation: Perspectives on the Philosophy of Donald Davidson*, ed. Ernest Lepore, Basil Blackwell, 1986, pp. 272–304.

Rosenberg, Alexander, *Philosophy of Social Science*, Westview Press, 1988.

Ross, L., Lepper, M. R. and Hubbard, M., "Perseverance and Self-Perception and Social Perception: Biased Attributional Processes in the Debriefing Paradigm," *Journal of Personality and Social Psychology*, 32 (1975), pp. 880–92.

Rossiaud, Jacques, "Prostitution, Youth, and Society in the towns of Southeastern France in the Fifteenth Century," in *Deviants and the Abandoned in French Society: Selections From the Annales Economies, Souétiés, Civilisations*, ed. Robert Forster and Orest Ranum, tr. Elborg Forster and Patriaz Ranum, Johns Hopkins University Press, 1978, pp. 1–46.

Ruse, Michael, "Definitions of Species in Biology," *British Journal of the Philosophy of Science*, 20 (1969), pp. 97–119.

Searle, John, *Speech Acts*, Cambridge University Press, 1969.

Sen, Amartya K., *On Ethics and Economics*, Basil Blackwell, 1987.

Sen, Amartya K., "Rational Fools: A Critique of the Behavioral Foundations of Economic Theory," in *Philosophy and Economic Theory*, ed. Frank Hahn and Martin Hollis, Oxford University Press, 1979, pp. 87–109.

Simon, Herbert, "From Substantive to Procedural Rationality," in *Philosophy and Economic Theory*, ed. Frank Hahn and Martin Hollis, Oxford University Press, 1979, pp. 65–86.

Sjoberg, G. and Nett, R., *A Methodology of Social Research*, Harper and Row, 1968.

Smith, Dorothy E., *The Everyday World as Problematic: A Feminist Sociology*, Northeastern University Press, 1987.

Sober, Elliot, "Holism, Individualism and the Units of Selection," in *Conceptual Issues in Evolutionary Biology*, ed. Elliot Sober, MIT Press, 1984.

Stanley, Liz and Wise, Sue, *Breaking Out: Feminist Consciousness and Feminist Research*, Routledge and Kegan Paul, 1983.

Storms, Michael and Nisbett, Richard E., "Insomnia and the Attribution Process," *Journal of Personality and Social Psychology*, 16 (1970), pp. 319–28.

Stout, A. K., "Free Will and Responsibility," in *Readings in Ethical Theory*, ed. Wilfred Sellars and John Hospers, Appleton-Century-Crofts, 1952, pp. 537–48.

Strawson, P. F., *Freedom and Resentment and Other Essays*, Methuen, 1974.

Suls, Jerry M. and Rosnow, Ralph L., "The Delicate Balance between Ethics and Artifacts in Behavioral Research," in *New Directions for Methodology of Social and Behavioral Sciences*, vol. 10, Jossey-Bass, 1981, pp. 56–67.

Thagard, Paul and Nisbett, Richard E., "Rationality and Charity," *Philosophy of Science*, 50 (1983), pp. 250–67.

Tversky, Amos and Kahneman, Daniel, "Rational Choices and the Framing of Decisions," *Journal of Business*, 59 (1986), pp. 251–78.

Tyler, Loena E. *Tests and Measurements*, 2nd edn, Prentice-Hall, 1971.

van Fraassen, Bas, *The Scientific Image*, Oxford University Press, 1980.

Vio Grossi, Francisco, "Socio-Political Implications of Participatory Research," *Convergence*, 14 (1981), pp. 43–51.

von Wright, Georg Henrik, *Explanation and Understanding*, Cornell University Press, 1971.

Waismann, Friedrich, "Verifiability," in *Logic and Language*, ed. Antony Flew, 1st and 2nd series, Doubleday, 1965, pp. 122–51.

Wasserstrom, Richard, "Racism, Sexism and Preferential Treatment: An Approach to the Topics," *UCLA Law Review*, 24 (1977), pp. 581–622.

Watkins, J. W. N., "Ideal Types and Historical Explanation," in *The Philosophy of Social Explanation*, ed. Alan Ryan, Oxford University Press, 1973, pp. 82–104.

Weber, Max, *Economy and Society*, ed. Guenther Roth and Claus Wittich, Bedminster Press, 1968.

Weber, Max, *Max Weber on Universities*, tr. and ed. Edward Shils, University of Chicago Press, 1973.

Weber, Max, *The Methodology of the Social Sciences*, tr. and ed. Edward Shils and Henry Finch, Free Press, 1968.

Weber, Max, *The Protestant Ethic and the Rise of Capitalism*, Allen and Unwin, 1930.

Weber, Max, "Science as a Vocation," in *From Max Weber*, ed. H. H. Gerth and C. Wright Mills, Oxford University Press, 1946, pp. 129–56.

Whyte, William Foote, Greenwood, Davydd J. and Lazes, Peter, "Participatory Action Research," *American Behavioral Scientist*, 32 (1989), pp. 513–51.

Winch, Peter, *The Idea of a Social Science*, Routledge and Kegan Paul, 1958.

Wood, Allen, *Karl Marx*, Routledge and Kegan Paul, 1981.

Wrong, Denis, (ed.), *Max Weber*, Prentice-Hall, 1970.

Author Index

Subject Index